roots

roots
family histories
of familiar words

by Peter Davies

McGraw-Hill Book Company

New York   St. Louis   San Francisco   Auckland
Bogotá   Hamburg   Johannesburg   London   Madrid
Mexico   Montreal   New Delhi   Panama   Paris
São Paulo   Singapore   Sydney   Tokyo   Toronto

Library of Congress Cataloging in Publication Data

Davies, Peter, date
    Roots—family histories of familiar words

    Bibliography: p.
    Includes index
    1. English language—Etymology.   I. Title.
PE1574.D3   422   80-24118
ISBN 0-07-015449-X

234567890   KPKP   8987654321

The editors for this book were Robert A. Rosenbaum and Margaret
Lamb, the designer was Mark E. Safran, and the production
supervisor was Thomas G. Kowalczyk. It was set in Garamond by
ComCom.

Printed and bound by The Kingsport Press.

contents

v

vi

preface

This book is an amateur's effort at popularizing a subject that has been regarded as difficult: the Indo-European fact, and its relevance and interest for everyone who speaks English. It brings together some of the findings of two separate and demanding specialties — historical linguistics and Old World archaeology. I am an untrained aficionado of both, with professional qualifications in neither. I may well have made errors of detail that will give pain or amusement to specialists, and if so I am sorry. But this book has not been written for specialists.

The Indo-European fact dominates the prehistoric background of our entire culture. It has often been distorted by politicians and racists, and partly for this reason many academics have soft-pedaled it for a generation or so. Also, both the linguistics and the archaeology of the subject have become so complex that each requires a formidable training; it is now all but impossible to aquire real proficiency in both in one reasonable lifetime, and the two groups of scholars often find it hard to even communicate with each other. These are not good reasons for the rest of us to ignore this fascinating subject.

The real Indo-Europeans still loom there in our past, and some appreciation of them ought to be a commonplace part of modern education. In some still obscure sense, they were prime movers in some of the major cultural surges of the human race, in India, in the Middle East, and in Europe. Their influence remains formative, for good or evil, in the present and future world-culture.

This book is intended to provide a simple but realistic way of looking at the Indo-Europeans and the continuities that connect them to us. Using well-established word-histories, with archeological and historical comments, it offers a series of glimpses of the ever-ramifying traditions by which Indo-European roots are present in the familiar words of our everyday speech.

Crescent, Georgia   PETER DAVIES

introduction

We are still speaking Indo-European.
    —Calvert Watkins

Some of our words are "native," inherited words, but most have been
acquired by borrowing from other languages. The English word
BOURGEOIS* = "middle-class person" is a borrowing of the French word
bourgeois = "townsperson." The word MATERNAL is a borrowing from Latin
māternus = "motherly." CYCLE is borrowed (via several intermediaries) from
Greek *kuklos* = "wheel." More than ninety percent of our huge modern
vocabulary has been built up over the years from such borrowings. The
more recently the borrowing occurred, the easier (usually) it is to recognize
as a borrowing. Some are also easily identifiable as borrowings by their
shapes; CONSTELLATION is obviously from Latin, and DIAGNOSIS could
only be from Greek. But many others, especially those that were acquired
several centuries ago, such as BIRTH, CATCH, JOIN, FOREST, GRAIN,
SEASON, SQUARE, have been so thoroughly assimilated into the fabric of the
language that they are to all appearances entirely English words.

Alongside the hordes of naturalized aliens are the true natives. While
they are relatively few in number (less than ten percent of the entries given
in the big modern dictionaries), among them are most of our commonest
and most basic words, including nearly all the common prepositions,
conjunctions, pronouns, and other function words, and all of the cardinal
numbers from ONE to HUNDRED. Also among the natives are such basic
nouns as MOON, STAR, and THUNDER; COW, FISH, and HOUND; MOTHER
and FATHER; SWEAT, WORK, and WORD; such basic verbs as KNOW, RIDE,
ROW, SEW, SOW, WEAVE; and such basic adjectives as NAKED, NEW,
SWEET, TAME, and WISE. These words have come down to us in unbroken
inheritance, owing nothing to other languages, from the Old English (or
Anglo-Saxon) spoken a thousand years ago in England, from the Germanic
language spoken a thousand years before that by the ancestors of the
Anglo-Saxons in northwestern Europe, and long before that from the
prehistoric language ancestral to Germanic.

These two components of our word stock, the native and the borrowed,
exist compatibly side by side, and few people but experts are or need to be
conscious of any great difference between them. Details of their individual
stories are readily available in the etymologies given in any good dictionary.
The languages of Europe, and their neighbors to the east, have been so
thoroughly studied by the science of historical and comparative linguistics
that the origins of most of our words, both native and borrowed, can be
reliably traced back not only throughout the centuries of recorded history
but also several thousand years into the undocumented past of prehistory.

*The histories of the English words cited in the introduction in small capitals are given under
their individual roots. See index of English words on page 210.

1

How this seemingly impossible feat has been done will not be described here; some references are given at the end of this Introduction. The picture revealed by the linguistic evidence is one of a parent language referred to as Indo-European, from which most of the languages of Europe, and various others of the Middle East and India, are descended. Judging from the earliest recorded forms of these languages, the common parent must have existed two or three thousand years before them. But this does not imply that it was a "primitive" language. Human speech and language is thought to be several hundred thousand years old, and all individual languages that have been observed in the present and recent world are of virtually equal sophistication. Nor, from the great spread and success of its descendants, can we infer that Indo-European was an especially superior language. Languages expand their domains and prosper not by any internal dynamic but by the efforts and fortunes of the people who speak them. Indo-European was merely one of the world's already numerous languages spoken some five or six thousand years ago. It had its own intricate grammatical structure, and a vocabulary of (at least) several thousand words; from these the structure of our modern speech, and the "native" component of our vocabulary, are directly inherited.

Of our more numerous *borrowed* words, on the other hand, the great majority are taken from languages neighboring to the English-speaking people, chiefly Norse, Dutch, French, Spanish, and Italian, and from the two "dead" cultural languages Latin and Greek. All of these are cousins of English, equally descended from the Indo-European parent language; each of their inherited vocabularies is selectively derived from the same original set of words. Thus it has come about that English has, in thousands of cases, both inherited an Indo-European word and later (unwittingly) borrowed a cognate word, one that is separately descended from the same original term.

This book sets out one hundred of the most interesting and impressive Indo-European roots represented in English. Each entry tells the story of one word or root and how it has come into modern English both by inheritance and by borrowing. Each entry has a diagram on the facing page, showing the story in a concise visual form. Continuity within a language tradition is shown by solid lines. Borrowing from one language into another is shown by broken lines with arrows. Modern English words are given in capitals at the bottom of the diagram. No other special conventions are used, and there are no abbreviations.

It will be seen that in many cases the inherited "native" word remains the basic one, while the borrowings have been built onto the vocabulary as subordinate terms of one kind or another. The Indo-European words *māter**

---

*All the Indo-European words or roots cited here are treated, in alphabetical order, in the body of this book.

="mother" and *pater* ="father" have been inherited as Modern English MOTHER and FATHER, and although they possess regular English derivative adjectives *(motherly* and *fatherly),* still our language tradition has found it necessary or convenient to borrow the more formal adjectives MATERNAL and PATERNAL from Latin.

This situation is repeated in case after case: BROTHER and FRATERNAL, NOSE and NASAL, NIGHT and NOCTURNAL, NAME and NOMINAL, MIND and MENTAL, TOOTH and DENTAL.

Similarly, the cardinal numbers from ONE to TEN are the native and basic words, but each has been supplemented with cognate borrowings from Latin and Greek. With native ONE there is Latin UNITY, with native TWO there are Latin DUAL and Greek DI-(prefix), with native THREE there are Latin TRIPLE and Greek TRI-(prefix); and so for the whole set.

Likewise, we have often inherited the name of a plant or animal, which we continue to use as the everyday name, and then subsequently borrowed its Latin or Greek cognate to serve as its scientific name, sometimes also providing a formal adjective. We inherit the everyday name of the BEECH tree, but as its formal botanical name we use the Latin cognate *Fagus,* yielding the (rare) botanical adjective *fagaceous* ="belonging to the family of the beech."

There are many other examples of this relationship, where the inherited word has remained the everyday word and its Latin or Greek cousins supply some important but less basic term or terms. This situation was not consciously striven for by those who coined the terms; nor on the other hand was it wholly an accident. It results, almost inevitably, from the cultural history of the European languages, in which the two "learned" languages Latin and Greek have been used together as an inexhaustible quarry for the making of elegant, scholarly, and scientific terms, so that by mere probability the often unrecognizable cognates have often come to be regrouped in modern speech. The word HEMP is our inherited name for the plant, and when the pioneer taxonomist Linnaeus came to give it its formal botanical name he naturally adopted the Greco-Latin word *Cannabis.* He could not, of course, have known that the German word *hanf* and the English word HEMP were the exact cognates of Greek *kannabis.* But the upshot is that we now employ the inherited word HEMP for the plant in some contexts and its borrowed cognate CANNABIS in others.

The results have not always been so neat. We have inherited the Indo-European word *kwon* ="dog" in the modern English word HOUND, but this is no longer the basic word for the animal. HOUND and its cognate adjective CANINE are a pair, but the word DOG, which is now the basic word for the animal, is not related. The Indo-European word *ekwos* = "horse" has not been retained in Modern English at all, though we have as usual adopted the Latin adjective EQUINE.

3

In thousands of other cases, the sets of cognates that have emerged in Modern English are of a more random and miscellaneous nature. It may be only a curiosity that we measure farmland by the ACRE, and that our formal word for farming, AGRICULTURE, contains the same ancestral word for "field"; that the words NAKED and NUDE are a cognate pair; and that LIBIDO is a fancy or "clinical" word for LOVE. Individually such situations look like mere oddments or coincidences. Collectively, as this book is intended to show, they are a significant and little-noticed theme running through the whole of our vast vocabulary.

It will have been noticed that the forms of the words change in a remarkable way within each language tradition. This is one of the fundamental discoveries of the linguistic scholars to whom we owe the entire body of Indo-European reconstruction. These sound-changes result ultimately from the inevitable small changes of pronunciation that occur in the language-learning of children from generation to generation. The sound-system of a language is an extremely coherent and self-regulating system, and the permanent changes that result are not random but regular. Thus, the Indo-European sound /p/ was reinterpreted in Germanic as /f/, and this happened not sporadically but in every word in which the sound was present. The Indo-European word *piskos* = "fish" became Germanic *fiskaz,* and Indo-European *pəter* = "father" became Germanic *fadar;* whence Modern English FISH and FATHER. But these particular sound-changes applied only to Germanic. In Latin, the Indo-European /p/ was retained as /p/: thus *piskos* and *pəter* emerge in Latin as *piscis* and *pater.* When such Latin derivatives were later borrowed into English they retained the /p/ sound, which in corresponding *inherited* words had become /f/. Thus to our native words FISH and FATHER correspond the borrowed cognates PISCATORIAL and PATERNAL. This regularity of sound-changes is a large subject and will not be further explored here. A selective table of the more important ones is given on page 208. Some of the more clear-cut changes are also explicitly described in the word histories in the body of the book.

This book is intended as a browsable collection of some of the more fascinating of these deeply buried correspondences in our stock of words. Although the great majority of them result from borrowings that English has taken from its fellow-Germanic languages, from the Romance languages, and from Latin and Greek, as mentioned above, they are yet further extended by scattered borrowings from the Celtic languages (Welsh, and the Gaelic of Ireland and Scotland), the Slavic languages (Russian, Polish, etc.), and the Indo-Iranian languages (Sanskrit, Hindi, Persian, etc.). These, too, are members of the great Indo-European language family, and their inherited vocabularies, too, are selectively descended from the same original vocabulary in the parent language. It is therefore again not entirely coincidental that when English borrows a Celtic word such as WHISKY, a

Slavic word such as VODKA, or an Indic word such as NIRVANA, these, too, turn out to contain Indo-European roots that are already present in other English words, both inherited and borrowed. A representative scattering of these somewhat remoter cognates has also been included.

(It is perhaps worth pointing out that English has not confined its borrowings to its Indo-European cousins, but has taken words from every language with which English-speakers have come into contact, including Hebrew and Arabic, Bantu and Amharic, Chinese and Japanese, Algonquian and Eskimo. Such languages being of families other than Indo-European, borrowings from them obviously could not give rise to any of the correspondences here examined, and they therefore do not appear in this book. And the same of course applies to the considerable number of English words whose origins are still unknown.)

At the same time as the vocabulary has been expanded by borrowings, the original native word stock of Old English has also been considerably eroded over the past thousand years. Numerous inherited words, such as Old English *eoh* = "horse," continuing the ancestral form *ekwos,* have for various reasons disappeared entirely. But the rate of loss has been slow, and a bedrock of native words is retained from generation to generation with astonishing persistence. Onto this slowly diminishing bedrock the language deposits ever newer strata of borrowings, most of which stem from the same ultimate source. A similar situation exists, in endlessly varying permutations, in the other modern Indo-European languages, which also borrow insatiably both from their influential neighbors and from ancient repositories of cultural prestige such as classical Sanskrit as well as Latin and Greek. The English vocabulary itself, owing to the current worldwide influence of the English-speaking peoples, is now being borrowed into every language in the world; thus a further already stratified layer is added.

The situation has so far been described and discussed as if it were a purely linguistic situation, but it actually of course results from and reflects several thousand years of human activities, and the endless interactions of the Indo-European–speaking peoples, and others. The full story, lying as it does at the intersection of history, linguistics, archaeology, and anthropology, and passing from the dimly seen world of prehistory into the overwhelmingly well-documented histories of many ancient nations, has never yet been coherently told. The subject itself is so vast and complex, and the implications so important and interesting, that the competing specialists have been unable to agree on even the main outlines. It has also been bedeviled by nationalism and racism.

Recently, however, the first convincing and well-grounded model of the fundamental and prehistoric part of the story has been set out. Acceptance of such a model can come only slowly, and controversy will doubtless continue beyond the present generation. But I for one am satisfied that this long-standing riddle has been essentially solved.

The Lithuanian-American archaeologist Marija Gimbutas points to a people who lived on the plains of southern Russia and the Ukraine between 5000 and 4000 B.C. She has named them the Kurgan people (from *kurgan,* the modern local name for their burial mounds). Their way of life, in the fifth millennium B.C., was Neolithic. They planted grain and other crops and herded cattle, horses, sheep, and pigs. They lived in low-lying villages and also built hill forts for security and for political control. Their society, unlike those of the contemporary rather egalitarian peoples living in Europe, was rigidly stratified: an aristocratic caste of warriors ruled a larger class of farmers.

Gimbutas asserts that the Kurgan people were the original speakers of the Indo-European language. The assertion rests on two separate bodies of evidence. First, the culture and environment of the Kurgan people fit the culture and environment indicated by the Indo-European vocabulary. Second, and in the long run more conclusive, the Kurgan people in the period 4000–2000 B.C. embarked on a massive series of expansions, westward into Europe and southward into the Middle East, and continuities can be shown running on from their original Neolithic culture to those of the Bronze Age peoples who later emerge into the light of documented history as the Greeks, the Romans, the Celts, the Germans, the Balts and Slavs, and the Aryans of Iran and India. Many of these peoples can be seen as originally Kurgan elites imposed on conquered peoples of non-Kurgan origin. To follow the archaeological identifications involved would fill a shelf of books, and not even an outline will be attempted here. But in many of the root histories given in this book, pertinent archaeological observations are briefly made, all tending to confirm the truth of Gimbutas's brilliant hypothesis.

If the Kurgan/Indo-European identification is correct, we can know more of this horse-loving people of the Eurasian grasslands than we can of any other people of their time, since we can scrutinize them with the binocular vision of linguistics combined with archaeology. Neither their language nor they themselves need be thought of as "primitive." We know something of their law, of their social structure, of their poetry, and of the metaphors by which they saw and described the world—many of which we are still using today. One of the most fascinating themes in the story of their endlessly successful aggressions is the part played by the trained horse harnessed to a wheeled vehicle, very possibly an original Kurgan/Indo-European development (*ekwos* = "horse," *wegh-* = "to travel, transport in a vehicle," and *kwekwlos* = "wheel"). There are also glimpses of their agriculture (*grənom* = "seed," *sē-* = "to sow seed," *ghordhos* = "garden"), of their animal husbandry (*gwōus* = "cow/bull," *owis* = "sheep," *sus* = "pig," *agros* = "pasture"), of their mathematics (*dekm* = "ten," *kmtom* = "hundred"), of their hospitality (*ghostis* = "guest"), strong drink (*medhu* = "mead"), and religion (*deiwos* = "god").

But the most compelling fact about this remote people is that they are our linguistic ancestors. We are a mixed race, and our modern culture is a revolutionary synthesis of ingredients from many sources, including Semitic, Mediterranean, African, and even Chinese elements as well as Indo-European ones, all many times transformed by the technological quantum jumps of the past two or three hundred years. But the long continuity of language, carrying with it unbroken threads of human consciousness, has a special place in the reckoning. Through all the world-moving and culture-shattering changes we have engendered and inflicted, these threads of language somehow mysteriously endure. Thanks to the scholars who have patiently and brilliantly unraveled the evidence and restored a fragmentary picture of the remote past, we can recognize that when we speak of the MOON and the STARS and the NIGHT we inherit the *mēn-* and *ster-* and *nekwt-* of our Neolithic forebears, that our homely terms SIT and SEW and WEAVE continue their *sed-* and *syū-* and *webh-*, and that our words SWEET and SWEAT and LOVE still faithfully echo their *swād-* and *sweid-* and *leubh-*. These ancient words, with the related borrowings that supplement them, are alive today in our everyday utterances. This book is a small sampling of these deep and wonderful continuities.

agros

1. The Indo-European word *agros* = "pasture, uncultivated land" appears in Germanic *akraz* = "cultivated field," Latin *ager, agr-* = "land, field, farmland," Greek *agros* = "open country," later also "farmland," and Sanskrit *ajras* = "open country, plain."

   The Indo-Europeans, living on the grasslands north and northeast of the Black Sea between 5000 and 4000 B.C., had a Neolithic mixed-farming economy. They used the plow, and planted a little grain, but their cattle were more important to them than their crops; they computed wealth in head of cattle, not in land. As seminomadic cattle-herders they made far-reaching migrations into Europe and the Middle East.

   The word *agros* is a noun regularly formed from the verb root *ag-* = "to drive cattle." It was originally a herdsman's term meaning "the place where you drive the cattle," i.e., "uncultivated grassland, pasture, the open range." In Sanskrit and the earliest Greek and Latin, this remained the basic meaning of the word, still perhaps recalling periods of migration when the cattle-herders were always in search of good pasture. In later Greek and Latin, and exclusively in Germanic, the word *agros* was transferred to the farmlands of settled communities, whether used for grazing or for plowing.

2. *Agros* regularly became Germanic *akraz* = "field, piece of cultivated land." This appears in Gothic *akrs,* Old Norse *akr,* Old High German *acker,* and Old English *æcer* was also used to mean a field of specific size, sometimes defined as the area that a team of oxen could plow in one day. In the thirteenth century it was officially defined as 4,840 square yards, so that 640 acres = 1 square mile. The word emerged as ACRE in Modern English, in the United States still the basic unit in which farmland is reckoned. In England, Australia, and elsewhere it has recently been abolished in the interests of worldwide conformity with the metric system.

3. Latin *ager,* originally "open country," meant both plowland and farmland in general, especially the *ager publicus* = "public or common land, the land belonging to a village or community." The adjective *agrārius* = "relating to farmland" was adopted into English (seventeenth century) as AGRARIAN. The noun *agricultūra* = "cultivation of land" (*cultūra* = "cultivation") was adopted (also seventeenth century) as AGRICULTURE, a term that now includes animal-raising as well as crop-growing.

4. Greek *agros,* originally "open country," likewise later meant "cultivated field, farmland." There was a term *agronomos* = "land-manager" (*-nomos* = "practitioner, manager"). From this the modern word AGRONOMY = "the science and profession of land management" was coined.

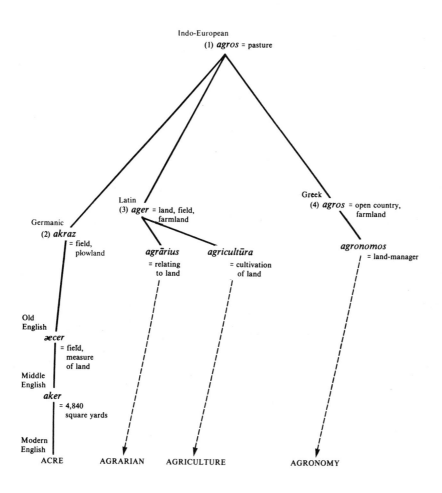

Indo-European
(1) *agros* = pasture

Latin
(3) *ager* = land, field, farmland

Greek
(4) *agros* = open country, farmland

Germanic
(2) *akraz* = field, plowland

agrārius = relating to land

agricultūra = cultivation of land

agronomos = land-manager

Old English
æcer = field, measure of land

Middle English
aker = 4,840 square yards

Modern English
ACRE AGRARIAN AGRICULTURE AGRONOMY

9

apo

1. The Indo-European adverb/preposition *apo* = "off, away, from," appears in Germanic *af* = "off," Latin *ab* = "from, by agency of," Greek *apo* = "off, from, away," and Sanskrit *ápa* = "away from."

2. Germanic *af* appears in Gothic *af,* Old Norse *af,* Old High German *aba,* and Old English *æf* = "from." Old English *æf* had an unstressed form *of,* which became Modern English OF, with a vast spread of prepositional meanings and functions.

    Late Middle English *of* also had a stressed variant OFF, which in the sixteenth century became a separate adverb/preposition meaning "away, separating from," etc.

3. A comparative form *apoter-* = "farther away" appears in Germanic *aftar-* = "coming after," Greek *apotero* = "farther away," and Sanskrit *apataram* = "farther away." Germanic *aftar-* appears in Gothic *aftra* = "again, back," Old Norse *aptr* = "back," Old High German *aftar* = "behind, after," and Old English *æfter* = "behind, after." Old English *æfter* became Modern English AFTER.

4. The Latin preposition *ab* = "from, by" was freely used as a prefix in hundreds of words such as *abdūcere* = "to take away, abduct," *abnormis* = "away from the norm, abnormal," and *abstractus* = "removed from reality, abstract." Many of these, including ABDUCT, ABNORMAL, ABSTRACT, have been adopted into English.

5. The Greek preposition *apo* = "off, away from," was likewise used to form hundreds of compounds, such as *apostatēs* = "one who stands away, a rebel," *apostolos* = "person who is sent away, envoy, apostle." Many of these, including APOSTATE and APOSTLE, have been adopted into English. APO-itself is used as a productive English prefix, as in APOMORPHINE = "a chemical compound derived from morphine."

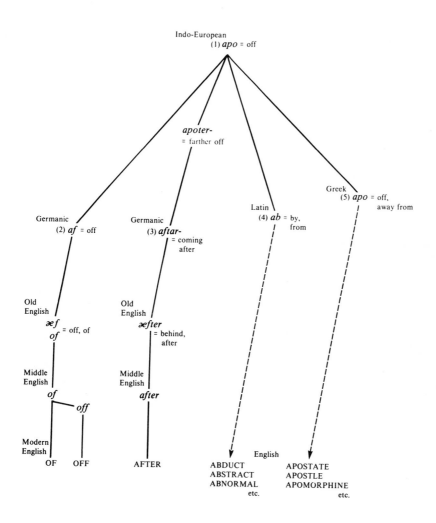

Indo-European
(1) *apo* = off

apoter-
= farther off

Greek
(5) *apo* = off,
away from

Germanic
(2) *af* = off

Germanic
(3) *aftar-*
= coming
after

Latin
(4) *ab* = by,
from

Old
English
æf
of = off, of

Old
English
æfter
= behind,
after

Middle
English
of   *off*

Middle
English
after

Modern
English
OF   OFF

AFTER

English
ABDUCT
ABSTRACT
ABNORMAL
etc.

APOSTATE
APOSTLE
APOMORPHINE
etc.

11

aus-

1.   The Indo-European noun *aus-*, also *awes-* = "dawn" appears in Germanic *aust-*, Latin *aurōra*, Lithuanian *aušra*, Greek *ēōs*, and Sanskrit *ushás*, all meaning "dawn, sunrise."

The Indo-Europeans worshiped the sun. Within their sun cult was a cult of the dawn. The rosy-colored light preceding the rising sun was recognized as a separate, and female, divinity.

2.   Germanic *aust-* = "dawn, east" appears in Old Norse *austan* = "from the east," Old High German *ost* (whence modern German *ost* = "east"), and Old English *ēast* = "east." Old English *ēast* became Modern English EAST.

3.   During the period A.D. 300–800, the Roman Church was working to convert the various peoples of western Europe to Christianity. When Roman missionaries encountered any especially strongly rooted "pagan" festival that they could not hope to eradicate entirely, they often used the stratagem of overriding it by founding a major Christian festival that would fall on or around the same date. Thus the Germanic midwinter festival of *Yule* was overridden by Christmas, and the Celtic autumn festival was overrun by Halloween and All Saints' Day.

Old English *Ēastre, Ēastron* = "Easter," first recorded in the ninth century, is clearly related to Old Frisian *āsteron* and Old High German *ōstarun*, also meaning "Easter." The English historian Bede comments that Old English *Ēastre* is derived from *Ēostre*, the name of a goddess whose festival was celebrated at the vernal equinox. Evidently this goes back to a Germanic form *Austrōn-*, one among many forms of the name of the Indo-European dawn goddess.

Old English *Ēastre, Ēastron* became Modern English EASTER.

4.   In Latin, an Indo-European *s* falling between two vowels regularly changed to *r*. Thus Latin *aurōra* is a regular descendant of Indo-European *aus-*. *Aurōra*, besides being the common noun for "dawn," was the name of the Roman goddess of dawn. In the seventeenth century it was adopted into scientific New Latin as the term for the electroluminescent effects called the "northern lights," *Aurora borealis* (*borealis* = "northern"); borrowed into English as AURORA.

5.   Indo-European *aus-* also became Greek *ēōs, eōs,* = "dawn," also the name of the Greek dawn goddess. In nineteenth-century paleontology, this was adopted to form the prefix EO-, as in EOLITH = "dawn-stone," i.e., one of the crudest and therefore presumably earliest stone artifacts, and EOHIPPUS = "dawn-horse," i.e., the fossil ancestor of the modern horse.

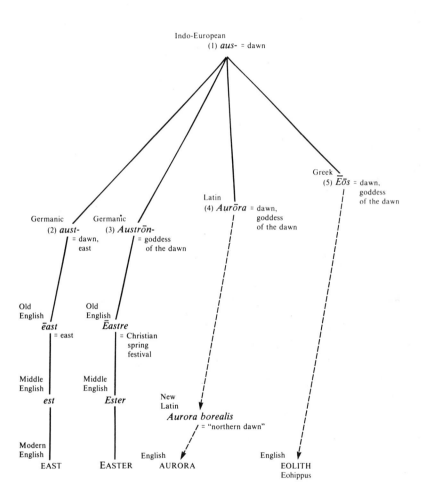

Indo-European
(1) *aus-* = dawn

Greek
(5) *Ēōs* = dawn,
goddess
of the dawn

Latin
(4) *Aurōra* = dawn,
goddess
of the dawn

Germanic
(2) *aust-*
= dawn,
east

Germanic
(3) *Austrōn-*
= goddess
of the dawn

Old
English
ēast
| = east

Old
English
Ēastre
| = Christian
spring
festival

Middle
English
est

Middle
English
Ester

New
Latin
Aurora borealis
= "northern dawn"

Modern
English
EAST

EASTER

English
AURORA

English
EOLITH
Eohippus

13

bhāgos

1.   The Indo-European word *bhāgos* = "beech tree" appears in Germanic *bōkō, bōkyō* = "beech," Gaulish Celtic *bāgos* = "beech" (only in place-names), Latin *fāgus* = "beech," and Greek *phēgos* = "edible oak."

The beech is a large deciduous tree yielding edible nuts that have been an important source of forest food since ancient times. The European beech, *Fagus silvatica,* is now native to most of Europe west of the Soviet Union. It has been argued that since the word *bhāgos* proves that the original Indo-Europeans knew the beech, their homeland must have been in central or western Europe. Two relatively recently established facts have nullified this argument. First, the closely related eastern beech, *Fagus orientalis,* still grows in the Caucasus, east of the Black Sea. Second, pollen counts from excavations have shown that both the European and the eastern beech grew on the plains of the Ukraine and south Russia at the time associated with the original Indo-Europeans (4500 B.C.).

2.   *Bhāgos* became Germanic *bōkō, bōkyō* = "beech," appearing in Old Norse *bōk,* Old High German *buohha* (whence Modern German *buche* = "beech"), Middle Dutch *boeke,* and Old English *bēce,* all meaning "beech." The Old English word became Modern English BEECH.

3.   The Germanic word *bōks* = "piece of writing," with plural *bōkiz* = "collection of writings, written document," appears in Old Norse *bōk,* Old High German *buoh* (whence Modern German *buch* = "book"), Old Frisian *bōk,* and Old English *bōc,* all meaning "written document, book."

The form of this Germanic word and its various forms in the individual languages strongly suggest that it is the same word as the word for "beech." It is therefore conjectured that the Germanic people of perhaps 200 B.C. used pieces of beechwood or possibly beech bark for writing on. No such documents have survived, but there is other evidence that the Germanic people used wooden—probably beech—staffs or sticks, on which they cut runic inscriptions (their alphabet of runes was modeled on the Etruscan alphabet). The German word *buchstabe* = "letter of the alphabet" is from Old High German *buohstap* = "beech staff." Probably, therefore, the conjecture is correct, and our word for "book" goes back to the very beginnings of writing in northwestern Europe.

By the early Middle Ages (say, eighth century A.D.), the Germanic peoples had adopted the Latin alphabet and the *codex,* or bound volume of sheets made of animal skin, also of Latin origin. Old English *bōc* thus meant "written document, parchment volume"; it became Modern English BOOK.

4.   Latin *fāgus* = "beech" was adopted in scientific New Latin as the name of the genus of beeches; hence *Fagus silvatica,* the European beech, and *F. orientalis,* the eastern beech, as above.

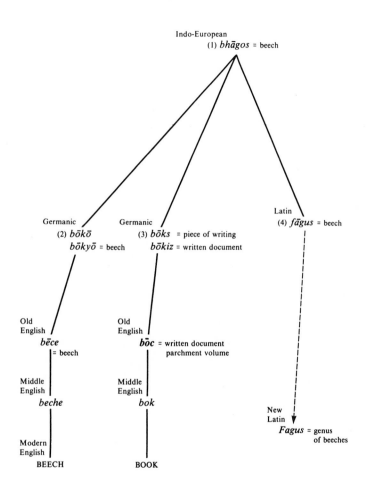

Indo-European
(1) *bhāgos* = beech

Germanic
(2) *bōkō*
bōkyō = beech

Germanic
(3) *bōks* = piece of writing
bōkiz = written document

Latin
(4) *fāgus* = beech

Old
English
bēce
= beech

Old
English
bōc = written document
parchment volume

Middle
English
beche

Middle
English
bok

Modern
English
BEECH

BOOK

New
Latin
Fagus = genus
of beeches

15

bher-

1. Indo-European *bher-* ="to carry" appears in Germanic *beran* ="carry," Old Irish *berim* ="take," Latin *ferre* ="carry," Old Slavic *bĭrati* ="take," Greek *pherein* ="carry," Armenian *berem* ="carry," Tocharian *pär-* = "carry," and Sanskrit *bhárati* ="carry."

This very basic word meant not only "carry" but also "bring forth offspring"; this is proved by the fact that many of the descendant words, including English BEAR itself, preserved both meanings.

2. Germanic *beran* =(a) "to carry" and (b) "to bring forth offspring" appears in Gothic *bairan,* Old Norse *bera,* Old High German *beran,* and Old English *beran.* The last became Modern English BEAR, with both of the original meanings still functioning fully.

3. Two other Germanic derivatives of the root are *barwōn* ="carrying frame, litter," and *burthinja* ="something carried, a load." These became Old English *bearwe* and *byrthen,* becoming Modern English (wheel)BARROW and BURDEN.

4. Two Germanic derivatives referring to procreation are *barnam* ="child" and *burthiz* ="the act or fact of childbearing, childbirth." *Barnam* appears in Gothic *barn,* Old Norse *barn,* Old High German *barn,* and Old English *bearn,* all meaning "child." Old English *bearn* survives in Scottish BAIRN. *Burthiz* appears in Gothic *ga-baurths* and Old Norse *byrdh,* both meaning "childbearing, nativity." Old Norse *byrdh* was borrowed into Middle English as *burth,* becoming Modern English BIRTH.

5. Latin *ferre* ="to carry, bring" had a large number of compounds and derivatives that yield English words, either by direct adoption or via French. Among them are *conferre* ="to bring together, contribute"; *differre* ="to carry apart, diverge"; *inferre* ="to bring in, make a logical deduction"; *offerre* ="to bring into the presence of, present as a sacrifice"; *referre* ="to bring back to, relate to"; *transferre* ="to carry across"; whence CONFER, DIFFER, INFER, OFFER, REFER, TRANSFER, as well as their derivatives CONFERENCE, DIFFERENT, etc.

6. The Latin adjective *fertilis* ="bringing forth, fruitful" (referring both to animals and plants, and to the earth) was adopted into English as FERTILE.

7. The Latin suffix *-fer* ="-bearing" occurs in adjectives such as *aurifer* = "gold-bearing," adopted into English as AURIFEROUS.

8. The equivalent Greek suffix *-phoros* ="-bearing" occurs in such compounds as *phōsphoros* ="light-bearing" (used of the evening star), which was adopted into New Latin (seventeenth century) as the name of the newly discovered element PHOSPHORUS (which shines in the dark). This suffix has been generalized to form new compounds such as French *sémaphore* (early nineteenth century)="signal-bearing system," borrowed into English as SEMAPHORE.

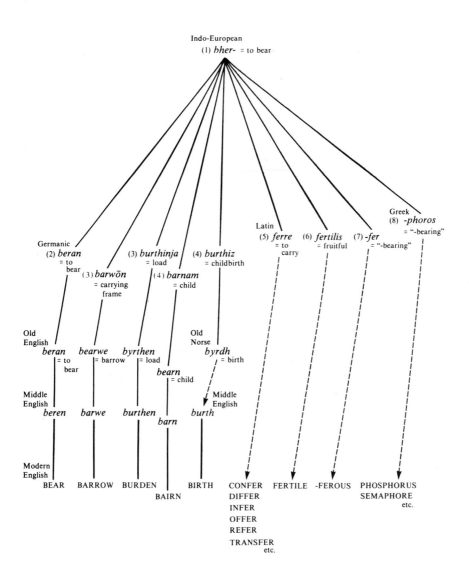

Indo-European
(1) *bher-* = to bear

Germanic
(2) *beran*
= to
bear

(3) *barwōn*
= carrying
frame

(3) *burthinja*
= load

(4) *barnam*
= child

(4) *burthiz*
= childbirth

Latin
(5) *ferre*
= to
carry

(6) *fertilis*
= fruitful

(7) *-fer*
= "-bearing"

Greek
(8) *-phoros*
= "-bearing"

Old
English
beran
= to
bear

bearwe
= barrow

byrthen
= load

bearn
= child

Old
Norse
byrdh
= birth

Middle
English
beren

barwe

burthen

barn

Middle
English
burth

Modern
English
BEAR

BARROW

BURDEN

BAIRN

BIRTH

CONFER
DIFFER
INFER
OFFER
REFER
TRANSFER
etc.

FERTILE

-FEROUS

PHOSPHORUS
SEMAPHORE
etc.

17

bhergh-

1. Indo-European *bhergh-* = "high" meant both physically high, as a hill, and also "exalted, high-ranking." It appears in Germanic *bergaz* = "hill, mountain," Middle Irish *brig* = "hill," Armenian *berj* = "height," Avestan *bərəzant-* = "high, hill," and Sanskrit *bṛhánt-* = "high, exalted."

2. Germanic *bergaz* appears in Old High German *berg,* Old Norse *berg,* Middle Dutch *berg,* and Old English *beorg,* all meaning "hill, mountain." Old English *beorg* meant both "hill, hillock" and "burial mound." It became Middle English *borewe,* Modern English BARROW, surviving only in (a) a few place-names, as Bull Barrow (= "hill") in Dorset, England, and (b) the local name in southwestern England for the numerous prehistoric burial mounds in Wiltshire and elsewhere. In sense (b) the word was picked up by archaeologists, who from the seventeenth century onward began to investigate the BARROWS, and has since been generalized to mean any burial mound of earth or stones. (It has no connection with *barrow* = "wheeled conveyance for loads".)

   Middle Dutch *berg* = "hill" was used by sailors in the compound noun *ijs-berg* = "ice-mountain," used of Arctic glaciers seen from the sea and then of detached sections of them floating in the sea. This was borrowed into English (eighteenth–nineteenth centuries) as ICEBERG.

3. Another Germanic derivative is *burgs* = "hill fort, fortified town." This appears in Gothic *baurgs* = "town, tower," Old High German *burg* = "castle," Old English *burg, burh* = "(fortified) town." The Old English word became Middle English *borowe, boroghe* = "town possessing a royal charter," Modern English BOROUGH. The word survives also in hundreds of place-names.

4. Germanic *burgs* was also borrowed into Late Latin as *burgus* = "fortified town." From this was formed *burgensis* = "townsperson," which was borrowed into Old French as *burgeis,* and thence into Middle English as *burgeis,* becoming Modern English BURGESS = "citizen of a town." Old French *burgeis* became Modern French *bourgeois* = "citizen of a French town, ranking midway between gentry and peasantry." This was borrowed into English as BOURGEOIS, given its sociopolitical value by nineteenth-century writers such as Marx.

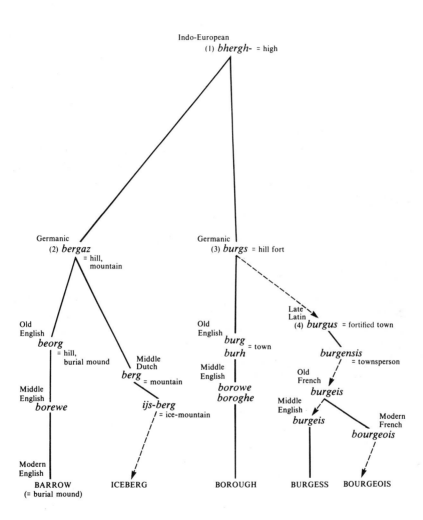

Indo-European
(1) *bhergh-* = high

Germanic
(2) *bergaz*
= hill,
mountain

Germanic
(3) *burgs* = hill fort

Old
English
beorg
= hill,
burial mound

Middle
Dutch
berg
= mountain

Old
English
burg
burh = town

Late
Latin
(4) *burgus* = fortified town

Middle
English
borewe

ijs-berg
= ice-mountain

Middle
English
borowe
boroghe

burgensis
= townsperson

Old
French
burgeis

Modern
English
BARROW
(= burial mound)

ICEBERG

BOROUGH

Middle
English
burgeis

Modern
French
bourgeois

BURGESS

BOURGEOIS

19

bhrāter

1. Indo-European *bhrāter* = "brother" appears in Germanic *brōthar*, Old Irish *brāthir*, Latin *frāter*, Old Slavic *bratrŭ*, Tocharian *prācar*, and Sanskrit *bhrā́tar*, all meaning "brother," and in Greek *phrātēr* = "member of a religious kin association."

   The original meaning of *bhrāter* was "clan member," rather than "sibling." In Indo-European social structure, the close-knit nuclear family (the two parents plus their children), which to us seems basic, was of relatively little importance. Their basic unit was a clan based on paternal kinship. Each of the males, whatever their individual blood relationships, was a *bhrāter*, equally subject to the clan chief, entitled *pəter*.

2. *Bhrāter* regularly became Germanic *brōthar*, which appears in Gothic *brōthar*, Old Norse *brōdhir*, Old High German *bruoder* (whence Modern German *bruder*), and Old English *brōthor*, all primarily meaning "male sibling," but also used more widely to mean "fellow-clansman, fellow-countryman," and "fellowman" in general. Old English *brōthor* became Modern English BROTHER.

3. Latin *frāter* also chiefly meant "male sibling." It also preserved vestiges of the Indo-European use, meaning "paternal first cousin" and "brother-in-law." In addition there were several religious cults in which members enrolled as *frātrēs* without necessarily being blood relations.

   The adjective of *frāter* was *frāternus* = "of or relating to a brother or brothers." This had a Medieval Latin extended form *frāternālis*, which was adopted into Middle English as FRATERNAL. The Medieval Latin noun *frāternitās* = (a) "the condition of being brothers" and (b) "a brotherhood" was adopted as Middle English *fraternite*, becoming Modern English FRATERNITY. This word, already in the late Middle Ages, was used not only of religious brotherhoods but also of trade associations such as guilds. The American idea of associations of university men was started in the late eighteenth century.

4. Latin *frāter* was inherited in Old French as *frere*. This was used especially of the members of the mendicant orders founded in the later Middle Ages—Augustinians, Franciscans, etc. It was borrowed into Middle English as *frere*, later becoming FRIAR.

5. The Gypsy people, originating in India and speaking an Indic language (Romany) derived from Sanskrit, began to arrive in Europe in the fourteenth and fifteenth centuries. Sanskrit *bhrā́tar* = "brother" was inherited in Romany as *pral* = "brother" (the form is recorded in the Turkish dialect of Romany). In English Romany the word became *pal*, which was adopted into the "cant" language of thieves and vagabonds, with whom Gypsies inevitably associated. PAL is first recorded in English cant in 1672, meaning "brother, friend, mate"; in the nineteenth century it became familiar in regular English slang.

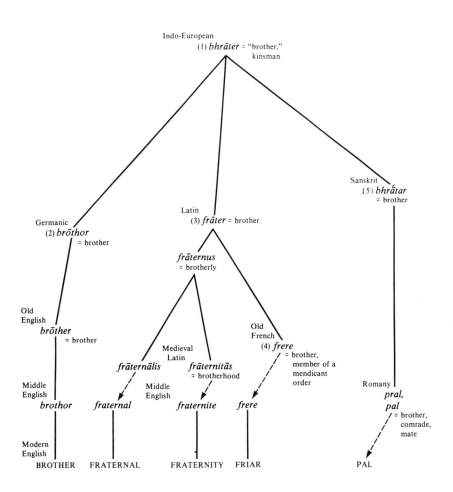

Indo-European
(1) *bhrāter* = "brother," kinsman

Sanskrit
(5) *bhrā́tar* = brother

Latin
(3) *frāter* = brother

Germanic
(2) *brōthor* = brother

frāternus = brotherly

Old English
brōther = brother

Old French
(4) *frere* = brother, member of a mendicant order

Medieval Latin
frāternālis

frāternitās = brotherhood

Middle English
brothor

Middle English
fraternal

fraternite

frere

Romany
pral, pal = brother, comrade, mate

Modern English
BROTHER   FRATERNAL   FRATERNITY   FRIAR   PAL

21

bhreg-

1. The Indo-European root *bhreg-* = "to break" appears only in Germanic *brekan* and Latin *frangere,* but there is a variant root form *bheg-,* also meaning "to break," which is found in Celtic, Armenian, and Sanskrit.

2. Germanic *brekan* appears in Gothic *brikan,* Old High German *brehhan,* Old Frisian *breka,* and Old English *brecan,* all meaning "to break." The last became Middle English *breken,* Modern English BREAK.

From Old High German *brehhan* was formed the noun *brehha, brecha* = "a breaking, a break." This was borrowed into Old French as *breche,* which in turn was borrowed into Middle English as *breche* = "breaking of anything, breaking of a law," Modern English BREACH.

3. The *n* in Latin *frangere* = "to break" is the "nasal infix" marking the present tense. The underlying stem is *frag-* or *frac-,* as in Latin *fractus* = "broken," *fragmentum* = "piece broken off," *fragilis* = "breakable."

From *fractus* were formed *fractiō* = "a breaking" and *fractūra* = "a breaking," adopted into Old French as *fraction* and *fracture,* and thence into (Middle) English as FRACTION and FRACTURE, each still expressing a somewhat different range of the concept "a breaking."

Latin *fragmentum* = "piece broken off" was adopted as (Middle) English FRAGMENT.

Latin *fragilis* = "breakable" became Old French *fraile,* which was borrowed into Middle English as FRAIL = "physically or spiritually weak." Latin *fragilis* was also adopted direct (seventeenth century—first used by Shakespeare) as FRAGILE, keeping the original sense of "breakable."

22

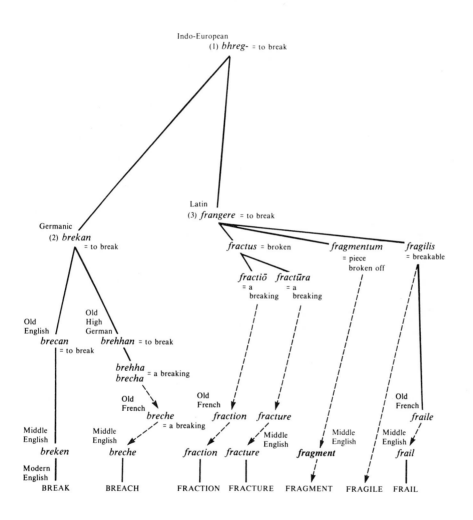

Indo-European
(1) *bhreg-* = to break

Germanic
(2) *brekan*
    = to break

Latin
(3) *frangere* = to break

fractus = broken   *fragmentum*   *fragilis*
                        = piece   = breakable
                        broken off

fractiō *fractūra*
= a   = a
breaking   breaking

Old English
brecan
= to break

Old High German
brehhan = to break

brehha
brecha = a breaking

Old French
breche = a breaking

Old French
fraction *fracture*

Old French
fraile

Middle English
breken

Middle English
breche

Middle English
fraction *fracture*

Middle English
fragment

Middle English
frail

Modern English
BREAK

BREACH

FRACTION FRACTURE FRAGMENT FRAGILE FRAIL

23

deiwos

1.   Indo-European *deiwos* ="god" appears in Germanic *Tiwaz* ="war god," Old Irish *dia* ="god," Latin *divus* ="divine, god" and *deus* ="god," Lithuanian *diēvas* ="god," and Sanskrit *dēvas* ="god."

The adjective/noun *deiwos* is formed from the verb root *deiw-* ="to shine." *Deiwos* therefore meant "shining, belonging to the bright sky." To the Indo-Europeans, the gods inhabited the upper air and were called "they of the sky," while humans were called "earthlings." *Deiwos* was both the general word for a god and specifically the name of the chief of the gods, who personified the bright or cloudy sky, controlled the weather, and wielded the lightning and thunderbolt. A variant form of the name *Deiwos* was *Dyeus;* the form of address to him used in prayer was *Dyeu-pəter,* which can be translated "O Sky-father!" (*See* **pəter**.)

2.   Indo-European *deiwos,* with regular sound-change of /d/ to /t/, became Germanic *Tiwaz,* sky god and war god. In the first century A.D. the Roman historian Tacitus regarded *Tiwaz* as the German equivalent of Mars, the Roman war god.

At some time between A.D. 100 and 400, the Germanic peoples, strongly influenced by the culture of the Roman Empire, adopted the Roman seven-day week, translating the Latin day-names. The third weekday was called in Latin *Martis diēs* ="Mars's day." This was accordingly translated as "Tiwaz's day" in the various Germanic dialects, which by then were splitting, or had already split, into separate languages.

Germanic *Tiwaz* appears in Old Norse as *Týr,* in Old High German as *Zio,* and in Old English as *Tiw.* "Tiwaz's day" was thus rendered as Old Norse *Týrsdagr,* Old High German *Ziestag,* and Old English *Tiwes-dæg.* The last became Modern English TUESDAY.

(In the German mythology of the early Middle Ages, Woden, originally god of the dead, had become the war god and had also taken over as chief of the gods. *Tiwaz* had become a secondary figure.)

3.   Latin *divus* ="of the gods," also "a god," had an adjectival form *divinus* ="of or relating to a god or gods." This was adopted into Old French as *divin,* which was borrowed into Middle English as *divin,* becoming Modern English DIVINE.

4.   Formed from Latin *deus* ="a god" was *deitās* ="godhead, divinity," also "a god." This was adopted into Old French as *deite,* which was borrowed into Middle English as *deite,* later DEITY.

5.   The Indo-European variant form *Dyeus* was inherited in Greek as *Zeus,* name of the chief of the Olympian gods; whence English ZEUS. He was addressed in Greek as *Zeu pater* ="O Zeus father!" exactly reproducing the Indo-European vocative *Dyeu-pəter.*

Dyeu-pəter was inherited in Sanskrit as *Dyāuh-pitā* ="Heaven-father," and in Latin as *Jūpiter,* chief of the Roman gods; whence English JUPITER. Both he and Zeus retained the original attributes of the Indo-European weather god, bringing rain and wielding the thunderbolt.

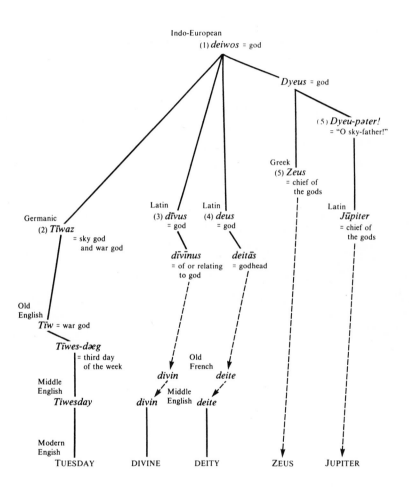

Indo-European
(1) *deiwos* = god

Dyeus = god

(5) *Dyeu-pəter!*
= "O sky-father!"

Germanic
(2) *Tīwaz*
= sky god
and war god

Latin
(3) *dīvus*
= god

Latin
(4) *deus*
= god

Greek
(5) *Zeus*
= chief of
the gods

Latin
Jūpiter
= chief of
the gods

dīvīnus
= of or relating
to god

deitās
= godhead

Old
English
Tīw = war god

Tiwes-dæg
= third day
of the week

Old
French
divin

deite

Middle
English
Tiwesday

divin

Middle
English *deite*

Modern
Engish
TUESDAY

DIVINE

DEITY

ZEUS

JUPITER

25

dekm

1. Indo-European *dekm* = "ten" appears in Germanic *tehun*, Old Irish *deich*, Latin *decem*, Greek *deka*, and Sanskrit *dásá*, all meaning "ten."

2. *Dekm* became Germanic *tehun*, with regular change of *d* to *t* and of *k* to *h*. *Tehun* appears in Gothic *taihun*, Old Norse *tiu*, Old High German *zehan* (whence modern German *zehn*), and Old English *tien*, all meaning "ten." *Tien* became Modern English TEN.

   Germanic *tehun* also appears as a suffix in Old English *thrēotīene* = "thirteen," *fēowertīene* = "fourteen," etc., becoming Modern English THIRTEEN, FOURTEEN, etc.

   Also related is the Germanic suffix *-tig* = "times ten," as in Old English *twentig* = "twenty," *thrītig* = "thirty," etc., becoming Modern English TWENTY, THIRTY, etc.

3. The ordinal adjective of Latin *decem* was *decimus* = "tenth." From this was formed the New Latin (seventeenth-century) word *decimalis* = "based on ten"; adopted into English as DECIMAL.

   In the original Roman calendar, in which March was the first month, the last month was named *December* = "tenth month." Later, January and February were added before March, but the name *December*, although no longer appropriate to the twelfth month, was never changed. It was adopted into Middle English as *Decembre*, Modern English DECEMBER.

4. From Greek *deka* = "ten" was formed the noun *dekas, dekad-* = "group of ten." This was adopted into Late Latin as *decas, decad-* = "period of ten years," and thence into English as DECADE.

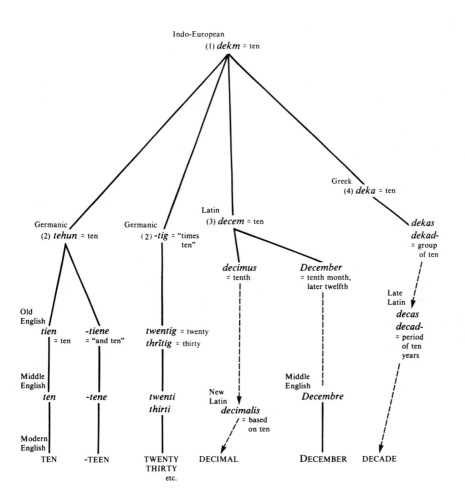

Indo-European
(1) *dekm* = ten

Greek
(4) *deka* = ten

Germanic
(2) *tehun* = ten

Germanic
(2) *-tig* = "times ten"

Latin
(3) *decem* = ten

dekas
dekad-
= group of ten

decimus
= tenth

December
= tenth month, later twelfth

Late Latin
decas
decad-
= period of ten years

Old English
tien
= ten

-tiene
= "and ten"

twentig = twenty
thrītig = thirty

Middle English
ten

-tene

twenti
thirti

New Latin
decimalis
= based on ten

Middle English
Decembre

Modern English
TEN

=TEEN

TWENTY
THIRTY
etc.

DECIMAL

DECEMBER

DECADE

27

demə-

1. The Indo-European word *demə-* ="to tame" appears in Germanic *tamjan* ="to tame" and *tamaz* (adjective) "tame," Old Irish *damnaim* ="I tame," Latin *domāre* ="to tame," and Sanskrit *dāmyati* ="is tame, tames."

This is originally a technical verb referring to highly significant Indo-European activities: the "breaking" and training of horses and the controlling of semiwild cattle. It was also extended to mean "subdue, overcome an enemy." In Homer the word *hippo-damos* ="horse-taming" is a frequent epithet of heroes. In the *Mahabharata* the word *arim-dama* = "enemy-taming, keeping one's enemies under control." Both horse-training and enemy-subduing were the proper and prestigious pursuits of the Indo-European warrior caste.

2. *Demə-* appears in the Germanic adjective *tamaz* ="tame," with regular change of *d* to *t*. This appears in Old High German *zam,* Old Norse *tamr,* and Old English *tam,* which became Modern English TAME (adjective).

3. Latin *domāre* ="to tame, subdue" had a "frequentative" form *domitāre,* also meaning "to tame, subdue." This was inherited in Old French as *danter* ="subdue," which was borrowed into Middle English as *daunten* = "subdue." The word later acquired the figurative meaning "subdue the spirit of, intimidate"; whence Modern English DAUNT.

Latin *domitāre* also formed a Late Latin adjective *indomitābilis* = "untamable, invincible," which was adopted into English as INDOMITABLE.

4. The post-Homeric Greek word *adamant-* ="hard metal, steel" appears to mean "invincible," from *a-* ="un-" + *dam-* ="to tame" (as in *damnāsthai* ="to tame"). Since the word refers to what was then a new substance, produced by a new technology (i.e., smelting steel), it may in fact be a borrowed foreign word, reshaped so as to "make sense" in Greek. In any case, *adamant-* was perceived as meaning "indestructibly hard, the hardest of all substances," and was applied, in Latin and Greek, to various hard crystals and gemstones.

In Latin, by coincidence, *adamant-* can also be the present participle of the verb *adamāre* ="to love, have a liking for, seek after." The word *adamant-* thus seemed to contain the meaning "seeking after," and acquired associations with the lodestone or magnet. In the alchemy and pseudoscience of the Middle Ages, the *adamant-* was a semimagical stone or substance both indestructibly hard and magnetic, as well as having other marvelous properties. It was adopted into Old French as *adamaunt,* whence Modern English ADAMANT, now chiefly used in its restored sense of "unyielding."

From Latin *adamant-* there appeared a Late Latin variant *diamant-,* "very hard gemstone," later "diamond," whence Old French *diamaunt,* Middle English *diamant,* Modern English DIAMOND.

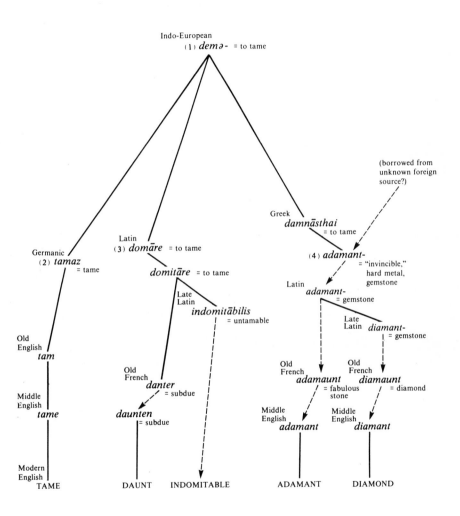

Indo-European
(1) *demə-* = to tame

(borrowed from
unknown foreign
source?)

Greek
damnāsthai
= to tame

Latin
(3) *domāre* = to tame

(4) *adamant-*
= "invincible,"
hard metal,
gemstone

Germanic
(2) *tamaz*
= tame

domitāre = to tame

Latin
adamant-
= gemstone

Late
Latin
indomitābilis
= untamable

Late
Latin
diamant-
= gemstone

Old
English
tam

Old
French
danter
= subdue

Old
French
adamaunt
= fabulous
stone

Old
French
diamaunt
= diamond

Middle
English
tame

Old
French
daunten
= subdue

Middle
English
adamant

Middle
English
diamant

Modern
English
TAME

DAUNT

INDOMITABLE

ADAMANT

DIAMOND

29

dent-

1. Indo-European *dent-* or *dont-* ="tooth" appears in Germanic *tanthuz,* Old Irish *det,* Latin *dent-,* Greek *odont-,* Lithuanian *dent-,* and Sanskrit *dant-,* all meaning "tooth."

   The existence of two forms of the root, containing the vowels *e* and *o,* is a typical Indo-European system of forming inflections and variants. The "basic" form *dent-* appears in Latin *dent-,* while the "o-grade" form *dont-* appears in Germanic *tanthuz.* All of the sound-changes from *dont-* to Germanic *tanth-* are regular: Indo-European /d/ always became Germanic /t/, /o/ always became /a/, /n/ was always retained, /t/ always changed to /th/.

2. Germanic *tanthuz* appears in Old High German *zan,* Old Norse *tonn,* Old Frisian *tōth,* and Old English *tōth,* all meaning "tooth."

   In some of the Germanic languages, the plural of this and other nouns came to be formed by internal vowel change. Old High German *zan* had plural *zeni* (whence Modern German *zahn, zähne*), Old Norse *tonn* had plural *tenn,* Old Frisian and Old English *tōth* had plural *tēth.* Old English *tō th, tēth* became Modern English TOOTH, TEETH.

3. Latin *dent-* (nominative singular *dens*)="tooth" was inherited into Old French and Modern French as *dent*="tooth." From this were formed the adjective *dental* (early sixteenth century)="relating to teeth," and the noun *dentiste* (eighteenth century)="tooth doctor." They were borrowed into English as DENTAL and DENTIST.

4. Greek *odont-* (nominative singular *odōn*) was used to form the New Latin noun *orthodontia* ="corrective dentistry" (*ortho-* from Greek *orthos* = "straight, correct"). This is the source of English ORTHODONTICS.

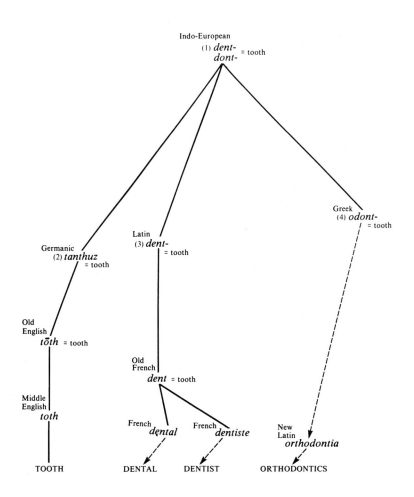

Indo-European
(1) *dent-*
dont- = tooth

Greek
(4) *odont-* = tooth

Latin
(3) *dent-* = tooth

Germanic
(2) *tanthuz* = tooth

Old
English
tōth = tooth

Old
French
dent = tooth

Middle
English
toth

French
dental

French
dentiste

New
Latin
orthodontia

TOOTH   DENTAL   DENTIST   ORTHODONTICS

31

dhwer-

1. The Indo-European noun *dhwer-* = "door" appears in Germanic *dur-*, Old Irish *dor*, Albanian *derë*, Lithuanian *durìs*, Old Slavic *dvĭri*, Greek *thura*, and Sanskrit *dvā́ras*, all meaning "door, gate."

The noun *dhwer-*, with its variant form *dhwor-*, referred particularly to the entrance to a house, including the gate in the enclosure surrounding the house. It was much used in the plural, and in adverbial expressions such as *dhworans* = "(going) out of doors" and *dhworois* = "(situated) out of doors." These appear in Latin as the adverbs *forās* = "(toward) outside" and *foris* = "(situated) outside."

2. In Germanic the word occurs in plural forms such as *duruns* and in singular forms such as *duram*, appearing in Gothic *daur*, Old High German *turi* and *tor*, and Old English *duru* and *dor*. The two Old English nouns survived as separate words in Middle English, *dur* and *dore*, both meaning "door"; in the sixteenth century they were combined as the single word DOOR.

3. Old French *forain* = "alien, from abroad," is assumed to be descended from a Latin adjective *forānus*, which has not been recorded but would be a natural derivative of the adverb *forās* = "outside." Old French *forain* was borrowed into Middle English as *forein, forren* = "alien, from abroad." The sixteenth-century spelling FOREIGN, somehow suggested by analogy with *sovereign*, became the standard spelling without affecting pronunciation.

4. The early medieval Latin term *silva forestis* meant "the outside woodlands" (*silva* = "woods"). It apparently referred to tracts of semiwilderness that were reserved for the king's hunting. The word *forestis* seems to have meant "outside, unenclosed," as opposed to enclosed parklands; it is therefore derived from the Latin adverb *foris* = "outside."

(Silva) forestis was adopted into Old French as *forest* and thence into Middle English as *forest*. It remained a legal term for royal game reserves such as the New Forest in Hampshire, but came to mean "thickly wooded land" in general, as in Modern English FOREST.

5. Another Indo-European derivative of the root was the noun *dhworom* = "forecourt, enclosure in front of a house (i.e., the place where the main entrance was)." This became Latin *forum*, originally meaning "enclosure," especially "forecourt or vestibule of a tomb," and later "marketplace." As the marketplace became the place of public business in Roman towns, the word *forum* rose in status, as seen above all in the *Forum Rōmānum*, the political nerve center of the city of Rome and of the empire. It was thus adopted into (Middle) English as FORUM. Its adjective *forensis* = "relating to public speaking or legal pleading" was adopted as FORENSIC = "relating to law courts or jurisprudence."

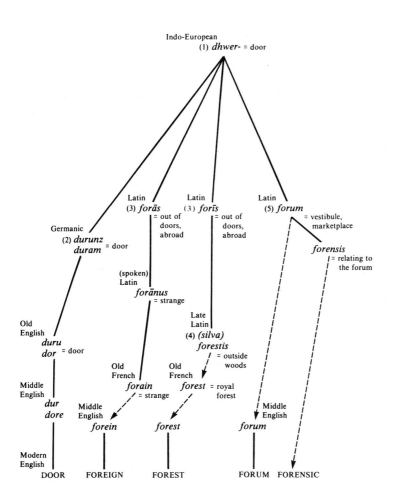

Indo-European
(1) *dhwer-* = door

Latin
(3) *forās*
= out of doors, abroad

Latin
(3) *forīs*
= out of doors, abroad

Latin
(5) *forum*
= vestibule, marketplace

forensis
= relating to the forum

Germanic
(2) *durunz*
duram = door

(spoken) Latin
forānus
= strange

Old English
duru
dor = door

Late Latin
(4) *(silva)*
forestis
= outside woods

Old French
forain
= strange

Old French
forest = royal forest

Middle English
dur
dore

Middle English
forein

Middle English
forest

Middle English
forum

Modern English
DOOR   FOREIGN   FOREST   FORUM   FORENSIC

33

dwō (I)

1. Indo-European *dwō*, also *duwo, du-*, ="two" appears in Germanic *twai*, Old Irish *dāu*, Latin *duo*, Lithuanian *dù*, Old Slavic *dǔwa*, Greek *duō*, and Sanskrit *dváu*, all meaning "two."

2. Germanic *twai* (with the regular change of *d* to *t*) appears in Gothic *twai*, Old Norse *tueir*, Old High German *zwei* (whence modern German *zwei*), and Old English *twegen* (masculine), *twā* (feminine), and *tū* (neuter). The masculine form survives as the now archaic word TWAIN, while the feminine form became the basic form of the numeral, Middle English *twa*, Modern English TWO. (The pronunciation changed from /twā/ to /twū/, and then the consonant *w* was eliminated because of its similarity to the following vowel *ū;* but the spelling was [illogically] standardized as TWO.)

3. In Indo-European languages generally, the numbers *eleven, twelve, thirteen,* etc., were formed from words meaning *one-and-ten, two-and-ten, three-and-ten,* etc. (e.g., Latin, see paragraph 5, below). In Germanic, for reasons unknown, the words for *eleven* and *twelve* (but no others) were formed on an entirely different principle: they were *ain-lif* and *twa-lif* = "one-left" and "two-left," respectively (*lif-* = "leave, left"), evidently meaning "one left over after ten," and "two left over after ten." Germanic *twa-lif* appears in Gothic *twalif*, Old Norse *tolf*, Old High German *zwelif*, and Old English *twelf*, all meaning "twelve." Old English *twelf* became Modern English TWELVE.

4. Latin *duo* = "two," in its feminine form *duae*, was inherited in Old French as *deus* = "two" (Modern French *deux*). *Deus* was borrowed into Middle English (fifteenth century) as DEUCE = "two at cards."

Latin *duo* was also inherited in Italian as *due* = "two." Formed from this was the noun *duetto* = "pair of musicians," borrowed into English in the eighteenth century, with much other Italian musical vocabulary, as DUET.

Latin *duālis* = "relating to two" was adopted in the seventeenth century as DUAL.

5. Latin *duodecim* = "twelve" (*decem* = "ten") was inherited in Old French as *doze*, from which came the noun *dozeine* = "group or batch of twelve." This was borrowed into Middle English as *dozein*, becoming Modern English DOZEN.

6. From the form *du-*, with two different suffixes, are the Latin adjectives *duplus* and *duplex*, both meaning "twofold." *Duplus* was inherited in Old French as *doble*, borrowed into Middle English, becoming Modern English DOUBLE.

From *duplex, duplic-* a verb *duplicāre* = "to make double" was formed, adopted into English as DUPLICATE. *Duplex* itself was adopted in the nineteenth century as DUPLEX.

34

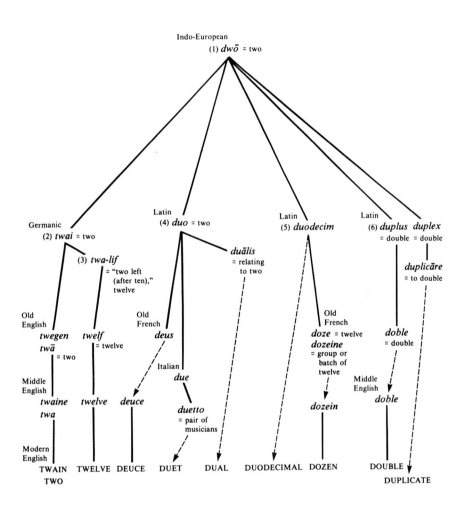

Indo-European
(1) *dwō* = two

Germanic
(2) *twai* = two

(3) *twa-lif*
= "two left
(after ten),"
twelve

Latin
(4) *duo* = two

duālis
= relating
to two

Latin
(5) *duodecim*

Latin
(6) *duplus duplex*
= double = double

duplicāre
= to double

Old
English
twegen
twā
= two

twelf
= twelve

Old
French
deus

Old
French
doze = twelve
dozeine
= group or
batch of
twelve

doble
= double

Middle
English
twaine
twa

twelve

deuce

Italian
due

duetto
= pair of
musicians

dozein

Middle
English
doble

Modern
English
TWAIN
TWO

TWELVE

DEUCE

DUET

DUAL

DUODECIMAL

DOZEN

DOUBLE

DUPLICATE

35

dwō (II)

A variant form of *dwō* was *dwi,* from which the adverb *dwis* = "twice" and the adjective *dwisnos* = "double" were formed.

1. Indo-European *dwi, dwis* appear in Germanic *twiyes,* Latin *bis, bi-,* Lithuanian *dvi,* Greek *dis, di-,* and Sanskrit *dvi-,* all meaning "two" or "twice."

2. Germanic *twiyes* appears in Old Frisian *twîa* and Old English *twige,* both meaning "twice." The latter was given the extra adverbial suffix *-s* (as in *nights* = "at night"), becoming *twiges,* Modern English TWICE.

3. Germanic *twegentig* = "two tens" (*-tig* = "ten") appears in Old High German *zweinzug* (Modern German *zwanzig*), Old Frisian *twintich,* and Old English *twentig,* all meaning "twenty." The last became Modern English TWENTY.

4. From Germanic *twihna* = "a pair" came the preposition *bi-twihna* = "in the middle of two things," appearing in Old English *betweonum,* Modern English BETWEEN.

Closely related was Germanic *twihnaz* = "double thread," appearing in Old Norse *tvinni* and Old English *twin,* both meaning "thread." The latter became Modern English TWINE.

5. Indo-European *dwi* became Latin *bi-,* with regular change of Indo-European *dw* to Latin *b.* Latin compounds such as *biennis* = "lasting two years" (*-ennis* from *annus* = "year") have been adopted into English: BIENNIAL. The prefix itself has also been adopted, forming new compounds such as BIFOCAL, BICARBONATE.

6. Indo-European *dwi* became Greek *di-,* used in compounds such as *dilemma* = "double (i.e., ambiguous) assumption" (*lemma* = "assumption, proposition"), adopted into English as DILEMMA. This prefix, too, has become an active one in English, forming such words as DICHLORIDE.

7. Indo-European *dwisnos* = "double" appears in Germanic *twisnaz* = "double," Latin *bīnī* = "two together," and Lithuanian *dvynu* = "twins."

Germanic *twisnaz* appears in Old Norse *tvinnr* and Old English *twinn,* both meaning "double." The latter became Modern English TWIN. This word does not seem to have been used of "two children born at a birth" until the sixteenth century.

Formed from Latin *bīnī* = "two together" was the Late Latin adjective *bīnārius* = "composed of two, based on two." This was adopted as BINARY. Also from Latin *bīnī* was the verb *combīnāre* = "to join two together" (*com-* = "together"), adopted as COMBINE.

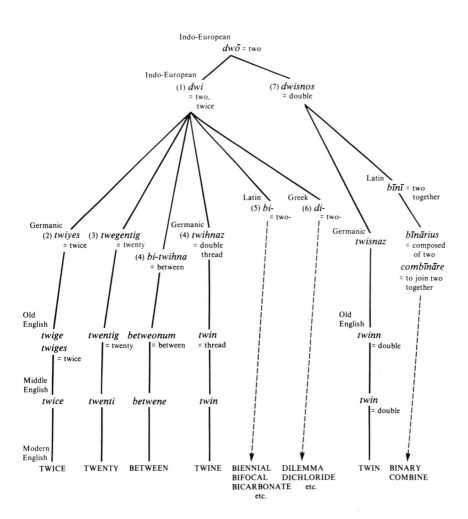

Indo-European
dwō = two

Indo-European
(1) *dwi*
= two,
twice

(7) *dwisnos*
= double

Germanic
(2) *twiyes*
= twice

(3) *twegentig*
= twenty

Germanic
(4) *twihnaz*
= double
thread

(4) *bi-twihna*
= between

Latin
(5) *bi-*
= two-

Greek
(6) *di-*
= two-

Latin
bīnī = two
together

Germanic
twisnaz

bīnārius
= composed
of two

combīnāre
= to join two
together

Old
English

twige
twiges
= twice

twentig
= twenty

betweonum
= between

twin
= thread

Old
English

twinn
= double

Middle
English

twice

twenti

betwene

twin

twin
= double

Modern
English

TWICE

TWENTY

BETWEEN

TWINE

BIENNIAL
BIFOCAL
BICARBONATE
etc.

DILEMMA
DICHLORIDE
etc.

TWIN

BINARY
COMBINE

37

ed-

1. Indo-European *ed-* = "eat" appears in Germanic *etan,* Irish *ith,* Latin *edere,* Lithuanian *edmi,* Greek *edein,* Sanskrit *admi,* all meaning "eat," and in Hittite *etir* = "they ate."

2. Germanic *etan* appears in Gothic *itan,* Old High German *ezzan* (Modern German *essen*), Old Norse *eta,* and Old English *etan,* all meaning "eat." *Etan* became Modern English EAT.

From Germanic *etan* was formed the causative verb *atjan* = "to cause to eat, to feed." This appears in Old High German *esjan,* becoming Modern German *ätzen* = "to eat away, corrode, etch." This was borrowed into Dutch as *etsen* and thence into English (seventeenth century) as ETCH.

3. Latin *edere* formed the Late Latin adjective *edibilis* = "eatable, fit to be eaten," adopted into English as EDIBLE.

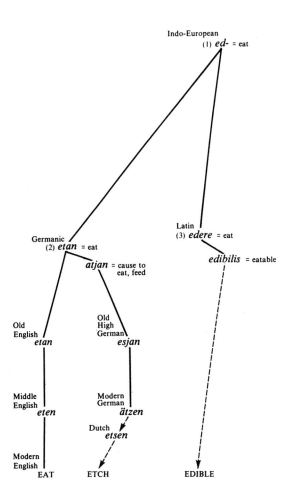

Indo-European
(1) *ed-* = eat

Germanic
(2) *etan* = eat

atjan = cause to
eat, feed

Latin
(3) *edere* = eat

edibilis = eatable

Old
English
etan

Old
High
German
esjan

Middle
English
eten

Modern
German
ätzen

Dutch
etsen

Modern
English
EAT

ETCH

EDIBLE

39

eg/me

1. Already at the earliest reachable Indo-European period, the pronoun of the first person singular was rendered by two unrelated roots; this situation has generally been inherited by the descendant languages, including English, down to our own time.

"I" was Indo-European *eg* or *ego;* "me" was Indo-European *me* or *mē.*

Indo-European *eg, ego* appears in Germanic *ek,* Latin *ego,* Lithuanian *eo,* Old Slavic *azŭ,* Greek *egō,* Hittite *uk,* Armenian *es,* and Sanskrit *ahám,* all meaning "I."

2. Germanic *ek* appears in Gothic *ik,* Old Norse *ek,* Old High German *ih* (whence Modern German *ich*), Old Frisian *ik,* and Old English *ic,* all meaning "I." Old English *ic* became Middle English *ic,* beginning to drop the *c* in the twelfth century, to become Modern English I.

3. Latin *ego* was used in the eighteenth century to form the word EGOTISM = "self-centeredness"; and *ego* itself was adopted in the nineteenth century as English EGO, a term for the self-conscious self used first in philosophy and then in psychology.

4. Indo-European *me, mē* had different inflected forms for the accusative, genitive, dative, and other cases of the pronoun, not fundamentally affecting English. It appears in Germanic *me, mē,* Old Irish *mé* = "I," Latin *mē,* Old Slavic *me,* Greek *me, eme,* and Sanskrit *mā,* all (except the Old Irish form) meaning "me."

5. Germanic *me* appears in Gothic *mik,* Old Norse *mik,* Old High German *mik* (becoming Modern German *mich*), and Old English *me, mē,* all meaning "me" (accusative case). In Old English the dative case was also *me, mē;* these coalesced in Middle English to become the all-purpose form ME, which in Modern English (unlike, for example, German) stands for all of the cases except the nominative (I).

6. Several possessive adjectives were formed from Indo-European *me,* including *meinos* = "my." This appears in Germanic *mīnaz* and Lithuanian *manas,* both meaning "my." Germanic *mīnaz* appears in Gothic *meins,* Old Norse *mínn,* Old High German *min* (whence Modern German *mein*), and Old English *mīn,* all meaning "my." From the twelfth century the *n* of Old English *mīn* began to be dropped before a following consonant: *mine enemy,* but *my friend.* Subsequently MY became the primary form of the possessive adjective, while MINE has been retained for predicative position, as in *This house is mine,* and in absolute uses, as in *That is his house; this is mine.*

7. Another possessive adjective from *me* was *meyos.* This appears in Latin *meus* and Hittite *mes,* both meaning "my." The Latin feminine form *mea* was inherited in Old French as *ma.* The Old French form of address *ma dame* = "my lady" was adopted into Middle English as *madame,* later MADAM.

40

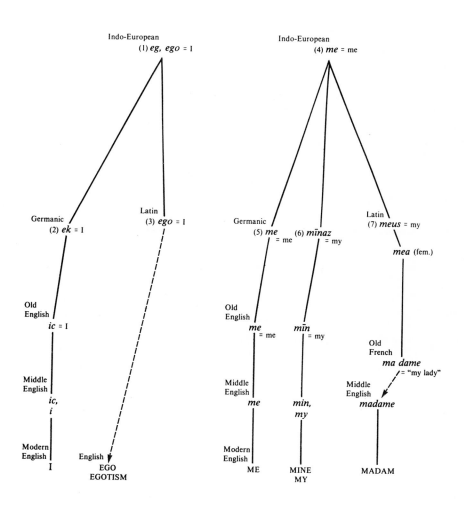

Indo-European
(1) *eg, ego* = I

Indo-European
(4) *me* = me

Germanic
(2) *ek* = I

Latin
(3) *ego* = I

Germanic
(5) *me* = me

(6) *mīnaz* = my

Latin
(7) *meus* = my

mea (fem.)

Old
English
ic = I

Old
English
me = me

mīn = my

Old
French
ma dame
= "my lady"

Middle
English
*ic,
i*

Middle
English
me

*min,
my*

Middle
English
madame

Modern
English
I

English
EGO
EGOTISM

Modern
English
ME

MINE
MY

MADAM

41

ekwos

1. The Indo-European word *ekwos* = "horse" appears in Germanic *ihwaz*, Old Irish *ech*, Latin *equus*, Lithuanian *asva*, Greek *hippos*, Tocharian *yakwe*, Avestan *aspa-*, and Sanskrit *asvah*, all meaning "horse."

The horse, which no longer exists as a genuinely wild animal, was native to the north-central parts of the Eurasian continent, including the grassland plains of southern Russia and Kazakhstan. In settlements of the Early Kurgan people (probably the original Indo-Europeans) in the Ukraine *c.* 4400 B.C., large quantities of horse bones have been found, clearly indicating that the animal was herded and eaten. These are the first known remains of the horse in any state of domestication. Stone horsehead figurines have also been found in Early Kurgan sites.

Much of the subsequent history of the Indo-European–speaking peoples, and their vast expansions into the Middle East, Europe, and even the Americas, is bound up with horse-breeding, horsemanship, and horse worship. The origin of riding remains obscure, but the Indo-Europeans were probably the first to harness horses to wheeled vehicles (*see* **kwekwlos** = "wheel" and **wegh-** = "to travel, carry by vehicle")—probably before 3000 B.C. From 2000 B.C., aggressive aristocracies of horse-loving Indo-European warriors were establishing themselves throughout the Middle East, the chariot-driving Aryans were on their way to India, and the Mycenaeans were bringing horses to Greece. Horse burials are found wherever the Indo-Europeans have spread, from Scandinavia to Turkestan.

2. *Ekwos* became Germanic *ihwaz*, with regular change of Indo-European *k* to Germanic *h*. Ihwaz appears in Gothic *aihwa-*, Old Norse *ior*, Old Saxon *ehu-*, and Old English *eoh*, all meaning "horse."

The Old English word *eoh* died out completely, being replaced by the unrelated Germanic word *horse*. The philologist-novelist J.R.R. Tolkien in *The Lord of the Rings* amused himself by using the Old English word *eoh* in some of the names of the royal family of the horse-loving people of Rohan: the name *Eowyn* (a princess) would mean "horse-friend" in Old English.

3. *Ekwos* became Latin *equus* = "horse," whence the adjective *equinus* = "like a horse, relating to horses," adopted into English as EQUINE. Also from Latin *equus* was the noun *equester* = "horseman, knight," which was adopted as EQUESTRIAN. Latin *equus* has also been used in scientific New Latin as the name of the genus of horses, *Equus*.

4. *Ekwos* became Greek *hippos* = "horse." When the Greeks heard of a large river-living animal in Egypt, they called it *hippos potamios*, later *hippopotamos* = "river-horse" (*potamos* = "river"). This was adopted into Latin as *hippopotamus* and thence into English as HIPPOPOTAMUS.

Greek *hippos* has also been used in New Latin to form the name *Eohippus* = "dawn-horse" (Greek *eos* = "dawn"), the name of the genus of the ancestor of horses, asses, and zebras.

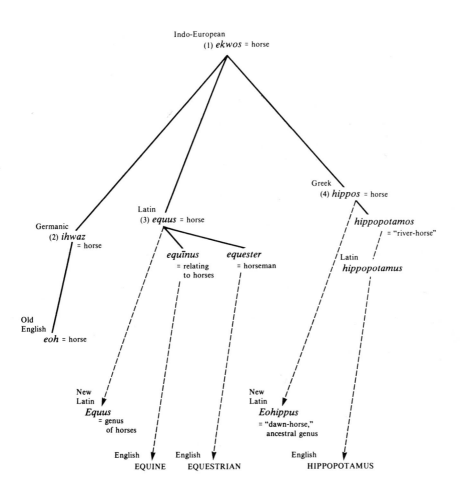

Indo-European
(1) *ekwos* = horse

Germanic
(2) *ihwaz*
= horse

Latin
(3) *equus* = horse

Greek
(4) *hippos* = horse

hippopotamos
= "river-horse"

equīnus
= relating
to horses

equester
= horseman

Latin
hippopotamus

Old
English
eoh = horse

New
Latin
Equus
= genus
of horses

New
Latin
Eohippus
= "dawn-horse,"
ancestral genus

English
EQUINE

English
EQUESTRIAN

English
HIPPOPOTAMUS

43

en

1. The Indo-European adverb/preposition *en* = "in" appears in Germanic *in,* Old Irish *in-,* Latin *in,* Lithuanian *i,* Old Slavic *vŭn-,* and Greek *en,* all meaning "in."

2. Germanic *in* appears in Gothic *in,* Old Norse *i,* Old High German *in* (whence Modern German *in*), and Old English *in* (preposition) and *inn* (adverb), becoming Modern English IN (preposition and adverb).

   The Old English adverb *inn* was used in a prepositional phrase *inn tō* = "moving or directed to within." This became the Modern English preposition INTO.

3. Latin *in* = "in, on, into, toward" was widely used as a prefix, in such words as *incarcerāre* = "to put in prison" (*carcer* = "prison"), *inclīnāre* = "to lean toward" (*clīn-* = "to lean"), *inclūdere* = "to shut in" (*claudere* = "to shut"). Several hundred such Latin words have been adopted into English, including the above, as INCARCERATE, INCLINE, INCLUDE. In Old French, Latin *in-* became *en-,* as Latin *inclūdere* became Old French *enclos-,* borrowed into English as ENCLOSE. Many of these Latin *in-* words thus appear in English spelled with EN-.

4. A suffixed form of the word, *en-ter-* = "within," appears in the Latin preposition *inter* = "between, among." This likewise appears in compounds such as *intervenīre* = "to come between" (*venīre* = "to come"), many of which have been adopted into English, such as INTERVENE. The prefix itself has also been adopted as INTER-, chiefly meaning "among," as in INTERNATIONAL.

   Closely related is the Latin adverb *intrā* = "inside." This, too, has been adopted as the English prefix INTRA- = "inside," as in INTRAVENOUS = "inside a vein or veins."

5. Greek *en* = "in" was also used as a prefix, as in *enkephalon* = "(organ) inside the head, brain" (*kephalē* = "head"); hence English ENCEPHALON = "brain," and others.

   The Greek adverb *endon* = "inside" has also been adopted as the scientific prefix ENDO-, as in ENDODONTICS = "dentistry dealing with the inner pulp of the teeth."

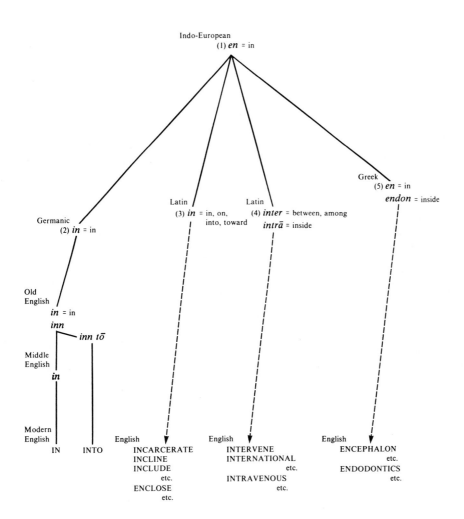

Indo-European
(1) *en* = in

Greek
(5) *en* = in
endon = inside

Germanic
(2) *in* = in

Latin
(3) *in* = in, on, into, toward

Latin
(4) *inter* = between, among
intrā = inside

Old
English
in = in
inn
inn tō

Middle
English
in

Modern
English
IN   INTO

English
INCARCERATE
INCLINE
INCLUDE
etc.
ENCLOSE
etc.

English
INTERVENE
INTERNATIONAL
etc.
INTRAVENOUS
etc.

English
ENCEPHALON
etc.
ENDODONTICS
etc.

45

gen-

1. Indo-European *gen-, genə-* = "to give birth to, be born," with its numerous derivatives such as *genos, gnyos* = "offspring, family," *genəter* = "parent," *gntis* = "family," *genətis* = "birth," appears in Germanic *kunjam* and *kunjaz* = "family," Old Irish *ro-gēnar* = "I was born," Latin *gēns* = "clan" and *genus* = "birth, origin, descent, race," Lithuanian *gentìs* = "relative," Greek *genos, genea* = "family, race" and *genesis* = "birth, origin," and Sanskrit *jánati* = "begets," *janitár-* = "father," and *janitrí* = "mother."

2. Germanic *kunjam* = "family, tribe, race" appears in Gothic *kuni,* Old Norse *kyn,* Old High German *chunni,* and Old English *cyn,* all meaning "family or race." Old English *cyn* became Modern English KIN.

3. From *kunjam* was formed *kuningaz* = "son of the kin" (the suffix *-ingaz* = "son of, descendant of" appears in hundreds of English family-names, such as *Fanning, Goring, Harding,* and place-names, such as *Nottingham*). *Kuningaz* was a title of Germanic tribal leaders, who did not automatically inherit by primogeniture but were elected from among the male descendants of former leaders. *Kuningaz* appears in Old Norse *konungr,* Old High German *chuning,* Old Frisian *kining,* and Old English *cyning,* all meaning "prince, ruler." The last became Modern English KING.

4. Germanic *ga-kundiz* = "family, birth" (*ga-* is a "collective" prefix, not affecting the meaning) appears in Old English *gecynd* = "birth, descent, family, race, class." This word was also used to mean "class, type, species," as of animals, plants, or similar objects. In Middle English it lost the prefix and became Modern English KIND (noun).

5. Germanic *ga-kundjaz* = "native, true-born" (also with the prefix *ga-*) appears in Old English *gecynde* = "nobly born, true-born, well-born," later also meaning "well-bred, courteous, gentle, benevolent." It also lost the prefix in Middle English and became Modern English KIND (adjective).

6. Latin *gēns,* stem *gent-,* = "family, clan" is exactly equivalent to Germanic *(ga)kundiz,* both descending from Indo-European *gntis* = "family." From Latin *gent-* was formed the adjective *gentīlis* = "belonging to a Roman *gens,* or clan," later also "of noble family." This was inherited into Old French as *gentil* = "of noble family," which was borrowed into Middle English as *gentil,* used in a specialized social sense to mean "of a family ranking below the peerage or nobility but entitled to bear arms." It also acquired the meanings "well-bred, courteous, honorable, generous, kind"; hence Modern English GENTLE, also GENTILITY, GENTLEMAN, etc.

7. Latin *genus* = "birth, family, race, class, kind" was used in New Latin (sixteenth century) in logic to mean a large class containing several smaller classes or *species;* this was adopted into English as GENUS.

From *genus* (stem *gener-*) was formed the adjective *generōsus* = "of noble family," hence also "of noble mind, magnanimous." This was adopted into Old French as *genereux,* borrowed thence into English as GENEROUS, now chiefly meaning "open-handed, liberal in giving."

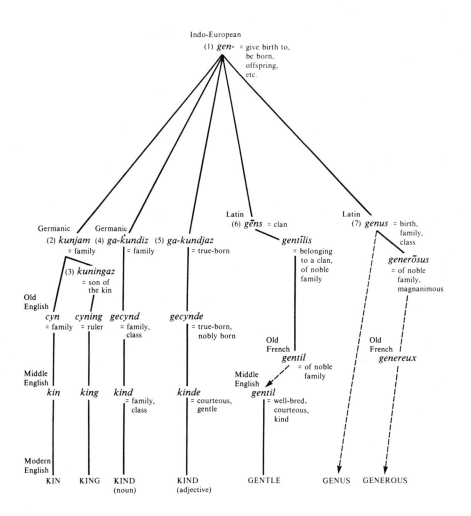

Indo-European
(1) *gen-* = give birth to, be born, offspring, etc.

Germanic
(2) *kunjam* = family

Germanic
(4) *ga-k̇undiz* = family

(5) *ga-kundjaz* = true-born

Latin
(6) *gēns* = clan

gentīlis = belonging to a clan, of noble family

Latin
(7) *genus* = birth, family, class

generōsus = of noble family, magnanimous

(3) *kuningaz* = son of the kin

Old English
cyn = family   *cyning* = ruler   *gecynd* = family, class   *gecynde* = true-born, nobly born

Old French
gentil = of noble family

Old French
genereux

Middle English
kin   *king*   *kind* = family, class   *kinde* = courteous, gentle

Middle English
gentil = well-bred, courteous, kind

Modern English
KIN   KING   KIND (noun)   KIND (adjective)   GENTLE   GENUS   GENEROUS

47

genu

1. The Indo-European noun *genu* or *gonu,* also *gnewom,* ="knee" appears in Germanic *kniwam,* Latin *genu,* Greek *gonu,* Hittite *gienu,* Tocharian *kenĭ ne,* and Sanskrit *janu,* all meaning "knee."

2. Germanic *kniwam* appears in Gothic *kniu,* Old Norse *knē,* Old High German *knio,* and Old English *cnēo,* all meaning "knee." Old English *cnēo* became Middle English *kneo, knee,* then (losing the initial /k/ sound but keeping the old spelling with *k*) Modern English KNEE.

   From Germanic *kniwam* was formed the verb *kniwljan* ="to go down on bent knee," appearing in Old English *cnēowlian,* becoming Middle English *knewlen, knelen,* Modern English KNEEL.

3. From Latin *genu* ="knee" was formed the Late (Christian) Latin verb *genuflectere* ="to bend the knee" (*flectere* ="to bend"). This was adopted into English as GENUFLECT, a liturgical word now used mainly by Catholics.

   Latin *genuĭnus* ="innate, native, authentic" derives from *genu* ="knee" in reference to an ancient custom by which a newborn child was acknowledged by its father by placing it on his knee. This was adopted into English as GENUINE.

4. Related to Greek *gonu* ="knee" is Greek *gōnia* ="corner, angle." From this were formed a number of terms used in geometry, including *polugōnon* ="figure with many angles" (*polus* ="many") and *diagōnios* ="crossing between angles, running from one angle of a polygon to another" (*dia* = "through, between"). These were adopted into Latin as *polygōnum* and *diagōnālis,* and thence into English (sixteenth century) as POLYGON and DIAGONAL.

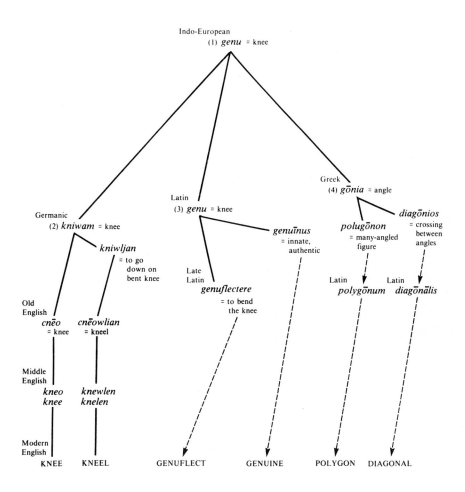

Indo-European
(1) *genu* = knee

Germanic
(2) *kniwam* = knee

kniwljan
= to go
down on
bent knee

Old
English
cnēo
= knee

cnēowlian
= kneel

Middle
English
kneo
knee

knewlen
knelen

Modern
English
KNEE   KNEEL

Latin
(3) *genu* = knee

genuīnus
= innate,
authentic

Late
Latin
genuflectere
= to bend
the knee

GENUFLECT   GENUINE

Greek
(4) *gōnia* = angle

polugōnon
= many-angled
figure

diagōnios
= crossing
between
angles

Latin
polygōnum

Latin
diagōnālis

POLYGON   DIAGONAL

49

ghordhos

1. The Indo-European word *ghordhos* or *ghortos* = "enclosure, garden" appears in Germanic *gardaz* = "enclosure, garden," Welsh *garth* = "garden," Latin *hortus* = "enclosure, garden," Lithuanian *gardas* = "enclosure, hurdle, cattle pen," Old Slavic *gradŭ* = "garden," also "city" (whence *Petrograd, Stalingrad,* etc.), and Hittite *gurtas* = "fortress."

Ghordhos/ghortos is a noun regularly formed from the verb root *gher-, gherdh-* = "to enclose." The basic meaning was therefore "fenced enclosure of any kind," including probably "cattle pen," and especially "fenced area attached to a house, garden." The original "garden" in this case would certainly not have been a flower garden, and may well have been a vegetable garden, fenced against foraging animals. On linguistic evidence, the Indo-Europeans grew an array of legumes, including peas, lentils, beans, and chick-peas.

2. *Ghordhos* regularly became Germanic *gardaz* = "enclosure, garden," with variant form *gardon* (same meaning). This appears in Gothic *garda* = "enclosure," Old Norse *gardhr* = "enclosure, garden," Old High German *gart* = "garden" (whence Modern German *garten*), and Old English *geard* = "enclosure, fence, farmyard, courtyard." Old English *geard* became Modern English YARD = "enclosure, house garden" (not related to *yard* = "three feet").

3. The Germanic compound *orti-gardaz* appears only in Gothic *aurtigards* and Old English *ortgeard*. Probably the first part of this compound is a borrowing of Latin *hortus, ortus,* which (unknown to the Germans) was an exact cognate of *gardaz*. The literal meaning was thus "garden-enclosure." The borrowing must reflect some interpenetration of Roman and German gardening practices in the time of the Roman Empire.

Old English *ortgeard* meant also specifically "fruit garden, plantation of fruit trees." By the late Middle Ages, this became its only meaning, as in Modern English ORCHARD.

4. Germanic *gardon* became Frankish *gardo,* a word that is not found in documents but is reliably inferred as the source of Provençal *gardi,* Old French *jardin,* and Old North French *gardin,* all meaning "garden." These three words are all clearly and regularly descended from a form *gardō, gardīno,* which must have existed in the variety of Latin spoken in postimperial Gaul, or France. Thus, just as the Germans had earlier borrowed the Latin word *hortus,* so now, the Romanized Gauls borrowed the Germanic word *gardō* from their Frankish overlords.

Gardino became *jardin* in Parisian French, but in the northern French dialects, it kept the "hard" *g.* It was the northern form *gardin* that was later (about the fourteenth century) borrowed by the English, becoming Modern English GARDEN.

5. Latin *hortus* = "garden" was used to form the seventeenth-century English word HORTICULTURE.

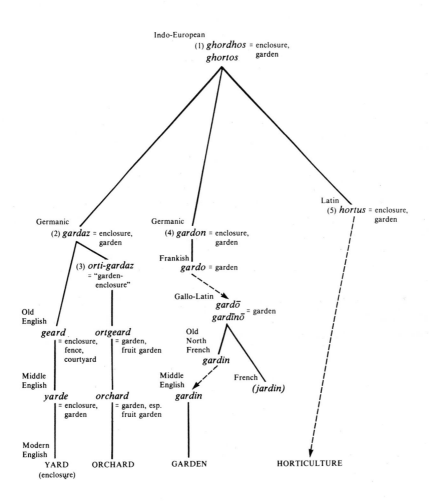

Indo-European
(1) *ghordhos* = enclosure, garden
ghortos

Germanic
(2) *gardaz* = enclosure, garden

(3) *orti-gardaz* = "garden-enclosure"

Germanic
(4) *gardon* = enclosure, garden

Frankish
gardo = garden

Latin
(5) *hortus* = enclosure, garden

Gallo-Latin
gardō
gardīnō = garden

Old English
geard = enclosure, fence, courtyard

ortgeard = garden, fruit garden

Old North French
gardin

French
(jardin)

Middle English
yarde = enclosure, garden

orchard = garden, esp. fruit garden

Middle English
gardin

Modern English
YARD (enclosure)

ORCHARD

GARDEN

HORTICULTURE

51

ghostis

1. Indo-European *ghostis* appears in Germanic *gastiz* ="guest," Latin *hostis* ="enemy," and Old Slavic *gostĭ* ="guest, friend." *Ghostis* seems to have meant "person who may be my guest or my host." It seems that it originally applied not to strangers but to members of a community or league bound by laws of hospitality and exchange.

2. In Germanic *gastiz,* the regular descendant of Indo-European *ghostis,* the word had narrowed, meaning chiefly "guest." It appears in Gothic *gasts,* Old Norse *gestr,* and Old English *giest,* all meaning "guest." The Old English word would have emerged in Modern English as *yest,* but it died out in the late Middle Ages, being replaced by the Old Norse equivalent *gestr,* with the "hard" /g/. The English word was later respelled GUEST, with the *u* added to show that the *g* was "hard."

3. Latin *hostis* means "enemy." But it has been shown that in the earliest Latin it meant "member of a people allied to the Romans." This meaning was a survival of Indo-European *ghostis* ="fellow-member of a hospitality-league." As the Romans conquered their neighbors, *hostis* ceased to mean "friendly non-Roman" and came to mean "enemy." Its adjective *hostīlis* was adopted into English as HOSTILE.

    In Medieval Latin, *hostis* was used to mean "an army." It thus passed into Old French as *host, ost,* which was borrowed into Middle English as HOST (="army").

4. The Indo-European compound noun *ghosti-pot-* or *ghos-pot-* was formed from *ghostis* + *-pot-,* a suffix meaning "he who presides over or represents." *Ghos-pot-* thus meant "guest-presider, hospitality-master, host."

    Ghos-pot- appears in Old Slavic *gospodĭ* ="lord" (Modern Russian *gospodin* ="sir") and in Latin *hospit-* ="host/guest." *Hospit-* must originally have meant only "host" in Latin; when *hostis* lost its old meaning, *hospit-* took them over.

    Latin *hospit-* was inherited in Old French as *hoste* ="host/guest." (Modern French *hôte*). When this was borrowed into Middle English, the word GUEST already existed; presumably for this reason, the borrowed word *hoste* was used only to mean "dispenser of hospitality," as in Modern English HOST (="entertainer").

5. Latin *hospit-* formed the adjective *hospitālis* ="pertaining to guests," with abstract noun *hospitālitās* ="the action or duty of providing for guests." This was borrowed into Middle English as *hospitalite,* now HOSPITALITY.

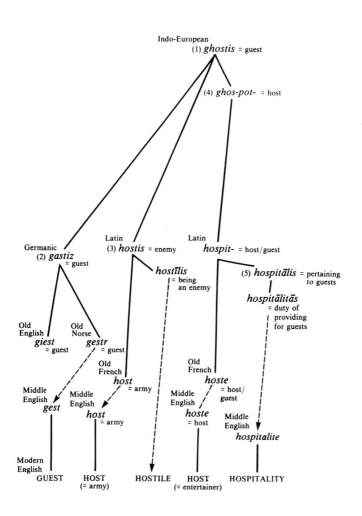

Indo-European
(1) *ghostis* = guest

(4) *ghos-pot-* = host

Germanic
(2) *gastiz*
= guest

Latin
(3) *hostis* = enemy

Latin
hospit- = host/guest

hostīlis
= being
an enemy

(5) *hospitālis* = pertaining
to guests

hospitālitās
= duty of
providing
for guests

Old
English
giest
= guest

Old
Norse
gestr
= guest

Old
French
host
= army

Old
French
hoste
= host/
guest

Middle
English
gest

Middle
English
host
= army

Middle
English
hoste
= host

Middle
English
hospitalite

Modern
English
GUEST

HOST
(= army)

HOSTILE

HOST
(= entertainer)

HOSPITALITY

53

gnō-

1. Indo-European *gnō-* = "to know" appears in Germanic *knōw-*, Old Irish *-gnin-*, Latin *gnōscere*, Lithuanian *žinaū*, Greek *gignōskein*, Tocharian *knā-*, and Sanskrit *jānắmi*, all meaning "to know."

2. Indo-European *gnō-* became Germanic *knōw-*, with regular change of *g* to *k*. This appears in Old Norse *knā* = "I can," Old High German *cnāen* = "to know," and Old English *cnāwan* = "to know." Old English *cnāwan* became Middle English *knowen* and, losing the pronunciation of the *k-* but retaining the spelling, KNOW.

3. The root also appears in Germanic *kunnan* = "to know how to, be able to," with present tense *kan-* = "I know how to, I am able." This appears in Gothic *kunnan, kan,* Old Norse *kunna, kan,* Old High German *kunnan, kan* (whence Modern German *können, kann),* and Old English *cunnan, can.* In Middle English the infinitive disappeared, leaving the auxiliary verb CAN.

   The Middle English adjective and noun *conning* = "knowing, skillful, able" and "knowledge, skill, ability" became Modern English CUNNING, now narrowed in meaning to "guileful, guile."

4. Formed from Latin *gnōscere* = "to get to know," losing the *g-* to become *nōscere,* was the noun *nōtiōn-* = "a getting to know, conception in the mind." This was adopted into English (sixteenth century) as NOTION. A compounded form of the verb, *recognōscere* = "to know again (i.e., something that one had known before)," was inherited in Old French as *reconiss-* = "to recognize." This was borrowed into English (also sixteenth century) as *recogniss,* RECOGNIZE.

5. Also from the root is Latin *ignōrāre* (*i-* = "*in-,* un-, not")= "not to know," with a noun *ignōrāntia* = "lack of knowledge." This was adopted into Old French as *ignorance,* which was borrowed into Middle English as IGNORANCE.

6. Closely related to Latin *gnōscere* was Greek *gignōskein* = "to perceive, know" (the initial *gi-* being a reduplication of the initial sound of the root). A compound of this verb was *diagignōskein* = "to discern, to distinguish" (*dia-* = "through, all the way through"). The noun formed from this was *diagnōsis* = "discernment, the act of discerning," as in the medical analysis of a case. This was adopted into New Latin as *diagnōsis,* and thence into English (sixteenth century) as DIAGNOSIS.

54

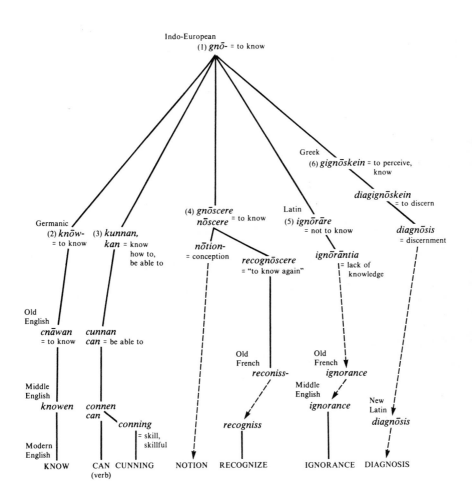

Indo-European
(1) *gnō-* = to know

Greek
(6) *gignōskein* = to perceive, know

diagignōskein
= to discern

Germanic
(2) *knōw-* = to know

(3) *kunnan, kan* = know how to, be able to

(4) *gnōscere nōscere* = to know

Latin
(5) *ignōrāre* = not to know

diagnōsis = discernment

nōtion- = conception

recognōscere = "to know again"

ignōrāntia = lack of knowledge

Old English
cnāwan = to know
cunnan can = be able to

Middle English
knowen
connen can

conning = skill, skillful

Old French
reconiss-

Old French
ignorance

Middle English
ignorance

New Latin
diagnōsis

Modern English
KNOW

CAN (verb)

CUNNING

NOTION

RECOGNIZE

recogniss

IGNORANCE

DIAGNOSIS

grənom

1. The Indo-European noun *grənom* = "seed, grain" appears in Germanic *kornam*, Old Irish *grān*, Latin *grānum*, and Old Slavic *zrŭno*, all meaning "seed, grain."

2. Indo-European *grənom* became Germanic *kurnam*, which appears in Gothic *kaurn*, Old Norse *korn*, Old High German *korn*, and Old English *corn*, all meaning "seed, grain, especially of the cereal grasses." Old English *corn* became Modern English CORN, still in British English referring basically to the cereal grasses (wheat, barley, oats, rye) in general. In the seventeenth century when the English encountered *mahíz*, or *maize*, in North America, they called it *Indian corn*. Later (eighteenth century) this was abbreviated to CORN, which in American English became exclusively the term for "maize"; the cereal crops therefore were collectively referred to as GRAIN (*see* paragraph 3, below).

A diminutive formed from Old English *corn* = "seed" was Old English *cyrnel* = "little seed," also "inner and edible part of a nut"; this became Middle English *kirnel*, Modern English KERNEL.

3. Latin *grānum* = "seed, grain" was inherited in Old French as *grain*, and borrowed thence into (Middle) English as GRAIN.

56

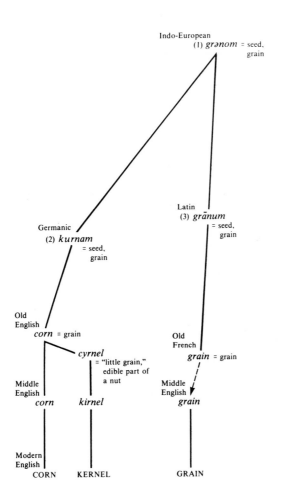

Indo-European
(1) *grənom* = seed, grain

Latin
(3) *grānum*
= seed, grain

Germanic
(2) *kurnam*
= seed, grain

Old French
grain = grain

Old English
corn = grain

cyrnel
= "little grain," edible part of a nut

Middle English
corn

kirnel

Middle English
grain

Modern English
CORN

KERNEL

GRAIN

gwei-

1. Indo-European *gwei-* = "to live," with its derivatives *gwiwos, gwīwos, gwiyos* = "alive" and *gwīwot-* = "life," appears in Germanic *kwiwaz* = "alive," Celtic *bivotut-* = "life," Latin *vīvus* = "alive" and *vīta* = "life," Lithuanian *gyvas* = "living," Old Slavic *žiti* = "live," Greek *bios* = "life" and *zōon* = "living thing," and Sanskrit *jivās* = "alive" and *jivātah* = "life."

   The sound-changes resulting from Indo-European /gw/ in the various languages are particularly surprising at first sight, but they are supported by plentiful comparative evidence. Indo-European /gw/ regularly became Germanic /kw/, Celtic /b/, Latin /v/, etc., and according to circumstances it could become /b/ or /z/ in Greek.

2. Indo-European *gwiwos* = "living" regularly became Germanic *kwiwaz,* with variant *kwikwaz,* appearing in Old Norse *kvikr,* Old High German *quek,* and Old English *cwicu,* all meaning "alive, living."

   Old English *cwicu* became Middle English *quik,* meaning "alive" and "lively, active, vigorous, sharp-witted," then also "moving rapidly, swift." It became Modern English QUICK.

3. Celtic *bivotuts* = "life," appears in Old Irish *bethu* = "life," becoming Modern Irish *beatha.* In the sixteenth century distilled alcohol suddenly became known all over Europe with the alchemical name (Latin) *aqua vītae* = "water of life." In Ireland and Scotland this was translated as *uisge beatha,* from *uisge* = "water" (*see also* under **wed-** = "water") + *beatha* = "life." This was borrowed into English as USQUEBAUGH, later shortened to WHISKY.

4. Latin *vīvus* = "alive" is from Indo-European *gwīwos.* From it were formed: the adjective *vīvidus* = "full of life," adopted into English as VIVID; and the verb *vīvere* = "to live," with Late Latin compounds *revīvere* = "to live again" and *supervīvere* = "to live beyond (others)." These became Old French *revivre* and *survivre,* and were borrowed into Middle English as *reviven, surviven,* Modern English REVIVE, SURVIVE.

5. Latin *vīta* = "life" is from Indo-European *gwīwota.* From it was formed the adjective *vītālis* = "relating to life, essential to life," which was adopted into Old French as *vital* and thence into (Middle) English as VITAL. In the early twentieth century the German scientist Casimir Funk identified certain biochemical compounds as essential to life and the prevention of specific diseases; believing (wrongly) that these chemicals were *amines* (a type of ammonia derivative), he named them *vitamine,* from Latin *vīta* = "life" + *amine.* This was borrowed into English as VITAMIN.

6. Greek *bios* = "life" is from Indo-European *gwiyos.* At the beginning of the nineteenth century it was used in German and French to coin the word *biologie* = "life science" (*-logie* from Greek *-logia* = "study, science"). This was borrowed into English as BIOLOGY.

7. Greek *zōon* = "living creature, animal" is from Indo-European *gwoyom.* In the seventeenth century this was used to coin the New Latin word *zoologia* = "animal science." This was borrowed into English as ZOOLOGY.

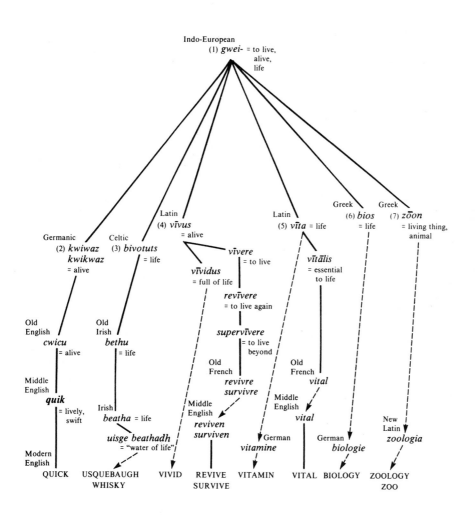

Indo-European
(1) *gwei-* = to live,
alive,
life

Germanic
(2) *kwiwaz*
kwikwaz
= alive

Celtic
(3) *bivotuts*
= life

Latin
(4) *vīvus*
= alive

vīvere
= to live

vīvidus
= full of life

revīvere
= to live again

supervīvere
= to live
beyond

Latin
(5) *vīta* = life

vītālis
= essential
to life

Greek
(6) *bios*
= life

Greek
(7) *zōon*
= living thing,
animal

Old
English
cwicu
= alive

Old
Irish
bethu
= life

Middle
English
quik
= lively,
swift

Irish
beatha = life

uisge beathadh
= "water of life"

Old
French
revivre
survivre

Old
French
vital

Middle
English
reviven
surviven

Middle
English
vital

German
vitamine

German
biologie

New
Latin
zoologia

Modern
English
QUICK

USQUEBAUGH
WHISKY

VIVID

REVIVE
SURVIVE

VITAMIN

VITAL

BIOLOGY

ZOOLOGY
ZOO

59

gwenā

1. Indo-European *gwenā,* also *gwēnis,* = "woman, wife" appears in Germanic *kwenōn, kwēniz,* Old Irish *ben,* Old Prussian *genna,* Old Slavic *žena* (whence Modern Russian *zhena*), Greek *gunē,* and Sanskrit *jāni-,* all meaning "woman" and/or "wife."

2. Germanic *kwenōn* (short /e/) appears in Gothic *qino,* Old Norse *kvinna,* Old High German *quena,* and Old English *cwene,* all meaning "woman." Old English *cwene,* sometimes used to mean "female servant," became Middle English *queyne, queine, quene* = "woman," used with an increasing sense of social/sexual disapproval: "impudent woman, slut, prostitute." This became Modern English QUEAN, now a relatively rare, rather literary word for a woman who is boldly and openly a prostitute. It is used in a short story (1921) of Somerset Maugham: "Her face was painted, her eyebrows were boldly black, and her lips were scarlet. She held herself erect. She was the flaunting quean they had known at first."

3. Germanic *kwēniz* (long /e/) appears in Gothic *qēns* = "wife," Old Norse *kvæn* = "woman, wife," and Old English *cwēn* = "lady, king's wife, sovereign lady." This became Middle English *quene, queene,* Modern English QUEEN. The striking divergence of meaning between QUEAN and QUEEN, formerly marked by a difference in pronunciation, is now marked only by a difference in spelling. The inevitable pun on the two was suitably made by the woman-obsessed poet Byron in *Don Juan* (1823): "This martial scold, This modern Amazon and queen of queans."

4. Indo-European *gwenā* also became Old Irish *ben* = "woman." (The sound-change from Indo-European /gw/ to Celtic /b/ is regular; *see also* **gwōus** = "cow," becoming Old Irish *bó* = "cow.") In Old Irish mythology, the *ben síde* = "woman of the fairies" (*síde* = "fairies") was a female spirit who warned of a coming death in a family by wailing near the house. This became Modern Irish *bean sídhe,* pronounced, approximately, *ban-shee.* It was borrowed into English in the eighteenth century as BANSHEE.

5. Indo-European *gwenā* also appears in Greek as *gunē* = "woman, wife." From this was formed the compound word *mīsogunēs* = "man who hates women" (*mīsein* = "to hate"). This was adopted into English in the seventeenth century as MISOGYNIST.

   Greek *gunē* had the stem *gunaik-;* in the Latinized spelling *gynec-* this was used to form the nineteenth-century medical term GYNECOLOGY = "branch of medicine specializing in the treatment of women."

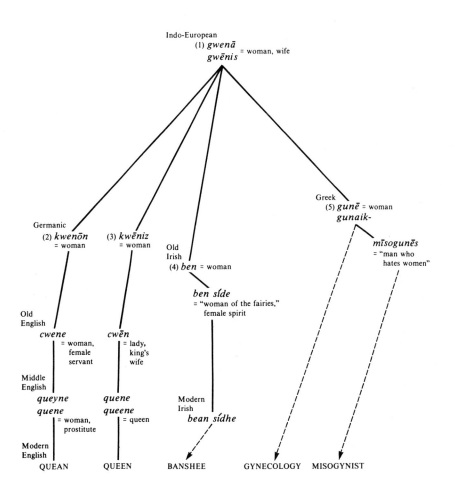

Indo-European
(1) *gwenā*
   gwēnis = woman, wife

Greek
(5) *gunē* = woman
  gunaik-

mīsogunēs
= "man who
  hates women"

Germanic
(2) *kwenōn*
= woman

(3) *kwēniz*
= woman

Old
Irish
(4) *ben* = woman

ben síde
= "woman of the fairies,"
  female spirit

Old
English
cwene
= woman,
  female
  servant

cwēn
= lady,
  king's
  wife

Middle
English
queyne
quene
= woman,
  prostitute

quene
queene
= queen

Modern
Irish
bean sídhe

Modern
English
QUEAN

QUEEN

BANSHEE

GYNECOLOGY

MISOGYNIST

61

gwōus

1. Indo-European *gwōus* = "cow or bull" appears in Germanic *kōuz,* Old Irish *bó,* Latin *bōs,* Latvian *gùovs,* Old Slavic *govędo,* Greek *bous,* Armenian *kov,* Tocharian *ko,* and Sanskrit *gáuh,* all meaning "cow" or "bull" or both.

While the horse (*see* **ekwos**) was the sacred animal of the Indo-Europeans, the cow was their animal of economic prestige. The earliest identifiable Indo-Europeans are the Kurgan people of southern Russia, who lived between 5000 and 4000 B.C. Cattle had then already been domesticated for at least two thousand years, and excavations have shown that the Kurgan people herded and ate them in quantity. Oxen were probably also yoked at a very early date, before horses were harnessed (*see* **yeug-**).

In their later migrations into Europe and the Middle East, the various Indo-European peoples undoubtedly took herds of cattle with them. Throughout the Bronze Age, their ruling caste of warriors reckoned their wealth in head of cattle and regarded cattle-raiding as a legitimate, in fact glorious, form of warfare and profit.

2. Germanic *kōuz* appears in Old Norse *kyr,* Old High German *chuo* (whence Modern German *kuh*), Old Frisian *kū,* and Old English *cū,* all meaning "cow." Old English *cū* became Modern English COW.

3. Indo-European *gwōus* would normally have become *vōs* in Latin, but actually appears as *bōs* = "cow or bull." This is accounted for by the fact that in some Italic dialects closely related to Latin, Indo-European *gw* regularly became *b.* The word *bōs* must therefore have been borrowed into early Latin from one of these dialects, perhaps Sabine, spoken by people who were neighbors of the early Romans.

The stem of Latin *bōs* was *bov-;* from this was formed the Late Latin adjective *bovīnus* = "oxlike, relating to cattle." This was adopted into English (sixteenth century) as BOVINE.

Latin *bov-* was inherited into Old French, including the dialect of Normandy, as *boef* (becoming Modern French *boeuf*). The Normans took their word *boef* into England, and it was borrowed into Middle English as *boef,* also BEEF, used primarily for the meat but also for the animal.

4. Greek *boukolos* = "cowherd" is formed from *bous* = "cow or bull" + *-kol-* = "tend, look after, herd." The highly literate urban Greeks and Romans of the Classical period had an almost romantic admiration for the simple country life, expressed by poets such as the Sicilian Greek Theocritus (third century B.C.). He and others called their rural poems *boukolikai aoidai,* literally meaning "cow-herding songs," but telling of idyllic country life in general, not specifically of cattle-herding. The adjective *boukolikos* thus came to mean "pastoral, praising country life," and was so adopted into Latin as *būcolicus,* and thence into English (sixteenth century) as BUCOLIC.

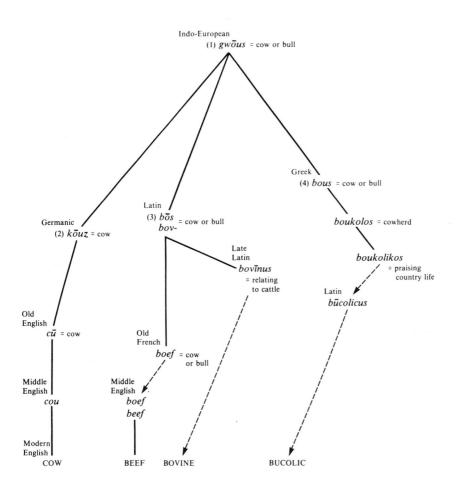

Indo-European
(1) *gwōus* = cow or bull

Greek
(4) *bous* = cow or bull

Latin
(3) *bōs* = cow or bull
bov-

Germanic
(2) *kōuz* = cow

boukolos = cowherd

Late
Latin
bovīnus
= relating
to cattle

boukolikos
= praising
country life

Latin
būcolicus

Old
English
cū = cow

Old
French
boef = cow
or bull

Middle
English
cou

Middle
English
boef
beef

Modern
English
COW   BEEF   BOVINE   BUCOLIC

63

kanabis

1. Germanic *hanapiz,* Lithuanian *kanapes,* Slavic *konoplja,* Albanian *kanep,* Greek *kannabis,* and Armenian *kanap,* all meaning "hemp," obviously derive from a common source. It cannot be a word inherited from Indo-European, because an original *k* changed to *s* when inherited in Slavic, Albanian, and Armenian.

The Germanic word, on the other hand, is clearly descended from a pre-Germanic *kanabis,* which must have existed before the Indo-European *k* became Germanic *h* and Indo-European *b* became Germanic *p*—presumably before 500 B.C.

The Greek word was first used by Herodotus in the fifth century B.C., reporting that the plant grew in Scythia (north of the Black Sea) both as a weed and under cultivation, and that the Thracians used it for making cloth. Probably the Greek word itself is borrowed from either Thracian or Scythian, two Indo-European languages of which little has been recorded. The plant is native to Asia, probably Central Asia. It grows wild around encampments of the nomads and is also cultivated by them. It could well have been brought to Europe by the Scythians, whose cultural influence was strong in the period 600–400 B.C.

2. Germanic *hanapiz* appears in Old Norse *hampr,* Old High German *hanaf* (whence Modern German *hanf*), and Old English *hænep,* all meaning "hemp." The last became Modern English HEMP.

3. Greek *kannabis* was adopted into Latin as *cannabis.* An unrecorded Latin adjective *cannabāceus* = "made of hemp" was inherited in the Romance languages: Italian *canvaccio,* Provençal *canabas,* Old French *chanevas,* and Norman French *canevas,* all meaning "hempen cloth, canvas." The last was borrowed into Middle English as *canevas,* becoming Modern English CANVAS. Some canvas is still made of hemp, but most is now made of linen or cotton.

4. Latin *cannabis* was adopted in New Latin (Linnaeus, eighteenth century) as the botanical name of the plant, *Cannabis sativa* (*sativa* = "cultivated"). This has recently been taken into the general English vocabulary as CANNABIS, the formal term for hemp used as a drug, otherwise known by informal terms such as *grass, marijuana,* etc.

Herodotus describes its use as a religious intoxicant by the Scythians, but this seems never to have spread to Europe until introduced in the nineteenth century from the Middle East and India. The plant has been cultivated for rope and cloth for at least two thousand years in Europe.

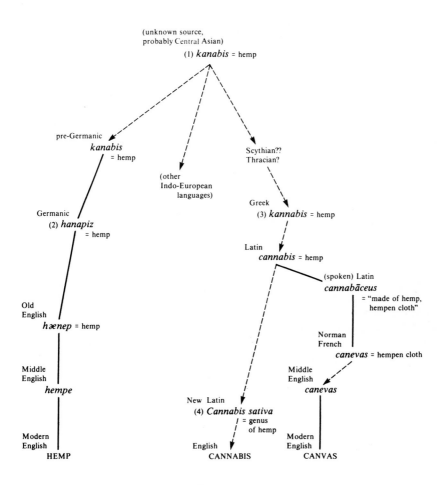

(unknown source,
probably Central Asian)
(1) *kanabis* = hemp

pre-Germanic
kanabis
= hemp

(other
Indo-European
languages)

Scythian??
Thracian?

Germanic
(2) *hanapiz*
= hemp

Greek
(3) *kannabis* = hemp

Latin
cannabis = hemp

(spoken) Latin
cannabāceus
= "made of hemp,
hempen cloth"

Old
English
hænep = hemp

Norman
French
canevas = hempen cloth

Middle
English
hempe

Middle
English
canevas

New Latin
(4) *Cannabis sativa*
= genus
of hemp

Modern
English
HEMP

English
CANNABIS

Modern
English
CANVAS

65

kap-

1. Indo-European *kap-* = "to grasp, take hold of" appears in Germanic *hafjan* = "to hold, lift" and *habben* = "to hold, possess," Latin *capere* = "to take" and *captus* = "taken," Latvian *kàmpju* (stem *kap-*) = "to seize," Greek *kaptein* = "to gulp down," and some other words.

2. Germanic *hafjan* = "to lift up" appears in Gothic *hafjan* = "to carry," Old Norse *hefja* = "to lift," Old High German *heffen* = "to lift," and Old English *hebban* = "to lift." The last became Middle English *heven*, Modern English HEAVE, now meaning primarily "to lift with great effort," or "to throw something heavy."

Formed from, or closely related to, Germanic *hafjan*, is Germanic *hafigaz* = "heavy," appearing in Old Norse *höfigr*, Old High German *hebig*, and Old English *hefig*, all meaning "heavy." The last became Middle English *hevi*, Modern English HEAVY.

3. Germanic *habben* = "to hold, possess" appears in Gothic *haban*, Old Norse *hafa*, Old High German *haben* (whence Modern German *haben*), and Old English *habban*, all meaning "to have." In Germanic this verb also came to be used as an auxiliary verb forming perfective tenses (*I have seen, I had seen,* etc.), just as Latin *habēre* = "to have" did in the Romance languages (French *avoir: j'ai vu,* etc.); but although their forms and meanings are so similar, the Latin and Germanic words are not the same— neither is borrowed from the other, nor are they descended from the same Indo-European root. Old English *habban* became Middle English *haven*, Modern English HAVE.

4. Latin *capere* = "to take," *captus* = "taken," and a number of closely related or derived Latin words are the source of over a hundred English words, borrowed through French or directly from Latin.

The noun *captūra* = "a taking" was adopted into Old French as *capture*, borrowed thence into English as CAPTURE (noun, hence verb). The Latin adjective *captīvus* = "taken prisoner" was adopted directly as CAPTIVE.

The "frequentative" Latin verb *captāre* meant "to seek to take, to lie in wait for, to hunt." A group of obviously related words in the Romance languages, Italian *cacciare*, Spanish *cazar*, Old French *chacier*, all meaning "to hunt," are descended from a Latin variant form *captiāre*, which is not recorded in surviving documents and is therefore assigned to the spoken "vulgar" Latin of the Roman Empire. Old French *chacier* (Modern French *chasser*) was borrowed into Middle English as *chasen* = "to hunt," becoming Modern English CHASE. While (spoken) Latin *captiāre* became standard Old French *chacier*, with regular change of *c-* /k-/ to *ch-* /sh-/, in the northern dialects of French it became *cachier*, retaining the "hard" *c-* /k-/. The Norman invaders of England thus brought with them their verb *cachier* = "to hunt," which was borrowed into Middle English as *cacchen* = "to pursue," also "to take, capture," becoming Modern English CATCH.

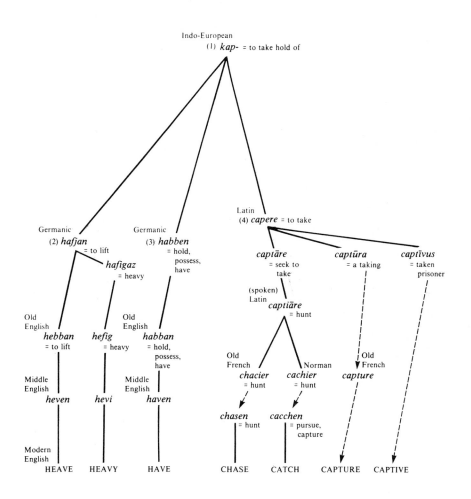

Indo-European
(1) *kap-* = to take hold of

Germanic
(2) *hafjan*
= to lift

hafigaz
= heavy

Germanic
(3) *habben*
= hold,
possess,
have

Latin
(4) *capere* = to take

captāre
= seek to
take

captūra
= a taking

captīvus
= taken
prisoner

(spoken)
Latin
captiāre
= hunt

Old
English
hebban
= to lift

hefig
= heavy

Old
English
habban
= hold,
possess,
have

Old
French
chacier
= hunt

Norman
cachier
= hunt

Old
French
capture

Middle
English
heven

hevi

Middle
English
haven

chasen
= hunt

cacchen
= pursue,
capture

Modern
English
HEAVE

HEAVY

HAVE

CHASE

CATCH

CAPTURE

CAPTIVE

67

ker-

1. The Indo-European root *ker-* = "horn, antler," with its derivatives *krnos* = "horn," *kerudos* and *kerwos* = "horned or antlered animal, stag," appears in Germanic *hurnaz* = "horn" and *herutaz* = "stag," Welsh *carw* = "deer," Latin *cervus* = "stag," Old Slavic *srŭna* = "roe deer," Greek *keras* = "horn," and Sanskrit *s̓rngam* = "horn."

2. Indo-European *krnos* regularly became Germanic *hurnaz* (the Germanic *h* being a /ch/ sound, as in Scottish *loch*). Germanic *hurnaz* appears in Gothic *haurn*, Old Norse *horn*, Old High German *horn*, and Old English *horn*, all meaning "horn." (Horns were used by the Germanic peoples both as musical instruments and as drinking vessels.) The last remains unchanged as Modern English HORN (as Modern German *horn* also remains unchanged).

3. Indo-European *kerudos* = "antlered animal, stag" became Germanic *herutaz* (with regular change of *k* and *d* to *h* and *t*), appearing in Old Norse *hjörtr*, Old High German *hiruz*, and Old English *heorot*, all meaning "stag" (note that the stag has antlers, the doe does not). Old English *heorot* became Middle English *hert*, Modern English HART, technically meaning a stag of the red deer over five years old.

4. Also from this root is Germanic *hrain-* = "horned animal," appearing in Old High German *(h)rind* = "bull or cow" (whence Modern German *rind*) and Old Norse *hreinn* = "reindeer" (a deer with conspicuously large antlers, and the only one of forty-one species of deer to have been domesticated, by various peoples in northernmost Eurasia). In Old Norse the animal was also known as *hreinn-dýri* (*dýr* = "deer"). This was borrowed into Middle English (fourteenth century) as *reyndere*, becoming Modern English REINDEER.

5. Closely related to Germanic *hurnaz* is Latin *cornū* = "horn." This was inherited in Old French as *corne* = "horn," also "horny growth of skin on the toe," which was borrowed into Middle English as *corne*, Modern English CORN (no connection with *corn* = "grain"). Formed from Old French *corne* was the diminutive *cornet* = "little horn," musical instrument of the horn or trumpet family, also "cone-shaped object." This was borrowed into (Middle) English as CORNET.

6. Latin *cervus* = "stag" is regularly from Indo-European *kerwos*. It was adopted in scientific New Latin as *Cervus*, name of the basic genus of deer, hence *Cervidae* = "the deer family" (including moose and elk), which was adopted into (scientific) English as CERVID.

7. Greek *keras, kerat-* = "horn" is the basis of numerous modern scientific words such as KERATIN = "fibrous protein in horn, skin, hair, etc." The Greek compound *rhinokerōs* (*rhis* = "nose") = "nose-horn, horned nose," name of an animal the Greeks heard of in Africa, was adopted into Latin as *rhinocerōs*. This was adopted into Middle English (thirteenth century) as *rynoceros*, corrected in Modern English to RHINOCEROS.

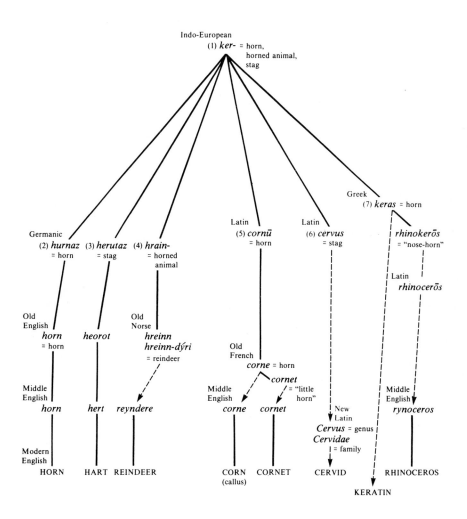

Indo-European
(1) *ker-* = horn,
horned animal,
stag

Germanic
(2) *hurnaz* (3) *herutaz* (4) *hrain-*
= horn   = stag   = horned
animal

Latin
(5) *cornū*
= horn

Latin
(6) *cervus*
= stag

Greek
(7) *keras* = horn

rhinokerōs
= "nose-horn"

Latin
rhinocerōs

Old
English
horn
= horn

heorot

Old
Norse
hreinn
hreinn-dýri
= reindeer

Old
French
corne = horn
cornet
= "little
horn"

Middle
English
horn

hert   *reyndere*

Middle
English
corne *cornet*

New
Latin
Cervus = genus
Cervidae
= family

Middle
English
rynoceros

Modern
English
HORN

HART REINDEER

CORN
(callus) CORNET

CERVID

RHINOCEROS

KERATIN

69

kerd-

1. Indo-European *kerd-* ="heart" appears in Germanic *hertōn-*, Old Irish *cride*, Latin *cor, cord-*, Lithuanian *širdìs*, Greek *kardia*, Armenian *sirt*, and Hittite *ka-ra-az*, all meaning "heart."

The Indo-European word already meant not only the heart as a physical organ but also the heart as the supposed residence of life, soul, or spirit.

2. *Kerd-* appears in Germanic *hertōn-* ="heart" (with regular change of Indo-European *k* to Germanic *h*, and with an added suffix). This appears in Gothic *hairto*, Old High German *herza*, Old Norse *hjarta*, and Old English *heorte*, all meaning "heart." *Heorte* became Middle English *herte*, Modern English HEART.

3. From Latin *cor, cord-* ="heart" was formed the Medieval Latin adjective *cordiālis* ="relating to the heart." This was borrowed into Middle English, later acquiring (chiefly) the sense "heartfelt," Modern English CORDIAL.

There are several words in the Romance languages meaning (approximately) "courage": Italian *coraggio*, Provençal *coratge*, Old French *corage*, Spanish *coraje*. They are obviously descended from a common ancestor, but no such Latin word has been preserved in records. It is known from numerous other examples that the ending *-aggio, -age*, etc., in the Romance languages descends from a Latin noun-ending *-āticum* (compare Old French *vayage*, from Latin *viāticum* ="journey"). The spoken Latin word *corāticum* has therefore been confidently reconstructed, as a derivative of *cor*, meaning (approximately) "heartiness, the quality of having a good heart or spirit." A reconstruction of this kind is assigned to the popular spoken Latin of the Roman Empire, much of which, when it differed from the literary Classical language, was never written down.

Old French *corage* was borrowed into Middle English as *corage*, becoming Modern English COURAGE.

4. Greek *kardia* ="heart," also "stomach," had the adjective *kardiakos* ="relating to the heart." This was adopted into Latin as *cardiacus* and thence into English (seventeenth century) as the medical word CARDIAC.

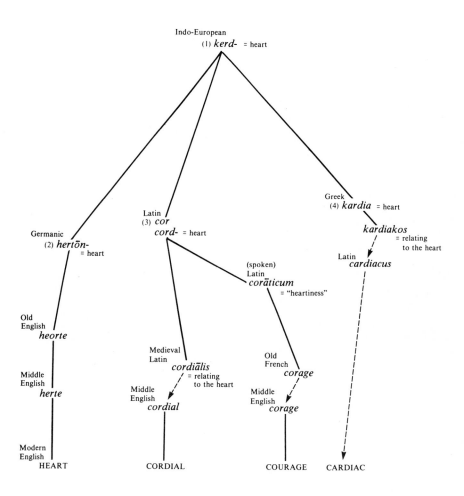

Indo-European
(1) *kerd-* = heart

Germanic
(2) *hertōn-*
       = heart

Latin
(3) *cor*
cord- = heart

(spoken)
Latin
corāticum
       = "heartiness"

Greek
(4) *kardia* = heart

kardiakos
       = relating
       to the heart

Latin
cardiacus

Old
English
heorte

Medieval
Latin
cordiālis
       = relating
       to the heart

Middle
English
cordial

Old
French
corage

Middle
English
herte

Middle
English
corage

Modern
English
HEART

CORDIAL

COURAGE

CARDIAC

71

klei-

1. The Indo-European root *klei-* = "to lean, slope, climb," with derivatives including *klein-, klin-* = "to lean, slope," *kleiwos* = "a slope, hill," and *kloitr-* = "inclined structure, climbing device, ladder," appears in Germanic *hlinēn* = "to lean" and *hlaidr-* = "ladder," Middle Irish *clíath* = "hurdle," Latin *-clīnāre* = "to lean" and *clīvus* = "a slope, hill," Lithuanian *šliēti* = "leans" and *šlite* = "ladder," Greek *klīnein* = "to lean," *klinē* = "bed," *klima* = "a slope," and *klīmax* = "ladder," and Sanskrit *śryati* = "leans on."

2. Indo-European *klin-* became Germanic *hlinēn* (with regular change of *k* to *h*, the latter representing a /ch/ sound, as in Scottish *loch*), appearing in Old High German *(h)linēn*, Old Frisian *lena*, and Old English *hlinian*, *hleonian*, all meaning "to lean." The Old English word as usual lost the initial *h-* before a consonant to become Middle English *lēnen*, Modern English LEAN, still precisely conserving the original meaning of the Indo-European root.

3. Germanic *hlaidr-* = "ladder" (from Indo-European *kloitr-*), appears in Old High German *leitara*, Middle Dutch *ledere*, Old Frisian *hledere*, and Old English *hlæder*, *hlædder*, all meaning "ladder." The Old English word became Modern English LADDER.

4. Latin *dēclīnāre* = "to go down, turn aside," *inclīnāre* = "to lean toward," and *reclīnāre* = "to lean back" became Old French *decliner, encliner, recliner*, which were borrowed into Middle English as *declinen, enclinen, reclinen*, becoming Modern English DECLINE, INCLINE, RECLINE.

5. From Greek *klinē* = "bed" was formed the adjective *klinikos* = "relating to the sickbed," whence *klinikē tekhnē* = "the practice of medicine upon patients in bed" (*tekhnē* = "art, craft"). This, shortened to *klinikē*, was adopted into Latin as *clinicē*, and thence into French (nineteenth century) as *clinique* = "teaching session in which a doctor instructs a class in a hospital ward using patients in bed as case studies." This was borrowed into English as CLINIC, with several subsequent extensions of meaning.

6. Greek *klima* = "slope of ground" was used in the technical geographical sense "one of the latitudinal zones of the earth in relation to the slope of its surface from the pole to the equator." This was adopted into Latin as *clima, climat-*, = "zone or region of the earth divided by lines of latitude." This was adopted into Old French as *climat* and thence into Middle English as *climat* = "zone of latitude, region characterized by specific weather (torrid, temperate, frigid, etc.)," becoming Modern English CLIMATE.

7. Greek *klimax, klimakt-* = "ladder" was used as a technical term in rhetoric to mean "a sequence of expressions progressively rising in intensity." This was adopted into English (sixteenth century) as CLIMAX. Subsequently the CLIMAX has been understood as being the final culminating point, the point of highest intensity or excitement.

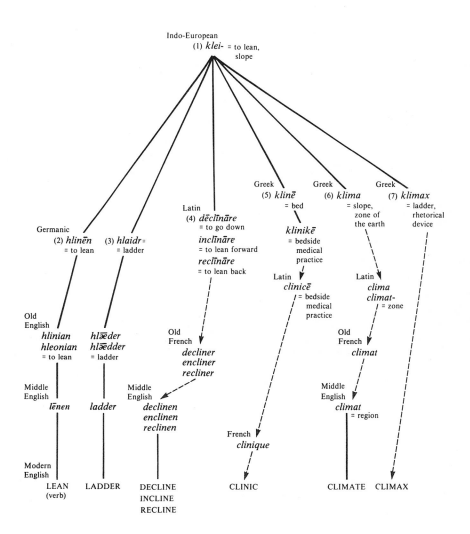

Indo-European
(1) *klei-* = to lean, slope

Germanic
(2) *hlinēn* = to lean

(3) *hlaidr* = ladder

Latin
(4) *dēclīnāre* = to go down
inclīnāre = to lean forward
reclīnāre = to lean back

Greek
(5) *klinē* = bed

klinikē = bedside medical practice

Latin
clinicē = bedside medical practice

Greek
(6) *klima* = slope, zone of the earth

Latin
clima
climat- = zone

Greek
(7) *klimax* = ladder, rhetorical device

Old English
hlinian
hleonian = to lean

hlǣder
hlǣdder = ladder

Old French
decliner
encliner
recliner

Old French
climat

Middle English
lēnen

ladder

Middle English
declinen
enclinen
reclinen

Middle English
climat = region

French
clinique

Modern English
LEAN (verb)

LADDER

DECLINE
INCLINE
RECLINE

CLINIC

CLIMATE CLIMAX

kmtom

1. The Indo-European numeral *kmtom* = "hundred" appears in Germanic *hundan,* Old Irish *cēt,* Latin *centum,* Lithuanian *simtas,* Greek *hekaton,* and Sanskrit *satám,* all meaning "hundred."

Within Indo-European, *kmtom* is derived from *dekmtom,* a noun form of the adjective *dekmtos* = "tenth," from *dekm* = "ten" (*see* **dekm**). The underlying meaning of *(de)kmtom* was thus "ten groups of ten" or "the tenth ten." It is the highest number for which an Indo-European original word can be reconstructed.

2. *Kmtom* became Germanic *hundan,* with regular change of *k* to *h* and of *t* to *d.* The Germanic word was used in a compound form *hunda-rath* = "the number hundred" (*rath* = "number"), appearing in Old Norse *hundradh,* Middle High German *hundert* (whence Modern German *hundert*), and Old English *hundred*—whence Modern English HUNDRED.

3. The Germanic term for "thousand" was the compound word *thus-hundi* = "swollen hundred" (*thus-* = "swell"). This appears in Gothic *thusundi,* Old Norse *thusund,* Old High German *thusunt* (whence Modern German *taus-end*), and Old English *thūsend,* becoming Modern English THOUSAND.

4. *Kmtom* became Latin *centum* = "hundred." Note that the Classical Latin *c* represented the sound /k/; in later Latin, and in Old French, *c* before *e* changed to the sound /s/. Thus Latin *centum* /kentum/ was inherited in Old French as *cent,* pronounced (approximately) /sont/. This treatment of Latin *c* was followed by English in numerous borrowings from French.

Latin *centūria* = "group of a hundred" was adopted into English (sixteenth century) as CENTURY.

5. In Greek *hekaton* = "hundred" the initial *he-* is from Greek *hen* = "one."

In the French Revolutionary system of weights and measures, for which Greek and Latin words were adopted, Greek *hekaton* was used to form the prefix *hecto-* = "× 100." The basic unit of land was the *are* (from Latin *ārea* = "piece of ground"), defined as 10 meters square (100 square meters). With the prefix *hecto-,* this produced the word *hectare* = "100 *ares,*" or 10,000 square meters (2.471 acres). The *hectare* later became the most frequently used unit of land in agriculture and planning, and if the U.S. Metric Board has its way, the borrowed word HECTARE is destined to replace the native word ACRE (*see* **agros**).

74

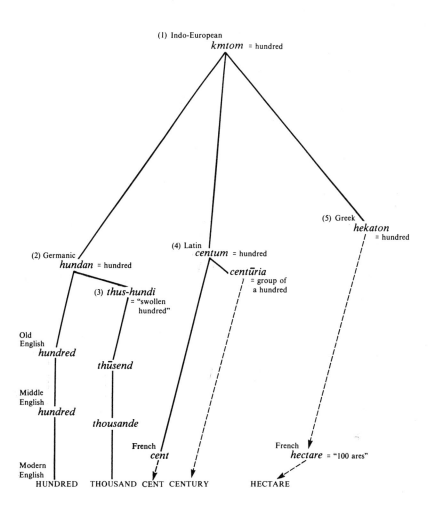

(1) Indo-European
kmtom = hundred

(5) Greek
hekaton
= hundred

(4) Latin
centum = hundred

centūria
= group of
a hundred

(2) Germanic
hundan = hundred

(3) *thus-hundi*
= "swollen
hundred"

Old
English
hundred

thūsend

Middle
English
hundred

thousande

French
cent

Modern
English
HUNDRED   THOUSAND CENT CENTURY

French
hectare = "100 ares"

HECTARE

kwekwlos

1. Indo-European *kwekwlos* ="wheel, circle" appears in Germanic *hwehulaz* ="wheel," Greek *kuklos* ="circle, wheel," Tocharian *kukäl* ="vehicle," and Sanskrit *cakrás* ="wheel, circle."

The noun *kwe-kwl-os* is derived by a regular Indo-European process from the verb root *kwel-* ="to revolve." *Kwekwlos* was thus literally "that which revolves."

The exact time and place of the invention of the wheel are not yet known, but the Indo-Europeans were among its very earliest users. The Kurgan people living north and northeast of the Black Sea, who were probably the original Indo-Europeans, were making vehicles with two and four solid wheels as early as 3000 B.C. and possibly much earlier. They may have invented the wheel themselves, or they may have learned of it from the Mesopotamians, who were also making wheeled vehicles at the same period. The idea could have been transmitted in either direction via the metal-using peoples of the Caucasus region, east of the Black Sea.

When a piece of strikingly new technology is borrowed from foreigners, foreign terms are usually borrowed with it. Not only is *kwekwlos* a native Indo-European term, clearly coined for the new device, but most if not all of the other Indo-European terms relating to vehicles are also native, not borrowed. (*See* **nobh-**="navel," *yugom* ="yoke" [given under **yeug-**= "to join"] and **wegh-**="to travel, carry by vehicle.")

To judge solely from the impressive linguistic evidence, therefore, the Indo-Europeans are certainly strong candidates as inventors of this momentous contrivance. But this remains to be proved or disproved by archaeology.

2. *Kwekwlos* became Germanic *hwehulaz,* with regular change of *k* to *h* (the Germanic *h* having a /ch/ sound, as in Scottish *loch*). *Hwehulaz* appears in Old Norse *hvel,* Middle Dutch *wiel,* Old Frisian *hwel,* and Old English *hwēol,* all meaning "wheel." Old English *hwēol* became Middle English *whele,* Modern English WHEEL.

3. *Kwekwlos* became Greek *kuklos* ="circle, wheel." This was borrowed into Late Latin as *cyclus,* which was adopted into English as CYCLE in the sixteenth century, meaning "circular path or orbit in astronomy," also "recurrent round of events, period."

Late Latin *cyclus* was also adopted into French as *cycle.* In the nineteenth century various human-powered vehicles were invented in Europe, chiefly in France; hence French *bicycle,* borrowed into English as BICYCLE.

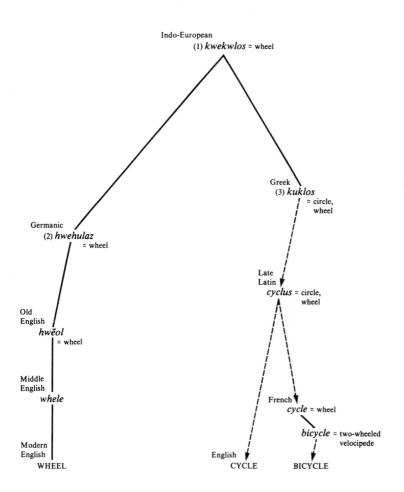

Indo-European
(1) *kwekwlos* = wheel

Greek
(3) *kuklos*
= circle,
wheel

Germanic
(2) *hwehulaz*
= wheel

Late
Latin
cyclus = circle,
wheel

Old
English
hwēol
= wheel

Middle
English
whele

French
cycle = wheel

bicycle = two-wheeled
velocipede

Modern
English
WHEEL

English
CYCLE

BICYCLE

77

kwetwer (I)

1. Indo-European *kwetwer,* also *kwetr,* ="four" appears in Germanic *fedwor,* Old Welsh *petguar,* Latin *quattuor,* Lithuanian *keturi,* Old Slavic *četyri,* Greek *tessares,* and Sanskrit *catúr-,* all meaning "four."

2. Germanic *fedwor* appears in Gothic *fidur-,* Old Norse *fjorir,* Old High German *fior* (whence modern German *vier*), and Old English *fēower,* all meaning "four." The last became Modern English FOUR.

3. Latin, besides the basic numeral *quattuor* ="four," had a number of words based on the Indo-European form *kwetr:* (a) *quadruplus* ="fourfold," adopted into French as *quadruple,* borrowed thence into English as QUADRUPLE; (b) *quadrāginta* ="forty," which was inherited in Italian as *quaranta* ="forty," hence *quarantina* ="period of forty days," specifically "period of isolation of possibly contagious ships or travelers arriving at a port or town"—this was borrowed into English (seventeenth century) as QUARANTINE; (c) *quadrāns, -ant-* ="fourth part," adopted into Middle English (fifteenth century) as QUADRANT ="navigational instrument embodying an arc of ninety degrees, or one fourth of a circle"; (d) *quadrus* ="four-sided figure, square." The Romance languages have a group of clearly related words meaning "square"—Italian *squadra,* Spanish *escuadra,* Old French *esquare;* they are derived from an unrecorded Latin noun *exquadra* ="square," from an also unrecorded verb *exquadrāre* ="to square out, make something square," from *ex* ="out" + *quadrus* ="square," as above.

Formed from Italian *squadra* was *squadrone* ="square formation of troops," also "unit of troops or ships"; this was borrowed into English (sixteenth century) as SQUADRON.

Old French *esquare* was borrowed into Middle English as SQUARE.

4. Indo-European *kwetr* also regularly appears in Greek as *tetra-* ="four," in (among other compound words) the Late Greek geometric term *tetrahedron* ="figure having four surfaces" (*hedra* ="surface"). This was adopted into English (sixteenth century) as TETRAHEDRON.

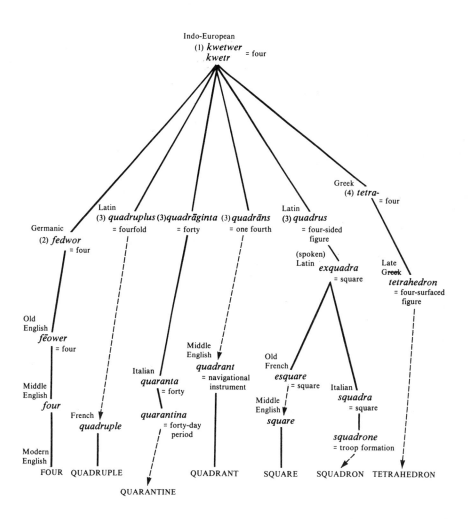

Indo-European
(1) *kwetwer*
kwetr = four

Germanic
(2) *fedwor*
= four

Latin
(3) *quadruplus*
= fourfold

(3)*quadrāginta*
= forty

(3)*quadrāns*
= one fourth

Latin
(3) *quadrus*
= four-sided figure

Greek
(4) *tetra-*
= four

Old English
fēower
= four

(spoken) Latin
exquadra
= square

Late Greek
tetrahedron
= four-surfaced figure

Middle English
quadrant
= navigational instrument

Old French
esquare
= square

Italian
quaranta
= forty

Italian
squadra
= square

Middle English
four

French
quadruple

quarantina
= forty-day period

Middle English
square

squadrone
= troop formation

Modern English
FOUR   QUADRUPLE

QUADRANT

SQUARE

SQUADRON   TETRAHEDRON

QUARANTINE

79

kwetwer (II)

1. Indo-European *kweturtos* = "fourth" is the ordinal adjective of *kwetwer* = "four" (*see* **kwetwer, I**). It appears in Germanic *fidworth-*, Old Welsh *petuerid*, Latin *quartus*, Lithuanian *ketvirtas*, Greek *tetartos*, and Sanskrit *caturtha-*, all meaning "fourth."

2. Germanic *fidworth-*, *fiworth-* appears in Old Norse *fiordhi*, Old High German *fiordo*, and Old English *feowertha*, all meaning "fourth." Old English *feowertha*, simplified to *feortha*, became Modern English FOURTH.

   Formed from Old English *feortha* was *feorth-ing* = "fourth part," specifically "a quarter of a penny." This became Middle English *ferthing*, Modern English FARTHING, a coin only recently (1950s) made obsolete by inflation, and still in figurative use as "the smallest possible amount of money."

3. Latin *quartus* = "fourth," in *quarta (pars)* = "fourth (part)," was inherited in Old French as *quarte* = "one fourth of a gallon." This was borrowed into Middle English as QUART = "two pints, one fourth of a galion," a unit that has been abolished in Britain in the interest of metric conformity, and is now in the process of being similarly abolished in the United States.

   A derivative of Latin *quartus* was *quartarius* = "fourth part of anything." This was inherited in Norman French as *quarter*, which was borrowed into Middle English (thirteenth century) as QUARTER.

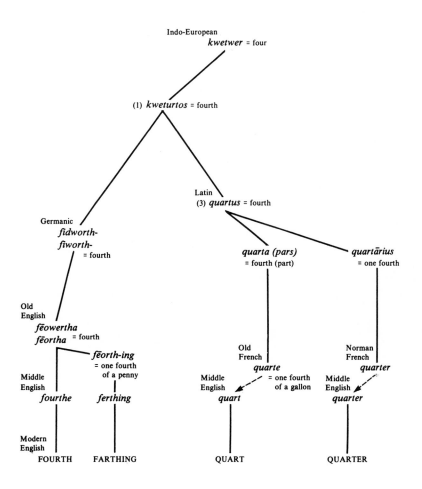

Indo-European
kwetwer = four

(1) *kweturtos* = fourth

Latin
(3) *quartus* = fourth

Germanic
fidworth-
fiworth-
= fourth

quarta (pars)
= fourth (part)

quartārius
= one fourth

Old
English
fēowertha
fēortha = fourth

fēorth-ing
= one fourth
of a penny

Old
French
quarte

Norman
French
quarter

Middle
English
fourthe

ferthing

Middle
English
quart
= one fourth
of a gallon

Middle
English
quarter

Modern
English
FOURTH

FARTHING

QUART

QUARTER

81

kwo-

1.   Many of the Indo-European interrogative words are formed on the stem *kwe* or *kwo-*. Among them are the pronoun *kwos* ="who?" (with accusative case *kwom* ="whom?" and genitive *kweso* ="whose?"), the adverb *kwei* = "for what cause?" and the adverb *kwū* ="in what way?" These and other derivatives of *kwo-* are the sources of interrogative/relative words in every branch of the language family, e.g.: Germanic *hwas* ="who," Old Irish *cuin* ="when," Latin *quis* ="who," Lithuanian *kàs* ="who, what," Greek *pōs* = "how," Hittite *kuiš* ="who," Sanskrit *kás* ="who."

2.   The personal pronoun *kwos, kwom, kweso* (="who, whom, whose") became Germanic *hwas, hwam, hwasa,* with the regular change of Indo-European *k* to Germanic *h*. The Germanic pronoun appears in Gothic *hwas,* Old High German *hwer,* and Old English *hwā, hwæm, hwæs.* The latter became Middle English *hwo/who, whom, whos,* whence Modern English WHO, WHOM, WHOSE.

   From the Germanic pronoun *hwas* was formed the compound word *hwa-līk-, hwe-līk-* ="of what form?" or, "what individual?" (with *līka* = "form, body"), appearing in Gothic *hvileiks,* Old High German *hwelīh,* Old Norse *hvílíkr,* and Old English *hwilc,* all meaning "of what kind?" or "what individual?" Old English *hwilc* became Middle English *whilk,* Modern English WHICH.

3.   The Indo-European pronoun *kwos* had the neuter form *kwod* ="which thing?" This regularly became Germanic *hwat,* appearing in Gothic *hwa,* Old High German *hwaz,* Old Norse *hvat,* and Old English *hwæt.* The last became Modern English WHAT.

4.   Indo-European *kwei* ="for what cause?" became Germanic *hwī,* appearing in Old Norse *hví,* Old Saxon *hwī,* and Old English *hwȳ,* becoming Modern English WHY.

5.   Indo-European *kwū* ="in what way?" became Germanic *hwō,* appearing in Old High German *wuo,* Old Frisian *hū,* and Old English *hū;* whence Middle English *hou,* Modern English HOW. Alone of the derivatives, this word lost its *w* in English, owing to the *w*-like influence of the following vowel *u*.

6.   Among the Latin derivatives of Indo-European *kwo* is *quālis* ="of what kind?" From this the Roman scholar Cicero coined the abstract noun *quālitās* ="the intrinsic nature of a thing"; the formation and meaning of this word were modeled on those of its Greek equivalent *poiotēs* ="intrinsic nature," abstract noun of *poios* ="of what kind?" Latin *quālitās* was adopted into Old French as *qualite,* borrowed into Middle English as *qualite,* becoming Modern English QUALITY.

7.   Similarly from Latin *quantus* ="how much? how big?" was formed the noun *quantitās* ="the size or amount of something." This was likewise adopted into Old French as *quantite,* whence Modern English QUANTITY.

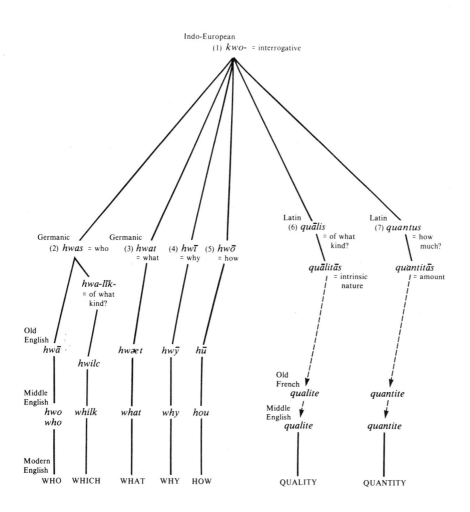

Indo-European
(1) *kwo-* = interrogative

Germanic
(2) *hwas* = who

Germanic
(3) *hwat* = what

(4) *hwī* = why

(5) *hwō* = how

Latin
(6) *quālis* = of what kind?

Latin
(7) *quantus* = how much?

hwa-līk- = of what kind?

quālitās = intrinsic nature

quantitās = amount

Old English
hwā   *hwæt*   *hwȳ*   *hū*

hwilc

Middle English
hwo   *whilk*   *what*   *why*   *hou*
who

Old French
qualite   *quantite*

Middle English
qualite   *quantite*

Modern English
WHO   WHICH   WHAT   WHY   HOW

QUALITY   QUANTITY

83

kwon

1. Indo-European *kwon* = "dog" appears in Germanic *hundaz,* Old Irish *cū, con,* Latin *canis,* Lithuanian *šu, šuñs,* Greek *kuōn,* Tocharian *ku, kon,* and Sanskrit *śvā, śun-,* all meaning "dog." The change of Indo-European *k* to *s* in Lithuanian and Sanskrit is regular.

  The dog had already been domesticated several thousand years before the time of the Indo-Europeans. Dog bones have been found in association with their earliest known settlements (north of the Black Sea, *c.* 4500 B.C.).

2. Germanic *hundaz* appears in Gothic *hunds,* Old Norse *hundr,* Old High German *hunt,* and Old English *hund,* all meaning "dog." Old English *hund* became Modern English HOUND. This word, originally the general word for all dogs, was in the Middle Ages especially applied to those bred for hunting in packs—the foxhounds, staghounds, beagles, and some others. The English word *dog,* first appearing from unknown origins in the eleventh century, at first designated some particular breed of dog, possibly of the mastiff type. As *hund* was increasingly restricted to foxhounds, etc., *dog* became the primary general word.

3. Old High German *hunt* became Modern German *hund,* remaining the general word for the animal, without specialization as in English. Hence *dachshund* = "badger-dog" (*dachs* = "badger"); this breed was probably so named, not because the badger was its exclusive quarry, but because the dog itself, with its pointed head and its digging power, resembled the badger. It was adopted into English as DACHSHUND.

4. Indo-European *kwon* is well represented in the Celtic languages: Old Irish *cū,* Cornish *ki,* Welsh *ci.* Hence Welsh *corgi* = "dwarf-dog" (*corr* = "dwarf"), a short-legged spitz type closely resembling the Swedish spitz. It was so named in contrast to the larger Welsh sheepdogs. It was adopted into English (nineteenth century) as CORGI.

5. Latin *canis,* almost certainly related to this root, is an aberrant form. Indo-European *kwon* should normally yield Latin *quon-.*

  In New Latin the word *Canis* has been adopted as the zoological name of the genus of dogs—*Canis familiaris* = "the domestic dog" (in all its hundreds of varieties), *C. lupus* = "the wolf," and *C. aureus* = "the jackal."

  The adjective *caninus* = "being a dog, relating to dogs," has been adopted into English as CANINE.

6. Italian *canile* and Old French *chenil,* both medieval words meaning "a shelter for a dog or dogs," are regularly descended from a Latin word *canile,* which has not survived in documents but is clearly a straightforward derivative of *canis* = "dog." The Middle English word *kenel* = "shelter for dogs," is likewise assumed to be from an unrecorded source, Norman French *kenil,* corresponding to Old French *chenil. Kenel* became Modern English KENNEL.

84

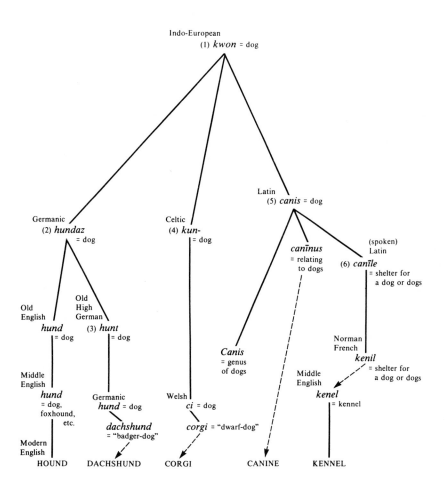

Indo-European
(1) *kwon* = dog

Germanic
(2) *hundaz*
= dog

Celtic
(4) *kun-*
= dog

Latin
(5) *canis* = dog

Old
English
hund
= dog

Old
High
German
(3) *hunt*
= dog

Middle
English
hund
= dog,
foxhound,
etc.

Germanic
hund = dog

dachshund
= "badger-dog"

Welsh
ci = dog

corgi = "dwarf-dog"

canīnus
= relating
to dogs

(spoken)
Latin
(6) *canīle*
= shelter for
a dog or dogs

Canis
= genus
of dogs

Norman
French
kenil
= shelter for
a dog or dogs

Middle
English
kenel
= kennel

Modern
English
HOUND   DACHSHUND   CORGI   CANINE   KENNEL

85

leubh-

1. The Indo-European word *leubh-* ="to love, like, desire" appears in Germanic *lubo* ="love," Latin *libīdo* ="desire," Old Slavic *lyubu* ="dear," and Sanskrit *lubhyati* ="feels desire."

2. Germanic *lubo* appears in Old High German *luba,* Old Frisian *luba,* and Old English *lufu,* all meaning "love." *Lufu* became Modern English LOVE.

3. In Germanic, several specialized meanings occur. From the notion of "love, like" came the notion "approve of, praise" and "favor, approval." The Germanic noun *laubo* meant "approval, permission," appearing in Middle High German *loube* and Old English *lēaf* ="permission." This became Modern English LEAVE (noun)="permission" (not related to the verb *leave* ="depart").

4. Another Germanic development was the meaning "to cherish, hold dear, trust, put one's faith in." This appears in the Germanic verb *ga-laubjan* (*ga-* being an "intensive" prefix, not affecting the meaning), becoming Gothic *galaubjan,* Old High German *gilouben,* and Old English *gelēfan,* all meaning "to trust, have faith in." Old English *gelēfan* gave way to the variant form *belēfan* (*be-* being a prefix of the same nature as *ge-*), which became Modern English BELIEVE.

5. Latin *libīdo,* on the other hand, was specialized in the sense of "desire, erotic love." It was adopted into English in the early twentieth century as the psychoanalyst's term for sexual desire, LIBIDO.

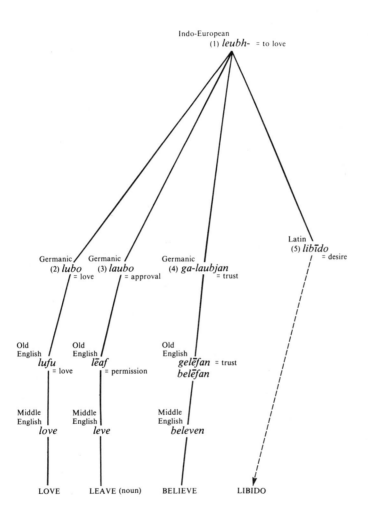

Indo-European
(1) *leubh-* = to love

Latin
(5) *libīdo*
= desire

Germanic / Germanic
(2) *lubo*   (3) *laubo*
= love   = approval

Germanic
(4) *ga-laubjan*
= trust

Old
English
lufu
= love

Old
English
lēaf
= permission

Old
English
gelēfan = trust
belēfan

Middle
English
love

Middle
English
leve

Middle
English
beleven

LOVE   LEAVE (noun)   BELIEVE   LIBIDO

87

leuk-

1.   Indo-European *leuk-* = "to shine, bright, light" appears in Germanic *liuhtam* = "light," Old Irish *luchair* = "brightness," Latin *lux, lūc-* = "light" and *lucēre* = "to shine (etc.)," Lithuanian *laũkas* = "pale," Greek *leukos* = "white," Armenian *lois* = "light," Hittite *lukk-* = "to shine," Tocharian *luk-* = "to shine," and Sanskrit *rócate* = "shines" and *roká* = "light" (with regular change of Indo-European *l* to Indic *r*).

2.   Germanic *liuhtam* is from the Indo-European noun form *leuktom* = "light." *Liuhtam* appears in Old High German *lioht* (whence modern German *licht*), Old Frisian *liacht,* and Old English *lēoht, līht,* all meaning "light." The last became Modern English LIGHT, with the archaic *gh* spelling left over from the original velar sound, which is still present in German *licht* and Scottish *licht.*

3.   From Latin *lūmen* = "light" were formed: (a) the adjective *lūminōsus* = "full of light, shining, bright," adopted into Middle English as *luminose,* Modern English LUMINOUS; (b) the verb *illūmināre* = "to shine light upon, brighten" (*il-, in-* = "upon"), adopted into English as ILLUMINATE.

4.   From Latin *lucēre* = "to shine" were formed: (a) the adjective *lucidus* = "shining, bright," adopted into English (sixteenth century) as LUCID, originally meaning "shining, brilliant," now chiefly meaning "very clearly intelligible"; (b) the Late Latin verb *ēlucidāre* = "to make bright" (*e-, ex-* = "out"), adopted into English as ELUCIDATE, now likewise meaning "to render intelligible."

5.   Latin *lustrāre* = "to brighten" was inherited in Italian as *lustrare,* forming the noun *lustro* = "brilliance, brightness," which was borrowed into French as *lustre* and thence into English as LUSTER, now meaning "richly diffused light," also figuratively "human splendor," also "glittering piece of glass."

From Latin *lustrāre* also was formed the compound verb *illustrāre* = "to shine light on" (*il-, in-* = "upon"). This was adopted into English (sixteenth century) as ILLUSTRATE, now meaning "to elucidate with examples" or "to embellish a written text with pictures." Latin *illustris* = "shining, noble" was also used figuratively to mean "eminent, glorious, noble," and was so adopted into English (sixteenth century) as ILLUSTRIOUS, now specifically meaning either "of famous and exalted family" or "famous for brilliant achievement."

6.   Latin *lūna* = "moon, moon goddess" is from an Indo-European form *louk-sna* = "the shining one" (feminine). The original Indo-European name for the moon (*see* **mēn-**) was masculine, as it remains in the Germanic languages. In both Latin and Greek it was replaced by feminine nouns (Latin *lūna,* Greek *selēnē*), no doubt reflecting acceptance by the Latins and Greeks of Mediterranean matriarchal moon cults. The adjective of *lūna* was *lūnāris,* adopted into English (seventeenth century) as LUNAR.

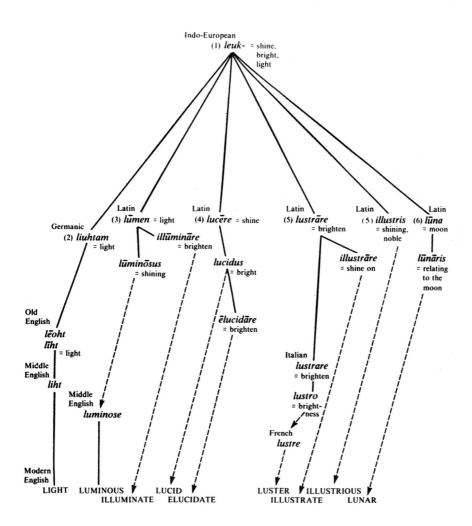

89

magh-

1. Indo-European *magh-* = "to be able, to have power," with its derivative noun *maghtis* = "power," appears in Germanic *magan* = "to be able," *mahtiz* = "power," and *magena* = "power," Old Slavic *mogǫ* = "I can" and *mošti* = "power," Greek *mākhanā, mēkhanē,* = "that which enables, a device, engine, machine," Tocharian *mokats* = "powerful," and Sanskrit *maghá-* = "power."

2. Germanic *magan* appears in Gothic *magan,* Old Norse *mega,* Old High German *magan* (whence Modern German *mögen*), and Old English *magan,* all meaning "to have the power, to be able." This verb was used as a "modal auxiliary," like the verb *can.* The Old English inflections *mæg* = "I am able, she/he is able" and *mihte* = "was/were able" became Middle English *may* (present tense) and *mighte* (past tense), Modern English MAY and MIGHT. This verb is now used chiefly to express possible action or permission to act, rather than power or ability to act.

3. Germanic *mahtiz* appears in Gothic *mahts,* Old High German *maht* (whence Modern German *macht*), and Old English *miht,* all meaning "power, strength." The last became Modern English MIGHT, now a somewhat archaic or rhetorical noun.

4. Germanic *magena* appears in Old Norse *megin,* Old High German *magan,* and Old English *mægen,* all meaning "power, strength." The last became the noun MAIN, now surviving solely in the traditional phrase *with might and main.*

Both Old English *mægen* and Old Norse *megin* were used in compound nouns such as Old English *mægenstrengo* = "mighty-strength," Old Norse *meginland* = "large-landmass." From a number of these expressions in both Old English and Old Norse (during the centuries when Norse people settled in Scotland and England) arose the Middle English adjective *mayn* or *maine* = "great," becoming Modern English MAIN (adjective) = "principal, most important."

5. The corresponding noun in Greek is *mākhanā* (Doric dialect), *mēkhanē* (Attic, or Athenian, dialect) = "that which enables, a contrivance, device, engine." The Doric form, used in Doric Greek cities in Italy, was borrowed into early Latin as *māchina* = "device, engine." This was adopted into French as *machine,* and thence into English in the sixteenth century as MACHINE. From the Attic form (the usage of Athens, Classical Greek), the adjective *mēkhanikos* = "relating to machines" was formed. This was adopted into Latin as *mēchanicus,* and thence into Middle English (fifteenth century) as *mechanicelle,* becoming Modern English MECHANICAL.

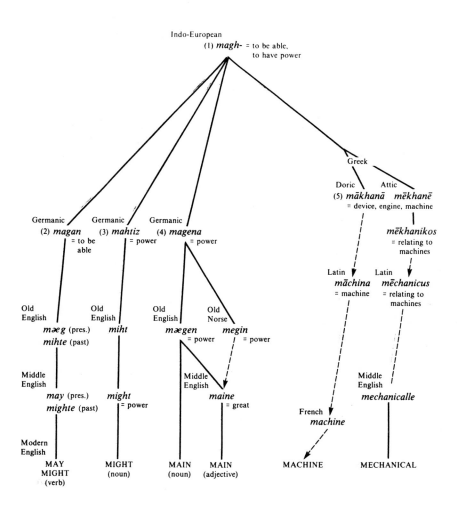

Indo-European
(1) *magh-* = to be able,
to have power

Germanic
(2) *magan*
= to be able

Germanic
(3) *mahtiz*
= power

Germanic
(4) *magena*
= power

Greek

Doric
(5) *mākhanā* *mēkhanē*
= device, engine, machine

Attic

mēkhanikos
= relating to
machines

Old
English

mæg (pres.)
mihte (past)

Old
English

miht

Old
English

mægen
= power

Old
Norse

megin
= power

Latin
māchina
= machine

Latin
mēchanicus
= relating to
machines

Middle
English

may (pres.)
mighte (past)

might
= power

Middle
English

maine
= great

Middle
English

mechanicalle

Modern
English

MAY
MIGHT
(verb)

MIGHT
(noun)

MAIN
(noun)

MAIN
(adjective)

French
machine

MACHINE

MECHANICAL

91

māter

1. Indo-European *māter* = "mother" appears in Germanic *mōthar*, Old Irish *māthir*, Latin *māter*, Old Slavic *mati*, Greek *mētēr*, Tocharian *mācar*, and Sanskrit *mātár*, all meaning "mother."

The baby-language syllable *mā* appears in words meaning "mother" and "breast" in languages all over the world. The Indo-European noun *māter* is formed from this syllable with the suffix *-ter*, which occurs also in the words *pəter* = "father," *bhrāter* = "brother," and *dhugəter* = "daughter." This suffix marks the whole set of words as formal kinship terms, belonging to the "high language" of religion, law, and social obligations. The word *māter* was the formal title of the married woman of full status, the female head of the household.

2. Indo-European *māter* regularly became Germanic *mōthar*, which appears in Old Norse *mōthir*, Old High German *muotar* (whence Modern German *mutter*), and Old English *mōdor*, all meaning "mother." Old English *mōdor* became Modern English MOTHER.

3. The Latin adjective *māternus* = "of or relating to a mother" was adopted into English as MATERNAL. The Medieval Latin noun *māternitās* = "the fact or condition of being a mother" was adopted as MATERNITY.

4. The Latin noun *mātrōna* meant specifically "married lady of high social status." It was adopted into Old French as *matrone*, borrowed thence into Middle English as *matrone*, becoming Modern English MATRON.

5. The Latin noun *mātrimōnium* meant "the legal institution that defines the *māter*, marriage." It was adopted into Norman French as *matrimonie*, borrowed into Middle English as *matrimoyne*, Modern English MATRIMONY.

6. The rigorously patriarchal Indo-Europeans did not originally worship female deities. But those Indo-European groups that settled in Mediterranean lands, where goddesses of fertility and agriculture had been worshiped for thousands of years before their arrival, were constrained to blend these powerful cults into their own.

The Roman deity Ceres presided over fruit-growing and agriculture. One of the titles given to her by the Romans was *Alma Māter* = "Nourishing Mother" (*māter* here being a term of respect as well as signifying the fertile "parent" of crops). In the seventeenth century this old title was taken over as an affectionate term for a university viewed as the (intellectually) nourishing mother of students (*alumni* = "those who are nourished," foster-children); hence English ALMA MATER.

7. Many of the oldest Mediterranean cities such as Athens were under the protection of female deities whose cults survived the Indo-European incursions. Thus a city itself could be seen as a female, as in the Greek term *mētropolis* = "mother-city" (*mētēr* = "mother" + *polis* = "city"). When a city such as Athens built up an extensive territory or empire, the *mētropolis* could

also be seen as the "mother" of its subject lands. The word was so borrowed by the Romans as Latin *mētropolis,* applied by them to the city of Rome, which itself was regarded as a goddess, *Rōma Māter,* with mother attributes—mother to the entire Roman Empire. The word was adopted into English as METROPOLIS in the sixteenth century.

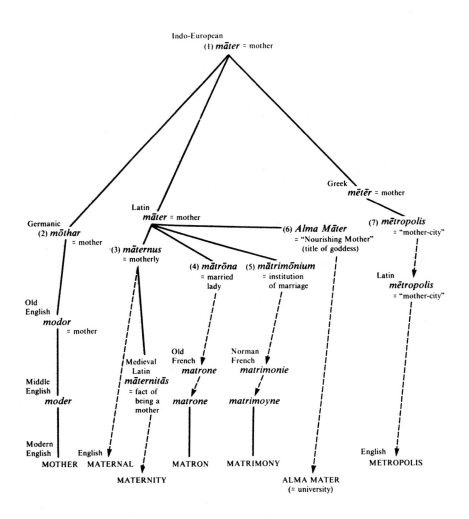

medhu

1. Indo-European *medhu* = "honey, mead" appears in Germanic *meduz* = "mead," Celtic *med-* = "mead," Russian *med-* = "mead," Latvian *medus* = "honey, mead," Greek *methu* = "wine, strong drink," and Sanskrit *madhu* = "honey, sweet intoxicating drink."

Mead is made of fermented honey and water, sometimes also with malted grain. It can be made as strong as strong beer or even wine.

The Indo-European peoples in eastern, northern, and western Europe (Slavs, Balts, Germans, Celts) continued to make mead into historical times, and perhaps still do in some country places. But the forerunners of the Greeks and Romans, when they settled in the already winemaking lands of the Mediterranean, gave up their traditional drink and took to the vine, adopting its local (non–Indo-European) name *woinom:* Greek *(w)oinos,* Latin *vinum* = "vine, wine." Latin discarded the word *medhu* entirely, but Greek kept it on as an archaic and poetical word for strong drink.

2. Germanic *meduz* appears in Old High German *metu,* Old Norse *mjodr,* and Old English *meodu,* all meaning "mead." The Gothic form *midus* was recorded by a Greek writer in 448 A.D. as the name of the drink used "instead of wine" at the court of the king of the Huns. To the Greeks and Romans, mead was the drink of barbarians. Old English *meodu* became Middle English *mede* and Modern English MEAD.

3. Formed from Greek *methu* = "wine, strong drink" are numerous words referring to drunkenness, such as *methuskein* = "to make drunk, intoxicate." It has recently been convincingly suggested that wine was not the only intoxicant used by the Greeks—that they used various inebriating and hallucinogenic herbs mixed with wine and water (see R. G. Wasson and others, *The Road to Eleusis* [New York, 1978]).

The name of a well-known bluish-violet gemstone was *lithos amethustos,* literally seeming to mean "the stone that wards off drunkenness": *lithos* = "stone" + *a-* = "un-" + *methustos* = "drunk-making" (from *methuskein*). *Amethustos* was adopted into Late Latin as *amethystus,* thence into Old French as *amatiste,* and thence into Middle English as *ametiste,* corrected to AMETHYST in Modern English.

Because of the apparent etymological meaning, it has long been imagined that the Greeks must have used the amethyst as a remedy or amulet against intoxication. The etymology is still given in most modern dictionaries, although it was long ago refuted by the Roman scientist Pliny, who pointed out that the name refers to the *color* of the stone, the color of red wine heavily cut with water. *Amethustos* was "the un-drunk-making drink, the beverage of moderation"; the *lithos amethustos* was "the watered-wine-colored stone."

Indo-European
(1) *medhu* = mead

Greek
(3) *methu* = wine, strong drink

methuskein = to make drunk

a-methustos = nonintoxicating

lithos amethustos
= bluish-violet
gemstone

Germanic
(2) *meduz*
= mead

Latin
amethystus
= amethyst

Old
English
meodu
= mead

Old
French
amatiste

Middle
English
mede

Middle
English
ametiste

Modern
English
MEAD

AMETHYST

medhyos

1. The Indo-European adjective *medhyos* = "middle" appears in Germanic *midjaz*, Old Irish *mid-*, Latin *medius*, Greek *mesos*, Armenian *mēj*, and Sanskrit *mádhya-*, all meaning "middle."

2. Germanic *midjaz* appears in Gothic *midjis*, Old Norse *midhr*, Old High German *mitti*, and Old English *midde*, all also meaning "middle." The last became Modern English MID, now relatively rare as a separate word, but used in combinations such as *midway, midsummer, midtown, midwest,* etc.

3. Alongside the common Germanic form *midjaz* there occurs in Western Germanic the form *middilaz* (with the "diminutive" suffix *-il-*, which in this case does not affect the meaning). This appears in Old High German *mittil* (whence Modern German *mittel*), Old Frisian *middel,* and Old English *middel,* which last became Modern English MIDDLE, now the basic and usual word for this basic concept.

4. Latin *medius* had a (post-Classical) extended form *mediānus* = "being in the middle," which was adopted into English (sixteenth century) as MEDIAN, used chiefly in technical contexts, as in mathematics. Latin *mediānus* was also inherited into the Romance languages as Italian *mezzano,* Spanish *mediano,* and Old French *meien* or *moien* (whence Modern French *moyen* = "middle"). Old French *meien* was borrowed into Middle English as *meen.* This became Modern English MEAN, which as adjective = "middling, intermediate" is now rare except in mathematics (*mean annual rainfall,* etc.), but has proliferated as a noun = (a) "middle point or state" (as in *the golden mean*) and (b) in the plural MEANS = "method, instrumentality."

   The neuter of Latin *medius* was *medium,* which was adopted into English (sixteenth century) as MEDIUM = "intermediate agency," later also especially "system of mass communication," with its much-used modern plural MEDIA. MEDIUM is also used as an adjective = "middling."

5. Greek *mesos* = "middle" has also been adopted into technical language to form numerous compounds such as MESOLITHIC = "Middle Stone Age," MESOTHORAX = "the middle part of an insect's thorax," and to form the noun MESON = "subatomic particle that is regarded as intermediate between the lepton and the baryon."

96

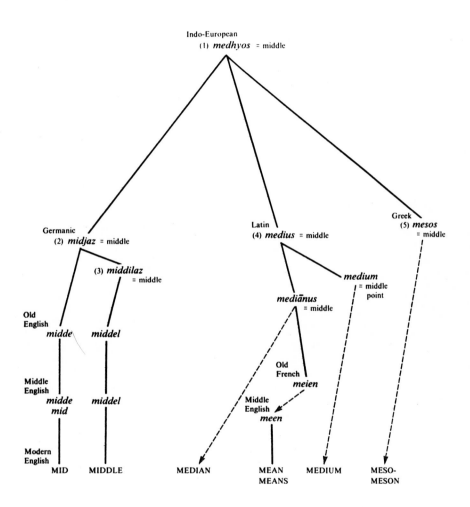

97

meg-

1. The Indo-European adjective root *meg-* ="great" appears in Germanic *mikilaz,* Old Irish *mochtae,* Latin *magnus,* Greek *megas,* Hittite *mekkis,* and Sanskrit *mahā,* all meaning "great, large" (both physically and abstractly).

2. Germanic *mikilaz* appears in Gothic *mikils,* Old Norse *mikill,* Old High German *michil,* and Old English *mycel,* all meaning "great." Old English *mycel* became Middle English *muchel,* losing its termination to become *muche,* Modern English MUCH.

3. Formed from Latin *magnus* ="great" was the abstract noun *magnitūdō* = "greatness," adopted into English as MAGNITUDE. Also formed from *magnus* was the compound adjective *magnificus* ="great-doing, great in deeds" (*-fic-* ="doing," from *facere* ="to do"). This was adopted into English as MAGNIFICENT, with a participial ending by analogy with adjectives like *beneficent.*

4. Latin *mājor* ="greater" (originally *mag-yos*) was used as the irregular comparative of *magnus.* It was adopted into English (sixteenth century) as the adjective MAJOR. In seventeenth-century French, the military rank *sergent-major* was that of a field officer ranking above a captain. Shortened to *major*, it was borrowed into English as MAJOR (noun). (*Sergent-major* was later reclassified as a noncommissioned rank, whence English SERGEANT MAJOR.)

5. Latin *maximus* ="greatest" (originally *mag-sam-os*) was likewise used as the irregular superlative of *magnus.* Its neuter form *maximum* ="greatest amount or degree" was adopted into English as MAXIMUM.

6. Latin *magister,* originally meaning "he who is great, man of high rank," was used as a title of high officials of the Roman Republic, including the consuls, and also as a general word for "man in authority, leader, owner." In the time of the Roman Empire, Latin *magister* was adopted by the German peoples on the northern border, becoming Old Norse *meistari,* Old High German *meister* (remaining *meister* in Modern German), and Old English *magister* ="ruler, chief, commander." Latin *magister* was also inherited in Old French as *maistre* (Modern French *maître*). Middle English *maister* is based partly on inheritance of the Old English form and partly on a borrowing of the Old French form; it became Modern English MASTER, with variant MISTER and feminine form MISTRESS, MRS.

7. Greek *megas* ="great," with alternate stems *mega-* and *megalo-,* has been adopted into English for the prefixes MEGA- and MEGALO-, used to form such compound words as MEGAPHONE and MEGALOMANIA.

8. Sanskrit *mahā* ="great" was inherited in Hindi and used to form the honorary title *mahārājā* ="great king" (*rājā* ="king"), used by some of the princes of the Mogul Empire, some later becoming sovereign rulers. This was borrowed into English (first in the seventeenth century) as MAHARAJA.

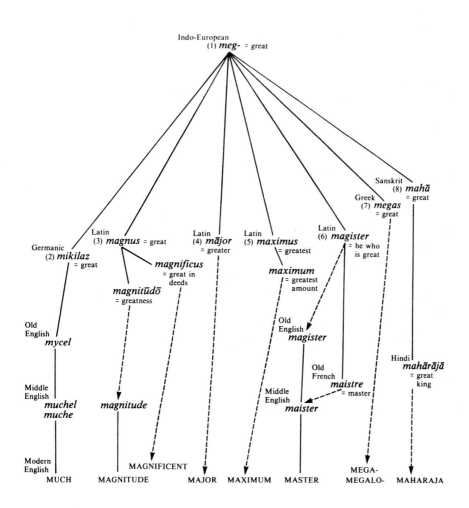

Indo-European
(1) *meg-* = great

Germanic
(2) *mikilaz*
= great

Latin
(3) *magnus* = great

magnificus
= great in
deeds

magnitūdō
= greatness

Latin
(4) *mājor*
= greater

Latin
(5) *maximus*
= greatest

maximum
= greatest
amount

Latin
(6) *magister*
= he who
is great

Greek
(7) *megas*
= great

Sanskrit
(8) *mahā*
= great

Old
English
mycel

Old
English
magister

Old
French
maistre
= master

Hindi
mahārājā
= great
king

Middle
English
muchel
muche

magnitude

Middle
English
maister

Modern
English
MUCH

MAGNITUDE

MAGNIFICENT

MAJOR

MAXIMUM

MASTER

MEGA-
MEGALO-

MAHARAJA

99

men-

1. The Indo-European root *men-* = (as verb) "to think, to reason, to call to mind" (and as noun) "mind, intellect, reason, thought" appears in Germanic *mun-* = "to think" and *ga-mundiz* = "mind," Old Irish *menme* = "mind," Latin *mēns, ment-* = "mind" and *meminisse* = "to remember," Lithuanian *menù* = "think" and *mintìs* = "thought," Old Slavic *mǐněti* = "think," Greek *mnāsthai* = "remember" and *mnēmōn* = "remembering," and Sanskrit *mányate* = "thinks" and *mántraḥ* = "counsel, hymn."

2. In Germanic *ga-mundiz,* the *ga-* is a "collective" prefix that has little effect on the meaning of the word. It appears in Gothic *gamunds,* Old High German *gimunt,* and Old English *gemynd,* all meaning "mind, intellect." Like all Old English words with the prefix *ge-, gemynd* lost it in Middle English, becoming *y-mund,* then *minde,* and in Modern English MIND.

3. Latin *mēns* (nominative) with stem *ment-* = "mind, intellect, intelligence" is exactly parallel to the Germanic form *ga-mundiz* (both representing an Indo-European noun *mntis* = "mind"). From *ment-* was formed a Late Latin adjective *mentālis* = "belonging or relating to the mind"; this was adopted into Old French as *mental,* and thence into (Middle) English as MENTAL.

4. In Latin *meminisse* = "to remember," the initial *me-* is a "reduplication" of the stem *min-* and does not affect the meaning. The imperative form of this verb was *memento* = "remember!" This was used in such medieval phrases as *memento mori* = "remember that you must die," a slogan associated with the practice of keeping a skull or "death's-head" as a reminder of human mortality. The word was thus borrowed into English as MEMENTO = "reminder," later merely = "a souvenir of some past time."

5. Another Latin derivative of the root is *reminiscī* = "to call back into mind, recollect" (*re-* = "back, again") forming a Late Latin noun *reminiscentia* = "recollection," adopted into English as REMINISCENCE.

6. Latin *monēre* is formed on *mon-,* the "o-grade" of the root, + the "causative" suffix *-ēyo-;* the underlying meaning is thus "to cause (someone) to think, to bring to someone's mind"; the actual meaning in Latin was "to warn." Among the compounds formed from this verb was *praemonēre* = "to forewarn" (*prae* = "before"), with Late Latin abstract noun *praemonitiō* = "a forewarning." This was adopted into English as PREMONITION.

7. Greek *mnāsthai* = "to remember" and *mnēmōn* = "remembering" contain an extended form of the root *mnā-.* From *mnēmōn* was formed the adjective *mnēmonikos* = "relating to memory, intended to aid the memory." This was adopted into Medieval Latin as *mnemonicus* and thence into English as MNEMONIC.

8. The underlying meaning of Sanskrit *mántraḥ* was "thought, formulated thought," hence (a) "advice, counsel" and (b) "sacred phrase or text, hymn of praise in the *Veda.*" In sense (b) it was adopted into English (early nineteenth century) as MANTRA, now enjoying a vogue in the West with neo-Hindu cults such as the movement for "Krishna consciousness."

100

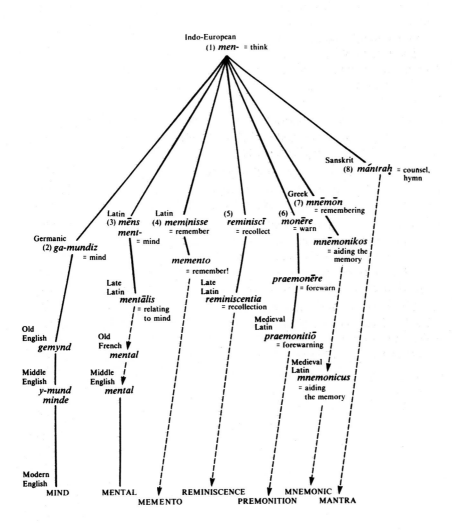

Indo-European
(1) *men-* = think

Sanskrit
(8) *mántraḥ* = counsel, hymn

Greek
(7) *mnēmōn* = remembering

Latin
(3) *mēns ment-* = mind

Latin
(4) *meminisse* = remember

(5) *reminiscī* = recollect

(6) *monēre* = warn

mnēmonikos = aiding the memory

Germanic
(2) *ga-mundiz* = mind

memento = remember!

Late Latin
mentālis = relating to mind

Late Latin
reminiscentia = recollection

praemonēre = forewarn

Medieval Latin
praemonitiō = forewarning

Old English
gemynd

Old French
mental

Medieval Latin
mnemonicus = aiding the memory

Middle English
y-mund minde

Middle English
mental

Modern English
MIND

MENTAL

MEMENTO

REMINISCENCE

PREMONITION

MNEMONIC

MANTRA

mēn-

1. Indo-European *mēn-* = both "moon" and "month" appears in Germanic *mǣnon-* = "moon" and *mǣnoth-* = "month," Old Irish *mí* = "month," Latin *mēnsis* = "month," Lithuanian *ménesis* = "moon/month," Old Slavic *měsęcǐ* = "moon/month," Greek *mēn* = "moon/month," Tocharian *mañ* = "moon/month," and Sanskrit *mā́s* = "moon/month."

    The word *mēn-* itself is an extension of the verb *mē-* = "to measure." The moon was thus known as "the measure" or "the measurer" (of days), and the lunar month was known by the same word. It was a masculine noun.

2. Germanic *mǣnon* = "moon" appears in Gothic *mēna*, Old Norse *máni*, Old High German *māno*, and Old English *mōna*, all meaning "moon." The last became Modern English MOON.

3. Germanic *mǣnoth-* = "month" appears in Gothic *mēnōths*, Old Norse *mánudhr*, Old High German *mānōd*, and Old English *mōnath*, all meaning "month." The last became Modern English MONTH.

4. Latin *mēnsis* = "month" had the plural form *mēnsēs* = "months," also "women's monthly discharges." This was adopted into medical English (sixteenth century) as MENSES. From *mēnsis* the adjective *mēnstruus* = "monthly" formed the verb *mēnstruāre* = "to discharge menses," which was adopted into English as MENSTRUATE.

5. Also from *mēnsis* = "month" was formed *sēmēstris* = "six-monthly" (*sē-, sex* = "six"). This was adopted into German as *semester* = "academic half-year," which was borrowed into English as SEMESTER. (Of similar origin is TRIMESTER = "one of three terms of an academic year.")

6. Greek *mēn* = "moon/month" was adopted into French to form the word *ménopause* = "cessation of menstruation" (Greek *pausis* = "cessation"). This was borrowed into English as MENOPAUSE.

7. From Greek *mēn* = "moon/month" was formed the diminutive *mēniskos* = "little moon, crescent moon," applied to things of crescent shape. This was adopted into New Latin as *meniscus* = "crescent-shaped object," especially "curved surface of a liquid held in a container"; borrowed into English as MENISCUS.

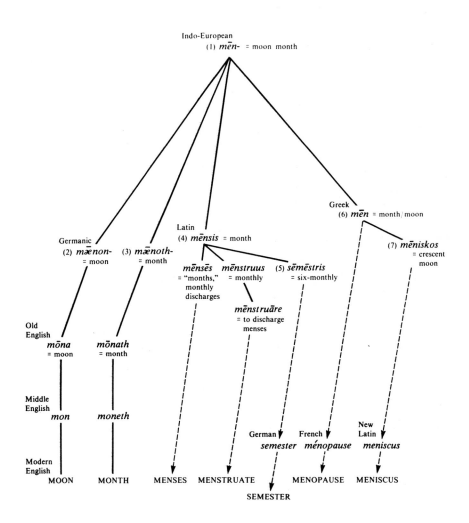

Indo-European
(1) *mēn-* = moon month

Greek
(6) *mēn* = month/moon

Germanic
(2) *mǣnon-*
= moon

(3) *mǣnoth-*
= month

Latin
(4) *mēnsis* = month

(7) *mēniskos*
= crescent
moon

mēnsēs
= "months,"
monthly
discharges

mēnstruus
= monthly

(5) *sēmēstris*
= six-monthly

mēnstruāre
= to discharge
menses

Old
English
mōna
= moon

mōnath
= month

Middle
English
mon

moneth

German
semester

French
ménopause

New
Latin
meniscus

Modern
English
MOON

MONTH

MENSES

MENSTRUATE

MENOPAUSE

MENISCUS

SEMESTER

103

mer-

1. Indo-European *mer-* = "to die," with its derivative noun *mrtis, mrtrom* = "death," appears in Germanic *murthram* = "homicide," Latin *mors, mort-* = "death," Lithuanian *mirstu* = "die" and *mirtis* = "death," Armenian *meranim* = "die," and Sanskrit *marati* = "dies" and *mrtis* = "death."

2. Germanic *murthram* appears in recorded form in only two of the Germanic languages, Gothic *maurthr* and Old English *morthor* = "criminal homicide."

The Old French word *murtre* = "criminal homicide" is obviously borrowed from Germanic; the reconstructed source is a Frankish form *murthr-*, which has not survived in recorded form.

Old English *morthor* became Middle English *morthre*, which would normally have become *morther* in Modern English. But the Middle English pronunciation was influenced by the contemporary Old French word *murtre* to emerge as *murdre*, Modern English MURDER.

3. From Latin *mors, mort-* = "death" was formed the adjective *mortālis* = "subject to death, human," with its reverse *immortālis* (*in-* = "not") = "not subject to death, divine"; these were adopted into (Middle) English as MORTAL, IMMORTAL.

4. The contrast between the human race, doomed to die, and the undying gods is an ancient conception of the Indo-European peoples (though not of course unique to them). At the Indo-European level itself, an adjective *mortos, mrtos* = "mortal" is reconstructible, and so is its complement *n-mortos* = "immortal" (*n-* being a negative prefix). The latter appears in Sanskrit *amrta* = Avestan *aməsa* = "immortal," and Greek *ambrotos* = "immortal" and *ambrosia* = "immortality."

Sanskrit *amrta* = "immortality" is used in the *Rig Veda* as a synonym or title of Soma, a divine substance that when ingested by devotees made them like the gods. The American mycologist R. Gordon Wasson has shown that Soma was the hallucinogenic mushroom fly agaric, which the Indo-Iranians must have known from central Asia, where shamanistic use of fly agaric is very ancient.

Greek *ambrosia*, also understood as meaning "immortality," was the name of the food of the gods, from which they derived or sustained their immortality; it was also given to divine horses and to heroes. It was also used as the name of various herbs.

It is thus possible that the original Indo-European–speaking people, who on archaeological grounds probably lived in south Russia before 4000 B.C., possessed or knew of a "divine" food, the ingestion of which was the center of a religion or cult. If, as Wasson suggests, this was fly agaric, the Indo-Iranians later migrated southward to countries where the mushroom does not grow; they retained the religion, and the hymns of the *Rig Veda* contain recognizable though cryptic descriptions of the mushroom and its effects; but substitutes were introduced to replace the mushroom itself. The Greeks likewise lost touch with the original substance, and with the cult also, remembering only an "immortal" food that was used by the gods.

Greek *ambrosia* was adopted into Latin as *ambrosia,* and thence into English (sixteenth century) as AMBROSIA.

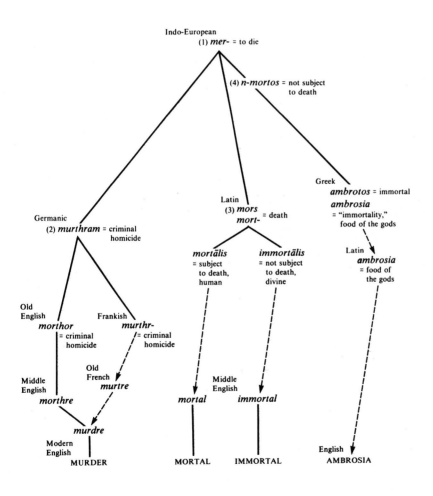

mori

1. Indo-European *mori* = "sea, lake" appears in Germanic *mari* = "sea, lake," Old Irish *muir* = "sea," Lithuanian *māre* = "sea," and Old Slavic *morje* = "sea."

This word is solidly represented in the western and northern sectors of the Indo-European world, while in Greek, and to the east, other terms are used. It seems impossible to determine whether the original meaning of *mori* was "sea" or "lake." The only real seas that the earliest Indo-European–speakers are likely to have known (assuming that they were in the region of the Ukraine before 4000 B.C.) are the Black Sea and the Caspian.

2. Germanic *mari* = "sea, lake" appears in Gothic *marei* = "sea," Old Norse *marr* = "sea," Old High German *mari* = "lake," and Old English *mere* = "sea, lake, pond." The Old English word survives in Modern English only as the archaism MERE, and in place-names such as *Haslemere*, *Windermere*.

(The word SEA is Old English *sǣ*, from Germanic *saiwiz*, which appears in all the Germanic languages and nowhere else; possibly, therefore, borrowed by the earliest Germanic-speakers from the indigenous inhabitants of northwestern Atlantic Europe.)

3. From Germanic *mari* was formed *mariskaz* = "marsh, swamp" (*-iskaz* being a diminutive suffix), appearing in Middle Low German *maras*, Middle Dutch *mersche*, and Old English *merisc*, *mersc*, all meaning "marsh, swamp." The last regularly became Modern English MARSH.

Germanic *mariskaz* was also borrowed (probably via Frankish) into Old French as *marais*, and this was borrowed into Dutch as *marasch*, later *moeras*. This last Dutch word was borrowed into English in the seventeenth century as MORASS, no doubt brought to England by the Dutch engineers working on the draining of the fens, or marshes, of East Anglia. The word survives now only archaically in the literal sense of "marsh," but remains in familiar use as a metaphor, or cliché, for a situation full of trouble.

4. From Latin *mare* = "sea" was formed the adjective *marīnus* = "relating to the sea." This became Old French *marin* and was borrowed thence into Middle English (fifteenth century) as *maryn*, becoming Modern English MARINE. From Latin *marīnus* came a Medieval Latin noun *marīnārius* = "seaman, sailor." This became Old French *marinier*, Norman French *mariner*, and was borrowed into Middle English as *maryner*, Modern English MARINER.

Another Latin adjective from *mare* was *maritimus* = "relating to the sea" (*-timus* being an adjectival suffix, as in *lēgi-timus* = "lawful," from *lēg-* = "law"). This was adopted into English (sixteenth century) as MARITIME.

106

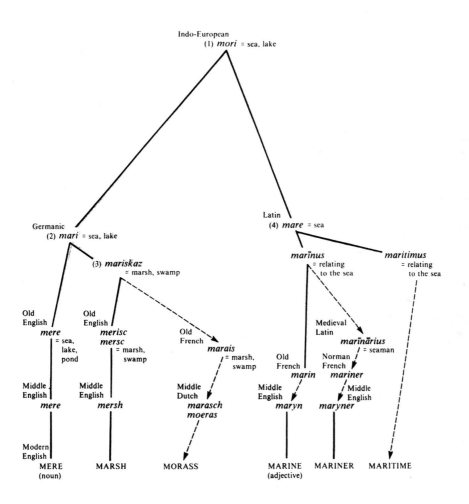

Indo-European
(1) *mori* = sea, lake

Germanic
(2) *mari* = sea, lake

Latin
(4) *mare* = sea

(3) *mariskaz*
= marsh, swamp

marīnus
= relating
to the sea

maritimus
= relating
to the sea

Old
English
mere
= sea,
lake,
pond

Old
English
merisc
mersc
= marsh,
swamp

Old
French
marais
= marsh,
swamp

Medieval
Latin
marīnārius
= seaman

Old
French
marin

Norman
French
mariner

Middle
English
mere

Middle
English
mersh

Middle
Dutch
marasch
moeras

Middle
English
maryn

Middle
English
maryner

Modern
English
MERE
(noun)

MARSH

MORASS

MARINE
(adjective)

MARINER

MARITIME

107

nas-

1. Indo-European *nas-* = "nose" appears in Germanic *nas-*, Latin *nāsus*, Lithuanian *nósis*, Old Slavic *nosŭ*, and Sanskrit *nasa-*, all meaning "nose."

2. Germanic *nas-* appears in Old Norse *nos*, Old High German *nasa* (whence Modern German *nase*), Old Frisian *nose*, and Old English *nosu*, all meaning "nose." Old English *nosu* became Modern English NOSE.

Formed from Old English *nosu* was the compound noun *nos-thyrl* = "nose-orifice" *(thyrl* = "hole," related to *through)*. This became Middle English *nostrill*, Modern English NOSTRIL.

3. Formed from Latin *nāsus* = "nose" was Medieval Latin *nāsālis* = "relating to the nose." This was adopted into English as NASAL.

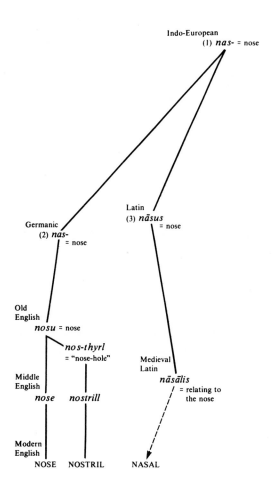

Indo-European
(1) *nas-* = nose

Germanic
(2) *nas-*
= nose

Latin
(3) *nāsus*
= nose

Old
English
nosu = nose

nos-thyrl
= "nose-hole"

Middle
English
nose   *nostrill*

Medieval
Latin
nāsālis
= relating to
the nose

Modern
English
NOSE   NOSTRIL   NASAL

109

ne

1. The Indo-European negative particle *ne,* also *n-,* appears in Germanic *ne,* Old Irish *ni, nī,* Latin *ne-,* Old Slavic *ne,* Greek *nē-,* Hittite *natta,* and Sanskrit *ná,* all meaning "not."

2. Germanic *ne* appears in Gothic *ni,* Old Norse *né,* Old High German *ni,* and Old English *ne,* all meaning "not."

Old English *ne* was used to form a number of negative compound words, including: (a) *ne* + *ā* = "ever," combined as *nā* = "never, not at all," becoming Middle English *na, no,* Modern English NO (adverb—used as the opposite of *yes*); (b) *ne* + *ān* = "one," combined as *nān* = "not one, none," becoming Middle English *nan, non,* Modern English NONE; Middle English *nan, non* was also reduced to *na, no* when occurring before a consonant, hence Modern English NO (adjective—as in *There is no wine*); (c) *ne* + *wiht* = "creature, thing," combined as *nōwiht, nāwiht* = "nothing," becoming Middle English *naught, nought,* Modern English NAUGHT; Middle English *nought* was also reduced to NOT, becoming the most general adverb or particle of negation in English.

3. Latin *ne-* was similarly used to form negative compounds, including (a) *ne* + *uter* = "either," combined as *neuter* = "neither," especially "neither masculine nor feminine," adopted into Old French as *neutre,* borrowed into Middle English as *neutre,* corrected to NEUTER in Modern English; (b) *ne* + *ūllus* = "any," combined as *nūllus* = "none," adopted into Old French as *nul, nulle,* borrowed into English (sixteenth century) as NULL.

4. Formed from Latin *negāre* = "to say no, deny" were the adjective *negātīvus* = "denying" and the abstract noun *negātiō* = "denial." These were adopted into (Middle) English as NEGATIVE (fourteenth century) and NEGATION (sixteenth century).

5. Latin *nōn* = "not" was originally also a compound, formed from *ne* + *oinom* = "one thing." It has been adopted into English as the widely used prefix NON-, as in NONFERROUS, NONSTANDARD.

6. The Indo-European particle *ne* had also a reduced form *n-,* used to form such Indo-European compounds as *n-mortos* = "undying, not subject to death" (*see* **mer-** = "to die"). This form of the particle was also regularly inherited by the various languages, as Germanic *un-,* Old Irish *in-, an-,* Latin *in-,* Greek *an-, a-,* and Sanskrit *an-, a-,* all meaning "not-."

7. Germanic *un-* appears in Gothic *un-,* Old Norse *u-,* Old High German *un-,* and Old English *un-,* all meaning "not-." Old English *un-* survives as Modern English UN-, as in UNTRUE, UNWISE, etc. (But note that there is another English prefix *un-,* not related to *ne,* expressing not mere negation but reversal of an action, as in *undo, untie.*)

8. Latin *in-* = "not-" appears in numerous compounds such as *incrēdulus* = "not credulous," *infīnītus* = "not finite," which have been adopted into English: INCREDULOUS, INFINITE, etc.

9. Greek *an-*, also reduced before a consonant to *a-*, ="not-" similarly appears in compounds such as *a-summetria* ="lack of symmetry," *an-ōnumos* ="nameless" (*see* **nomen**="name"); many of these, too, have been adopted into English: ASYMMETRY, ANONYMOUS, etc.

(Note that the three resulting English negative prefixes UN-, IN-, AN- (A-), have often subtly different functions of negation: for example, *unmoral, immoral, amoral;* to which *nonmoral* might be added.)

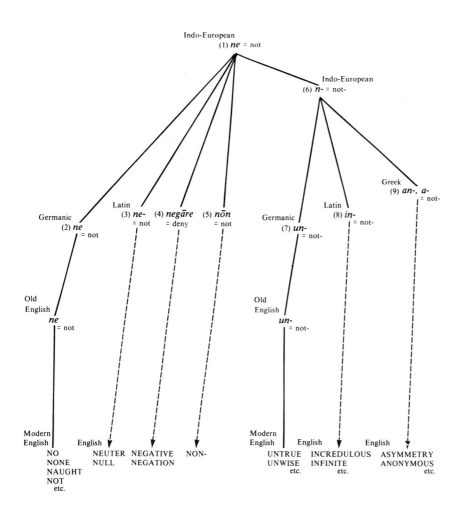

111

nekwt-

1. Indo-European *nekwt-,* also *nokwt-,* = "night" appears in Germanic *naht-,* Old Irish *nocht,* Latin *nox, noct-,* Lithuanian *naktìs,* Old Slavic *nŏstĭ,* Greek *nux, nukt-,* and Sanskrit *naktā,* all meaning "night."

2. Germanic *naht-* appears in Gothic *nahts,* Old Norse *natt,* Old High German *naht* (whence Modern German *nacht*), and Old English *niht.* (Note that the Germanic *h* represents the sound /ch/, as in Scottish *loch.*) Old English *niht* became Modern English NIGHT. The /ch/ sound has disappeared from all words of this class, as also in *bright, light,* the archaic *gh* spelling being a vestige of it. In the Scottish form *nicht,* and in German *nacht,* the sound has been retained.

3. In Old English the phrase *fēowertiene niht* = "fourteen nights" was used as a customary term for a period of two weeks. This unusual method of reckoning time was noticed by the Roman historian Tacitus, who wrote of the Germans in the first century A.D.: "They do not count the number of days, as we do, but the nights." The Old English phrase became the Middle English noun *fourteniht,* Modern English FORTNIGHT.

4. From Latin *nox, noct-,* was formed the adjective *nocturnus* = "occurring at night." This was adopted into (Middle) English as NOCTURNAL.

Nocturnus was also adopted into (Old) French as *nocturne.* In the late eighteenth century, the musical term *pièce nocturne* was used for a dreamy composition, vaguely associated with night scenes and night thoughts. It was borrowed into English as NOCTURNE.

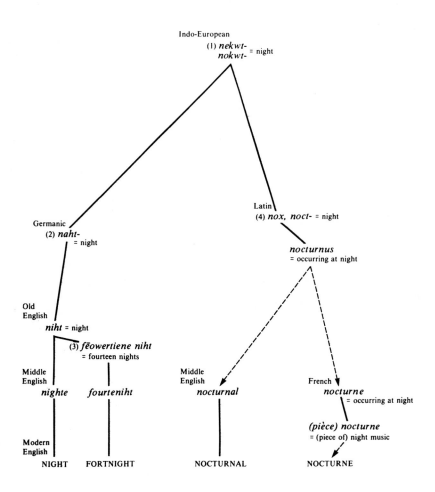

Indo-European
(1) *nekwt-*
   nokwt- = night

Latin
(4) *nox, noct-* = night

Germanic
(2) *naht-*
   = night

nocturnus
= occurring at night

Old
English
niht = night

(3) *fēowertiene niht*
   = fourteen nights

Middle
English
nighte   ***fourteniht***

Middle
English
nocturnal

French
nocturne
   = occurring at night

Modern
English
NIGHT   **FORTNIGHT**

NOCTURNAL

(pièce) nocturne
= (piece of) night music

NOCTURNE

113

newn

1. Indo-European *newn* = "nine" appears in Germanic *niwun, nigun,* Old Irish *nōi,* Latin *novem,* Albanian *nëndë,* Greek *enwa, ennea,* Tocharian *ñu,* and Sanskrit *náva,* all meaning "nine."

2. Germanic *niwun* or *nigun* appears in Gothic *niun,* Old Norse *nīo,* Old High German *niun* (whence Modern German *neun*), and Old English *nigon,* all meaning "nine." Old English *nigon* became Modern English NINE.

3. In the original Roman calendar of ten months, March was the first month and *November,* formed from *novem* = "nine," was the ninth. Later, when the calendar was expanded to twelve months by the addition of January and February, *November* became the eleventh month, but its now inappropriate name was not changed. It was adopted into Middle English as *Novembre,* Modern English NOVEMBER.

4. The Indo-European ordinal adjective *newnos* = "ninth" became Latin *nōnus* = "ninth." The phrase *nōna hōra* = "the ninth hour" referred, in the Latin system of reckoning the time of day, to the ninth hour after dawn (i.e., approximately 3:00 P.M.), when Christ was crucified and when the fourth Christian service of the day was held. This was borrowed into Old English as *nōn.* In the later Middle Ages this service was often held somewhat before 3:00 P.M., and for reasons that have not been fully explained, the word *nōn,* becoming Middle English *none,* came to mean "midday," emerging as Modern English NOON.

Also formed from Latin *nōnus* was *nōnāginta* = "ninety," whence the adjective *nōnāgēnārius* = "ninety years old." This was adopted as NONAGENARIAN.

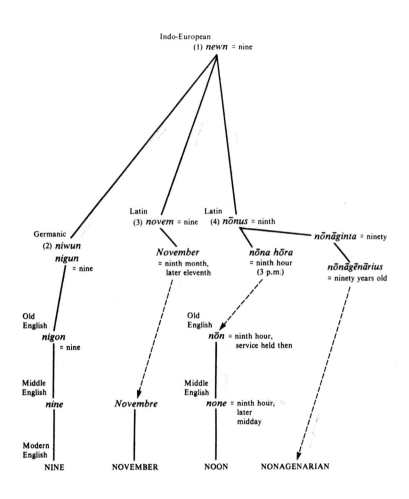

Indo-European
(1) *newn* = nine

Germanic
(2) *niwun*
nigun
= nine

Latin
(3) *novem* = nine

Latin
(4) *nōnus* = ninth

nōnāginta = ninety

November
= ninth month,
later eleventh

nōna hōra
= ninth hour
(3 p.m.)

nōnāgēnārius
= ninety years old

Old
English
nigon
= nine

Old
English
nōn = ninth hour,
service held then

Middle
English
nine

Novembre

Middle
English
none = ninth hour,
later
midday

Modern
English
NINE

NOVEMBER

NOON

NONAGENARIAN

115

newos

1. The Indo-European adjective *newos,* also *newyos,* ="new" appears in Germanic *newjaz,* Old Irish *nūe,* Latin *novus,* Lithuanian *navas,* Old Slavic *novŭ,* Greek *newos, neos,* Hittite *newa-,* Tocharian *ñu,* and Sanskrit *náva-,* all meaning "new."

2. Germanic *newjaz* appears in Gothic *niujis,* Old Norse *nyr,* Old High German *niuwi* (whence Modern German *neu*), and Old English *nīwe,* all meaning "new." (Note that the Germanic and Gothic *j* represent the sound /y/.) Old English *nīwe* became Middle English *newe,* Modern English NEW.

3. Latin *novus* had a "diminutive" form *novellus* ="new" (the meaning was not affected by the diminutive suffix *-ell-*). This was inherited in Old French as *novel* (becoming Modern French *nouveau*); *novel* was borrowed into (Middle) English as NOVEL (adjective).

    Latin *novellus* was also inherited in Italian as *novello* ="new." In the fifteenth century, short stories such as those of Giovanni Boccaccio were known as *storie novelle* ="new (or modern) stories"; hence the abbreviation *novella* ="story, work of fiction." Italian *novella* in this sense was borrowed into English (sixteenth century) as NOVEL (noun).

4. From Latin *novus* was formed the verb *novāre* ="to make new," with its compounds *innovāre* ="to bring in something new," and *renovāre* ="to make new again, renew." These have been adopted into English as INNOVATE, RENOVATE.

5. *Newos* appears in Greek *newos,* dropping the *w* to become *neos* ="new." This has been adopted into English to form the prefix NEO-, as in such words as NEOLITHIC="of the New Stone Age," NEOCLASSICAL="in a revived Classical style," etc.

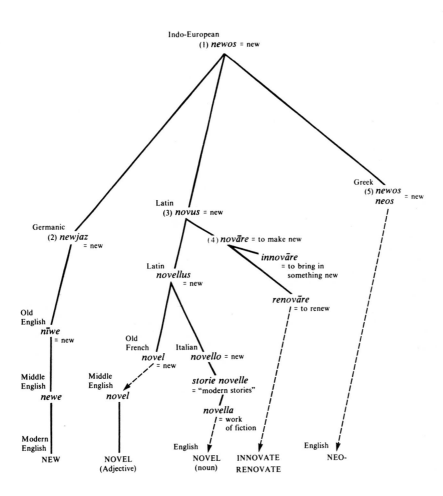

Indo-European
(1) *newos* = new

Germanic
(2) *newjaz*
= new

Latin
(3) *novus* = new

Greek
(5) *newos*
neos = new

(4) *novāre* = to make new

innovāre
= to bring in
something new

Latin
novellus
= new

renovāre
= to renew

Old
English
nīwe
= new

Old
French
novel
= new

Italian
novello = new

Middle
English
newe

Middle
English
novel

storie novelle
= "modern stories"

novella
= work
of fiction

Modern
English
NEW

NOVEL
(Adjective)

English
NOVEL
(noun)

INNOVATE
RENOVATE

English
NEO-

117

nizdos

1. The Indo-European noun *nizdos* is a compound, formed from the adverb *ni* = "down" + the verb root *sed-* (here reduced to *sd-, zd-*) = "sit." The literal meaning was therefore "a sitting down, a place where one sits down, a seat," which remained with little change in some branches of the language family; but in the European branches, at some very early date, the word acquired the specific meaning "bird's nest."

Nizdos appears in Germanic *nistaz* = "nest," Old Irish *net* = "nest," Latin *nīdus* = "nest," Armenian *nist* = "situation, residence," and Sanskrit *nida* = "resting place, couch."

2. Germanic *nistaz* appears in Old High German *nest* (Modern German *nest*), Middle Dutch *nest*, and Old English *nest*, becoming Modern English NEST.

The Germanic verb *nistilan* = "to nest, make a nest, sit on a nest" appears in Middle Dutch *nestelen* and Old English *nestlian*, later meaning also "to settle in snugly as a bird does on its nest," becoming Modern English NESTLE.

3. Old French *niche* was the term for a highly characteristic feature of Gothic architecture, "wall recess in which a statue is set." The word is formed from the verb *nicher* = "to nest," which is descended from an unrecorded Latin verb *nīdicāre* = "to nest," from the noun *nīdus* = "nest."

Old French *niche* was borrowed into English (seventeenth century) as NICHE, remaining an architectural term, but also taking on the meaning "a comfortable spot, a suitable position in life." Very recently a further meaning has been added, in ecology: "the place and function of an organism within its entire environment."

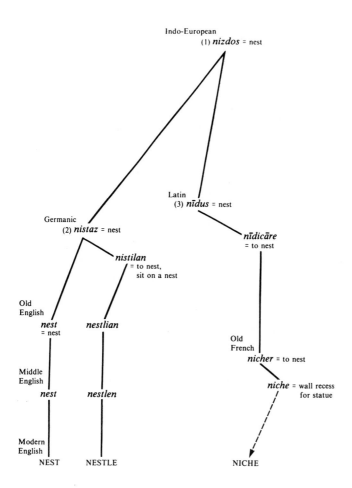

Indo-European
(1) *nizdos* = nest

Latin
(3) *nīdus* = nest

nīdicāre
= to nest

Germanic
(2) *nistaz* = nest

nistilan
= to nest,
sit on a nest

Old
English
nest
= nest

nestlian

Old
French
nicher = to nest

niche = wall recess
for statue

Middle
English
nest

nestlen

Modern
English
NEST   NESTLE

NICHE

119

nobh-

1. The Indo-European noun *nobh-* = "navel" existed also in the variant form *ombh-*. There were also two further forms with the noun suffix *-al-: nobhalos* and *ombhalos.*

The Indo-Europeans evidently thought of the navel as a protuberance rather than as a depression; in a very early and long-lasting metaphor, the word was used to mean (a) "the central knob or boss on a shield" and (b) "the hub of a wheel"; while also keeping the original meaning "navel."

The word appears in Germanic *nabō* = "wheel hub" and *nabilaz* = "navel," Old Irish *imbliu* = "navel," Latin *umbō* = "shield-boss" and *umbilicus* = "navel," Old Prussian *nabis* = "navel" and "wheel hub," Greek *omphalos* = "navel" and "shield-boss," and Sanskrit *nấbhis* = "navel" and "wheel hub," and *nabhīlam* = "navel."

2. Germanic *nabō* appears in Old Norse *noef,* Old High German *naba* (whence Modern German *nabe*), Middle Dutch *nave,* and Old English *nafu, nafa,* all meaning "wheel hub." Old English *nafa* became Modern English NAVE, long remaining the basic and technical term for the central wooden block of a wheel, into which the spokes are fitted. This word is now, however, all but obsolete, having been replaced by the unrelated word *hub,* for reasons unknown, in the nineteenth century.

A Germanic technical term formed from *nabō* = "wheel hub" + *gaizaz* = "spear, spike" was *nabōgaizaz* = "hub spike," the name of a presumably specialized tool for boring the hole in the central block of a wheel. The craft of the wheelwright remained a separate and highly specialized branch of woodworking throughout the long history of wooden wheels. Germanic *nabōgaizaz* appears in Old Norse *nafarr,* Old High German *nabugēr* (whence Modern German *näber*), and Old English *nafogār;* by the time these early medieval words are recorded, the tool had lost its specific association with the wheelwright, and was a basic part of the general woodworker's tool kit, remaining essentially unchanged to the present day: it consists of a metal spike, with a piercing and cutting point, set at right angles in a wooden bar or handle.

Old English *nafogār* became Middle English *nauger,* which from the fifteenth century began to lose its initial *n* by association with the indefinite article; so that *a nauger* was perceived as *an auger,* and the word was permanently reshaped to Modern English AUGER.

3. Germanic *nabilaz* appears in Old Norse *nafli,* Old High German *nabalo* (whence Modern German *nabel*), Old Frisian *navla,* and Old English *nafela,* all meaning "navel." Old English *nafela* became Modern English NAVEL.

4. Latin *umbilicus* = "navel" was adopted into English (seventeenth century) as the scientific term for the navel.

5. Greek *omphalos* appears in English as OMPHALOS, a word occasionally used for the navel, or for some central hub or point.

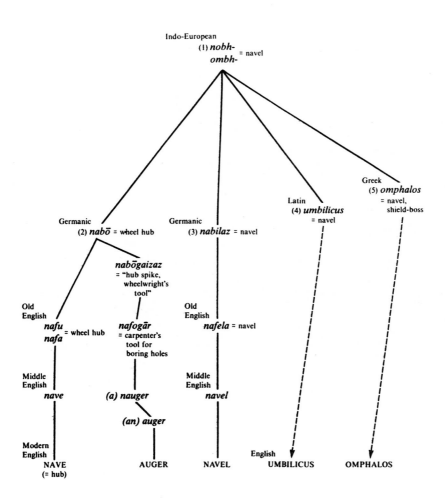

Indo-European
(1) *nobh-*
ombh- = navel

Germanic
(2) *nabō* = wheel hub

nabōgaizaz
= "hub spike,
wheelwright's
tool"

Germanic
(3) *nabilaz* = navel

Latin
(4) *umbilicus*
= navel

Greek
(5) *omphalos*
= navel,
shield-boss

Old
English
nafu
nafa = wheel hub

nafogār
= carpenter's
tool for
boring holes

Old
English
nafela = navel

Middle
English
nave

(a) nauger

Middle
English
navel

(an) auger

Modern
English
NAVE
(= hub)

AUGER

NAVEL

English
UMBILICUS

OMPHALOS

121

nogh-

1. Indo-European *nogh-* = "nail" had a variant form *ongh-*, and, with the noun suffix *-el-*, two further forms, *noghela-* and *onghela-*.

    The word was applied both to human fingernails and toenails, and to animal claws.

    It appears in Germanic *nagelaz* = "nail," Old Irish *ingen* = "nail," Latin *unguis* = "nail" and *ungula* = "claw, hoof," Lithuanian *nãgas* = "nail" and *nagà* = "hoof," Old Slavic *nogŭtĭ* = "nail," Greek *onux, onukh-* = "nail, claw," and Sanskrit *nakhás* = "nail, claw."

2. Germanic *nagelaz* meant (a) "fingernail, toenail" and (b) "metal spike used in carpentry." It appears in Old Norse *nagl* = "fingernail, toenail" and *nagli* = "carpenter's nail," Old High German *nagal* and Modern German *nagel* (both meanings), and Old English *nægl* became Modern English NAIL.

3. Latin *unguis* has been adopted into English as UNGUIS, the anatomical term for a claw, hoof, or nail. Latin *ungula* = "hoof" has also been adopted to form the word UNGULATE = "any of the hoofed animals—horses, cattle, deer, elephants, etc."

4. Greek *onux* = "variety of quartz in which flat bands of white alternate with dark" is probably a transferred use of *onux* = "fingernail," referring to the appearance of the white area at the base of a fingernail. (But it is also possible that the word for the quartz was really borrowed from a foreign language, and was reshaped so as to "make sense" in Greek.) Greek *onux* was borrowed into Latin as *onyx*, which was adopted into Old French as *onix*, borrowed thence into Middle English as *onix*, corrected to ONYX in Modern English.

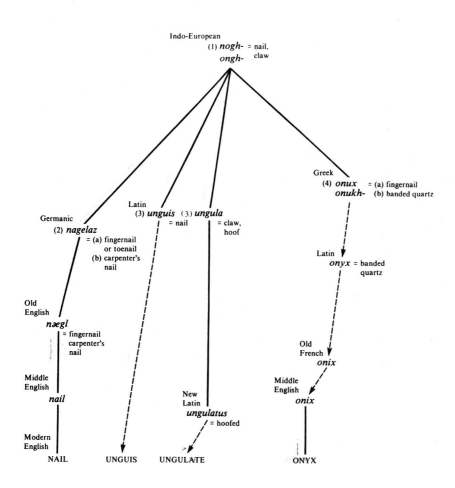

Indo-European
(1) *nogh-* = nail, claw
ongh-

Greek
(4) *onux* = (a) fingernail
onukh- (b) banded quartz

Latin
(3) *unguis* (3) *ungula*
= nail = claw, hoof

Germanic
(2) *nagelaz*
= (a) fingernail or toenail
(b) carpenter's nail

Latin
onyx = banded quartz

Old English
nægl
= fingernail carpenter's nail

Middle English
nail

Old French
onix

Middle English
onix

New Latin
ungulatus
= hoofed

Modern English
NAIL

UNGUIS

UNGULATE

ONYX

123

nogw-

1. Indo-European *nogw-* = "naked," with its adjectival forms *nogwedos*, *nogwdos*, and *nogwnos*, appears in Germanic *nakwedaz*, *nakwadaz*, Old Irish *nocht*, Latin *nūdus*, Lithuanian *nugas*, Old Slavic *nagŭ*, Hittite *nekumanzas*, and Sanskrit *nagnáh*, all meaning "naked."

2. Germanic *nakwedaz*, *nakwadaz*, appears in Gothic *naqaths*, Old Norse *noekkvithr*, Old High German *nackut* (whence Modern German *nackt*), Old Frisian *naked*, and Old English *nacod*, all meaning "naked." The last became Modern English NAKED.

3. Latin *nūdus* = "naked" (from Indo-European *nogwedos*, and therefore exactly parallel to Germanic *nakwedaz*) was adopted into English (seventeenth century) as NUDE.

4. The authorities generally agree that Greek *gumnos* = "naked" must belong to this root, but the details remain obscure. In Iranian and perhaps elsewhere, this word underwent "taboo deformation" (the initial *n* was changed to *m* in the Avestan form *magna-* = "naked"). In Greek, besides *gumnos*, a form *lumnos* appears once. This might possibly be a "differentiated" form of *numnos*, which could represent some Indo-European derivative of *nogwnos*. The whole argument may thus seem unconvincing. In its favor at least is that Greek alone of the major branches of the language family lacks a normal form of the common Indo-European adjective for "naked"; instead, it has *gumnos* in identical meaning. Probably the words are somehow related. Nakedness had an important ritual significance in some parts of the Indo-European world (Celtic warriors sometimes went into battle naked), and it would not be surprising for such a word to be irregularly altered by taboo.

Greek athletes performed naked (their games and contests, ritual in origin, were dedicated to gods). From *gumnos* = "naked man, athlete" the verb *gumnazein* = "to practice athletics" was formed; hence *gumnastēs* = "a trainer of athletes" and the noun *gumnasion* = "an athletic school." *Gumnastēs* was adopted into English (sixteenth century) as GYMNAST, at first meaning an expert athlete of any kind, now specifically one who practices certain generally calisthenic exercises. *Gumnasion* was adopted into Latin as *gymnasium*, and thence similarly into English as GYMNASIUM.

124

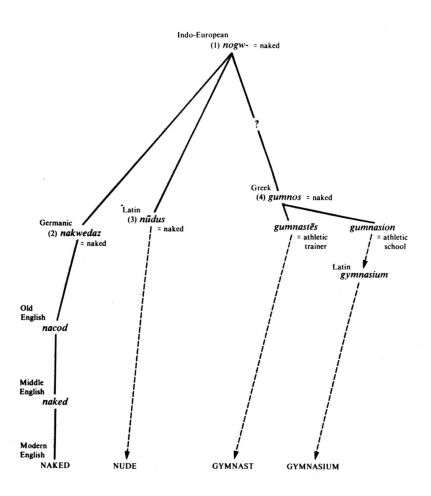

Indo-European
(1) *nogw-* = naked

?

Greek
(4) *gumnos* = naked

Germanic
(2) *nakwedaz*
= naked

Latin
(3) *nūdus*
= naked

gumnastēs
= athletic
trainer

gumnasion
= athletic
school

Latin
gymnasium

Old
English
nacod

Middle
English
naked

Modern
English
NAKED

NUDE

GYMNAST

GYMNASIUM

125

nomen

1. Indo-European *nomen,* with variant form *onomen,* = "name" appears in Germanic *namōn,* Old Irish *ainm,* Latin *nōmen,* Old Prussian *emnes,* Greek *onoma, onuma,* Tocharian *nem,* and Sanskrit *nāma,* all meaning "name."

2. Germanic *namōn* appears in Gothic *namo,* Old High German *namo* (whence Modern German *name*), and Old English *nama,* all meaning "name." Old English *nama* became Modern English NAME.

3. Latin *nōmen* = "name" was also used as a grammatical term for a word that is the name of a person or thing. It was inherited in Norman French as *noun,* which was borrowed into Middle English as *nowne,* becoming Modern English NOUN.

The adjective of Latin *nōmen* was *nōminālis* = "of or relating to a name or names." This was adopted into English as NOMINAL. Similarly, the Latin verb *nōmināre* = "to name" was adopted as NOMINATE.

4. From Greek *onuma* = "name" were formed the compound words *anōnumos* = "nameless" (*an-* = "not, un-") and *sunōnumos* = "having the same name" (*sun-* = "together, with"). These were adopted into Latin as *anōnymus* and *synōnymus,* and thence into English as ANONYMOUS, SYNONYMOUS.

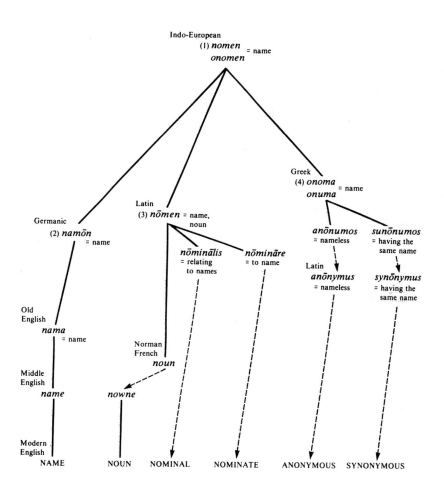

Indo-European
(1) *nomen*
onomen = name

Greek
(4) *onoma*
onuma = name

Latin
(3) *nōmen* = name, noun

Germanic
(2) *namōn* = name

nōminālis
= relating
to names

nōmināre
= to name

anōnumos
= nameless

sunōnumos
= having the
same name

Latin
anōnymus
= nameless

synōnymus
= having the
same name

Old
English
nama = name

Middle
English
name

Norman
French
noun

nowne

Modern
English
NAME

NOUN   NOMINAL   NOMINATE   ANONYMOUS   SYNONYMOUS

127

oinos

1. Indo-European *oinos* = "one" appears in Germanic *ainaz*, Old Irish *ōen*, Latin *ūnus*, Old Prussian *ains*, Old Slavic *inŭ*, all meaning "one," and in Greek *oinos* = "score of one at dice."

Oinos was originally an adjective meaning "one alone, single," but came to be used also as the numeral 1 and as an indefinite article.

2. *Oinos* regularly became Germanic *ainaz*, appearing in Gothic *ains*, Old Norse *ainn*, Old High German *ein* (whence Modern German *ein*), and Old English *ān*, all meaning "one."

Old English *ān* became Middle English *an, on, oon, own*, with a variety of spellings and pronunciations in different parts of the country. A form *won, wone, wun* developed in dialects of western and southwestern England, and by 1700 this became the standard pronunciation in London. The spelling, however, was standardized as ONE, originally representing the earlier pronunciation /ōn/ as in *bone*.

The adverbial genitive of Middle English *an, on*, was *anes, ones*, = "at one time." This also acquired the pronunciation with *w-*, emerging as /wuns/, spelled ONCE.

In early Middle English *an* was also used as an indefinite article, and before a vowel was reduced to *a*; hence Modern English A, AN.

3. In the thirteenth century the phrase *al one* = "all by oneself" became a solid adjective ALONE. It was also sometimes written as *a lone*, resulting in the separate adjective LONE, and later LONELY.

4. The Germanic words for the numerals 11 and 12 were *ain-lif-* = "one left (after ten)" and *twā-lif-* = "two left (after ten)," respectively. (*See twā-lif-* under dwō.) *Ain-lif-* appears in Gothic *ainlif*, Old High German *einlif* and Old English *endleofan, elefne*, all meaning "eleven." Old English *elefne* became Middle English *elevne*, Modern English ELEVEN.

5. From Latin *ūnus* = "one" was formed the verb *ūnīre* = "to make into one," adopted into Middle English as *uniten*, becoming Modern English UNITE. Also from Latin *ūnus* was *ūnitās* = "the state of being one," adopted via Old French into Middle English as *unite*, later UNITY.

6. An extended form of Indo-European *oinos* was *oinokos* = "one alone." This appears in Germanic *ainigaz* = "one, any," Latin *ūnicus* = "alone of its kind," and Old Slavic *inokŭ* = "solitary."

Germanic *ainigaz* appears in Old Norse *einigr*, Old High German *einag*, and Old English *ænig*. The Old English word *ænig* = "one (no matter which), any," became Middle English *eny*, Modern English ANY.

Latin *ūnicus* = "alone of its kind" was adopted into French as *unique;* this was borrowed into English as UNIQUE.

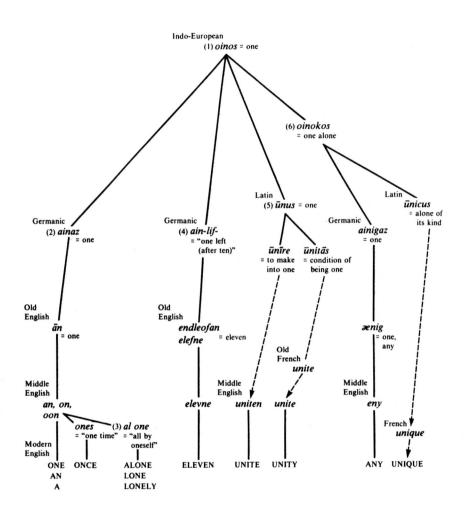

Indo-European
(1) *oinos* = one

(6) *oinokos*
= one alone

Germanic
(2) *ainaz*
= one

Germanic
(4) *ain-lif-*
= "one left
(after ten)"

Latin
(5) *ūnus* = one

Germanic
ainigaz
= one

Latin
ūnicus
= alone of
its kind

ūnīre
= to make
into one

ūnitās
= condition of
being one

Old
English
ān
= one

Old
English
endleofan
elefne = eleven

Old
English
ænig
= one,
any

Middle
English
an, on,
oon

ones
= "one time"

(3) *al one*
= "all by
oneself"

Old
French
unite

Middle
English
elevne

Middle
English
uniten

unite

Middle
English
eny

French
unique

Modern
English

ONE
AN
A

ONCE

ALONE
LONE
LONELY

ELEVEN

UNITE

UNITY

ANY

UNIQUE

oktō

1. Indo-European *oktō* = "eight" appears in Germanic *ahtō*, Old Irish *ocht*, Latin *octō*, Lithuanian *aštuoni*, Greek *oktō*, Tocharian *okt*, and Sanskrit *astāu*, all meaning "eight."

2. *Oktō* became Germanic *ahtō*, with regular change of *k* to *h* (the Germanic *h* originally representing a /ch/ sound, as in Scottish *loch*). This appears in Gothic *ahtau*, Old Norse *ātta*, Old High German *ahto* (whence Modern German *acht*), and Old English *ahta*, *eahta*, all meaning "eight." Old English *ahta*, *eahta* became Modern English EIGHT, with the archaic *gh* spelling still marking the Old English /ch/ sound, which has disappeared from the pronunciation.

3. In the original Roman calendar, March was the first month, and the eighth month was named *Octōber*, from *octō* = "eight." Later, January and February were added, so that October became the tenth month; the name, though now inappropriate, was never changed. It was borrowed into late Old English and has been transmitted to Modern English as OCTOBER.

4. Also from Latin *octō* was the ordinal adjective *octāvus* = "eighth." In Medieval Latin the musical term *(vox) octāva* meant "eighth note" (*vox* = "voice, note") in the diatonic scale; this was adopted into English (seventeenth century) as OCTAVE.

5. Formed from Latin *octōgintā* = "eighty" was *octōgēnārius* = "eighty years old," adopted as OCTOGENARIAN.

6. From Greek *oktō* the word *oktopous* = "eight-footed" (*pous* = "foot"; *see* ped- = "foot") was formed, for the well-known Mediterranean mollusk. This was adopted in zoological New Latin (eighteenth century) as *Octopus*, the genus name of those mollusks, whence English OCTOPUS.

7. A term used in Greek geometry was *oktagōnon* = "figure having eight angles" (*gōnia* = "angle"; *see* **genu** = "knee"), adopted into English as OCTAGON.

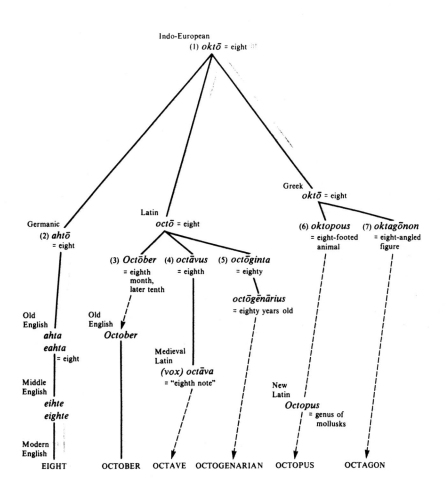

Indo-European
(1) *oktō* = eight

Greek
oktō = eight

Germanic
(2) *ahtō*
= eight

Latin
octō = eight

(6) *oktopous*
= eight-footed
animal

(7) *oktagōnon*
= eight-angled
figure

(3) *Octōber*
= eighth
month,
later tenth

(4) *octāvus*
= eighth

(5) *octōginta*
= eighty

octōgēnārius
= eighty years old

Old
English
ahta
eahta
= eight

Old
English
October

Medieval
Latin
(vox) octāva
= "eighth note"

New
Latin
Octopus
= genus of
mollusks

Middle
English
eihte
eighte

Modern
English
EIGHT

OCTOBER   OCTAVE   OCTOGENARIAN   OCTOPUS   OCTAGON

131

owis

1. Indo-European *owis* = "sheep" is very well represented throughout most of the language family: Germanic *awiz*, Old Irish *ōi*, Latin *ovis*, Lithuanian *avìs*, Old Slavic *ovica*, Greek *owis, ois*, Sanskrit *avis*, all meaning "sheep."

Words for lamb, yearling, and wool have also been reconstructed, so it is highly probable that the Indo-Europeans had domesticated sheep.

The sheep, possibly the first of the food animals to be domesticated by the human race, was already herded in the Middle East before 8500 B.C. The Early Kurgan culture of the Ukraine of about 4500 B.C. (thought to be speakers of Proto–Indo-European) left domestic sheep and goat bones in its middens, but in much smaller quantities than those of horses and cattle. Subsequently, sheep-herding has been continuous in most of the Indo-European world, and in many times and places has been the chief kind of farming practiced; but ownership of sheep has generally carried much less prestige than ownership of cattle.

2. Indo-European *owis* was of common gender, designating male or female sheep indifferently. In some of the language groups it became restricted to females, no doubt because the bulk of the herds were in fact females, since most of the males were killed young. One of these was Germanic *awiz*, appearing in Old High German *ouwi*, Old Norse *aer*, Old Frisian *ei*, and Old English *ēowu*, all meaning "female sheep." The last became Modern English EWE.

3. Latin *ovis* preserves the Indo-European form virtually unchanged. Its Late Latin adjective *ovīnus* = "relating to sheep" was adopted into English as OVINE.

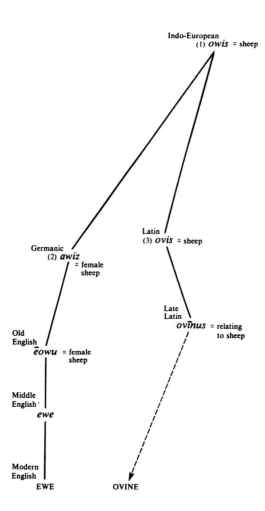

Indo-European
(1) *owis* = sheep

Latin
(3) *ovis* = sheep

Germanic
(2) *awiz* = female
sheep

Late
Latin
ovīnus = relating
to sheep

Old
English
ēowu = female
sheep

Middle
English
ewe

Modern
English
EWE

OVINE

133

ped-

1.   Indo-European *ped-* or *pod-* = "foot" appears in Germanic *fōt* = "foot," Latin *pēs, ped-* = "foot," Lithuanian *pedà* = "footstep," Greek *pous, pod-* = "foot," Hittite *pad* = "foot," and Sanskrit *pad-* = "foot."

The vowel variation in *ped-/pod-* is a basic Indo-European feature. There were also further variations with lengthened vowels, *pēd-/pōd-*.

The Indo-European word was also used from the earliest time, like its Modern English descendant, as a formalized measure of length.

2.   The lengthened form *pōd-* became Germanic *fōt-*, with regular changes from *p* to *f* and from *d* to *t*. This appears in Gothic *fōtus*, Old Norse *fōtr*, Old High German *fuoz* (whence Modern German *fuss*), and Old English *fōt*, all meaning "foot." Old English *fōt* became Modern English FOOT.

3.   The basic form of the root, *ped-*, appears in Latin *pēs, ped-* = "foot." Its adjective *pedālis* = "of or relating to the foot" was adopted into Italian (Renaissance period) to form the term *pedale d'organo* = "foot key of the organ," shortened to the noun *pedale*. This was borrowed into French as *pédale* and thence into English as PEDAL.

Also formed from Latin *pēs, ped-* was *pedester* = "going on foot," which was also used to mean "written in prose, prosaic, not poetic." This was adopted into English (eighteenth century) as PEDESTRIAN, meaning both "going on foot" and "prosaic, uninspired."

Latin *pēs, ped-* was also adopted into French to form the term *pédicure* = "surgical care of the feet" (*cure* from Latin *cūrāre* = "to take care of"). This was borrowed into English as PEDICURE.

4.   The *o*-form *pod-* appears in Greek *pous, pod-* = "foot." The compound word *tripous, tripod-* = "three-footed," also "vessel or caldron supported on three feet," was adopted into Latin as *tripūs, tripod-*, and thence into English as TRIPOD. Greek *pous, pod-* was also adopted directly into twentieth-century English to form the word PODIATRY = "foot-doctoring" (Greek *iatreia* = "medical care").

5.   The basic form of the root, *ped-*, regularly became Indo-Iranian *pad-*, appearing in Sanskrit *pad-* = "foot" and in Middle Persian *pāī* = "foot," also "leg." In the late Middle Ages when the Muslim Persians invaded India, numerous Persian words were borrowed into Urdu, the Indic language of the Mogul Empire. Among these words was *pāī*, used in the Urdu term *pāē -jāma* = "leg-garment, trousers" (*jāma* = "garment"). These loose trousers of linen or silk, tied around the waist, were worn by Muslim and Sikh men. In the eighteenth century or before, European traders and imperialists in India took to wearing these trousers as a relaxed "undress" garment for males, the word being borrowed into English as *paijamas*, PYJAMAS, (U.S.) PAJAMAS. It was the British of the Victorian period who introduced the pyjama suit into Europe as a sleeping garment (Europeans up to that time had slept naked or in nightgowns).

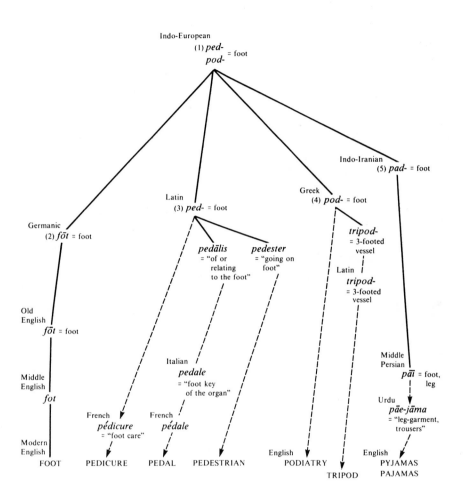

Indo-European
(1) *ped-*
pod- = foot

Indo-Iranian
(5) *pad-* = foot

Latin
(3) *ped-* = foot

Greek
(4) *pod-* = foot

tripod-
= 3-footed
vessel

Germanic
(2) *fōt* = foot

pedālis
= "of or
relating
to the foot"

pedester
= "going on
foot"

Latin
tripod-
= 3-footed
vessel

Old
English
fōt = foot

Middle
English
fot

Italian
pedale
= "foot key
of the organ"

Middle
Persian
pāi = foot,
leg

Urdu
pāe-jāma
= "leg-garment,
trousers"

Modern
English

French
pédicure
= "foot care"

French
pédale

English
PODIATRY

English
PYJAMAS
PAJAMAS

FOOT   PEDICURE   PEDAL   PEDESTRIAN

TRIPOD

penkwe (I)

1. Indo-European *penkwe* = "five" appears in Germanic *fimfi,* Gaulish Celtic *pempe,* Latin *quinque,* Lithuanian *penki,* Greek *pente,* Hittite *panta,* and Sanskrit *pañca,* all meaning "five."

(For other derivatives *see* **penkwe,** II.)

2. From the basic form *penkwe* occurred a variant form *pempe,* in which the original consonant cluster *kw* has been "assimilated" to the sound of the initial consonant *p,* thus (perhaps) making the word easier to pronounce. *Pempe,* with regular change of Indo-European *p* to Germanic *f,* became Germanic *fimfi.* This appears in Gothic *fimf,* Old Norse *fimm,* Old High German *fimf* (whence modern German *fünf*), and Old English *fíf,* all meaning "five." Old English *fíf* became Modern English FIVE.

3. Another variant of the basic form *penkwe* was *kwenkwe,* in which an exactly opposite "assimilation" has occurred, the initial sound /p/ being assimilated to the cluster *kw.* This became Latin *quinque* = "five." A compound word formed from this was *quinquennis* = "lasting five years" or "renewed every five years" (*-ennis* from Latin *annus* = "year"). This was adopted into English as QUINQUENNIAL.

4. *Penkwe* became Greek *pente* (with a regular sound-change of /kw/ to Greek /t/). Formed from *pente* was the Greek geometric term *pentagōnon* = "five-angled figure" (*gōnia* = "angle"; *see* **genu** = "knee"), adopted into English as PENTAGON. In the literature of medieval magic, several of the western European languages had words based on Medieval Latin *pentaculum* (formed from Greek *pente* + the Latin suffix *-culum*), meaning "five-pointed star," a mystical figure used in divination and sorcery. This in English (sixteenth century) became PENTACLE.

5. *Penkwe* became Sanskrit *pañca,* which was inherited into Hindi as *panch* = "five." In the seventeenth century, English merchants trading with India began to make a drink, usually hot, which they called PUNCH, by many different recipes on a base of brandy, rum, or arrack, typically mixed with such ingredients as milk, lime juice, tea, and nutmeg. It is probable, but cannot be definitively proved, that there were originally and basically five ingredients, and that the word was coined by the English merchants from Hindi *panch* = "five."

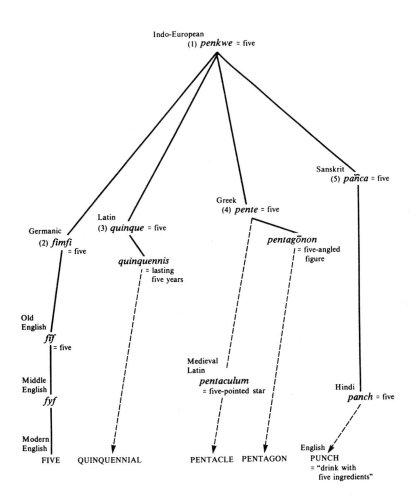

Indo-European
(1) *penkwe* = five

Germanic
(2) *fimfi*
= five

Latin
(3) *quinque* = five

quinquennis
= lasting
five years

Greek
(4) *pente* = five

pentagōnon
= five-angled
figure

Sanskrit
(5) *pañca* = five

Old
English
fīf
= five

Medieval
Latin
pentaculum
= five-pointed star

Hindi
panch = five

Middle
English
fyf

Modern
English

FIVE   QUINQUENNIAL   PENTACLE   PENTAGON

English
PUNCH
= "drink with
five ingredients"

137

penkwe (II)

1.   Formed from Indo-European *penkwe* = "five" was the ordinal adjective *penkwetos* or *penkwtos* = "fifth." This appears in Germanic *fimftaz*, Old Welsh *pimphet*, Latin *quin(c)tus*, Lithuanian *peñktas*, Greek *pemptos*, and Sanskrit *paktha-*, all meaning "fifth."

2.   Germanic *fimftaz* appears in Gothic *fimfta-*, Old Norse *fimti*, Old High German *fimfto*, and Old English *fifta*, all meaning "fifth." Old English *fifta* became Modern English FIFTH.

3.   Latin *quintus* = "fifth" was inherited in Italian as *quinto* = "fifth," from which came the noun *quintetto* = "group of five," especially "group of five musicians." This, along with many other Italian musical terms, was adopted into English in the seventeenth century as *quintetto*, later standardized (by analogy with *duet*) as QUINTET.

   In Greco-Roman science and medieval alchemy, it was held that there were four elements (earth, air, fire, and water), and beyond them a "fifth essence," of which the stars and planets were made and which was also latent in all other natural bodies. In Medieval Latin this was named *quinta essentia,* which was adopted into Middle English (fifteenth century) as QUINTESSENCE.

   Two further Indo-European derivatives of *penkwe* = "five" were *penkweros* = "one of a set of five," and *pnkstis* = "set of five."

4.   With regular sound-changes, *penkweros* became Germanic *fingwraz* = "finger," appearing in Gothic *figgrs*, Old Norse *fingr*, Old High German *finger* (whence Modern German *finger*), and Old English *finger*, all meaning "finger." The last remains unchanged as Modern English FINGER.

5.   Also with regular sound-changes, *pnkstis* became Germanic *funhstiz*, simplified to *fūstiz* = "fist." This appears in Old High German *fūst* (whence Modern German *faust*), Old Frisian *fēst*, and Old English *fyst*, all meaning "fist." The last became Modern English FIST.

138

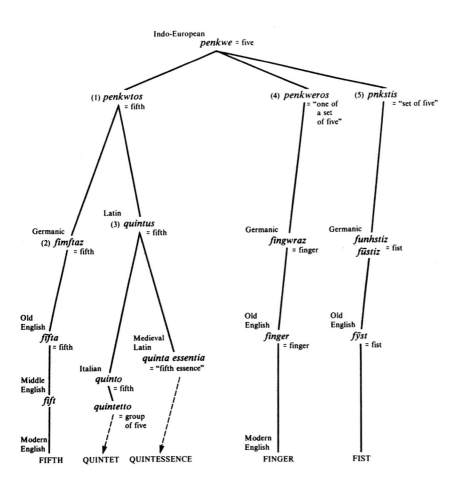

Indo-European
penkwe = five

(1) *penkwtos* = fifth

(4) *penkweros* = "one of a set of five"

(5) *pnkstis* = "set of five"

Latin
(3) *quintus* = fifth

Germanic
(2) *fimftaz* = fifth

Germanic
fingwraz = finger

Germanic
funhstiz
fūstiz = fist

Old English
fīfta = fifth

Medieval Latin
quinta essentia = "fifth essence"

Old English
finger = finger

Old English
fȳst = fist

Middle English
fift

Italian
quinto = fifth

quintetto = group of five

Modern English
FIFTH

QUINTET

QUINTESSENCE

Modern English
FINGER

FIST

139

pet-

1. Several slightly different Indo-European nouns for "bird's wing, feather" were formed from the verb root *pet-* = "to fly," which is widely attested throughout the language family. Among them were *pet-ra, pet-na,* and *pte-ro-,* appearing in Germanic *fethrō* = "feather," Old Welsh *eterin* = "bird" (with regular Celtic loss of *p*), Latin *penna* or *pinna* = "wing, feather," Greek *pteron* = "wing," Hittite *pattar* = "wing," and Sanskrit *páttram* = "wing."

2. Germanic *fethrō* appears in Old Norse *fjodhr,* Old High German *fedara* (whence Modern German *feder*), and Old English *fether,* all meaning "feather." Old English *fether* became Modern English FEATHER.

3. Latin *penna* or *pinna* = "wing, primary feather" also in Late Latin meant "quill used for writing." This was inherited in Old French as *penne* = "feather, quill," borrowed into Middle English as *penne,* becoming Modern English PEN (writing instrument).

   Old French *pignon* = "wing feather" is inherited from an undocumented Latin form *pinniōn-,* a derivative of *pinna. Pignon* was borrowed into Middle English as PINION (noun) = "wing feather." Hence the sixteenth-century verb PINION = "to cut a bird's wing feathers so that it cannot fly," hence also "to tie a man's arms so that he cannot move."

   Old French *penon* = "bunch of feathers used as a crest," also "long narrow flag or banner," is similarly inherited from an undocumented Latin form *pennōn-,* derived from *penna* = "feather." *Penon* was borrowed into Middle English as *penon,* becoming Modern English PENNON.

4. Greek *pteron* = "wing" was adopted in scientific New Latin to form the word *pterodactylus* = "wing-finger" (Greek *daktulon* = "finger"), the name given to the flying reptile that was found by geologists in the fossil strata of Europe early in the nineteenth century. This was borrowed into English as PTERODACTYL.

   Greek *pteron* was also adopted into French in the later nineteenth century to form the word *hélicoptère* = "spiral-wing" (Greek *heliko-* = "spiral"), a term coined for a possible flying machine that would be powered by horizontally revolving blades. The term was used by, among others, Jules Verne. In the twentieth century the machine became a reality, and the word was borrowed into English as HELICOPTER.

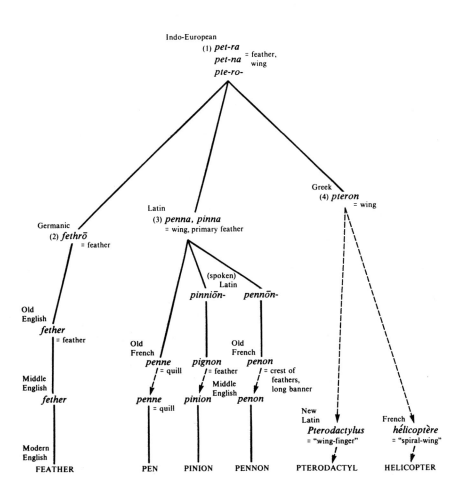

Indo-European
(1) *pet-ra*
pet-na = feather, wing
pte-ro-

Greek
(4) *pteron*
= wing

Latin
(3) *penna, pinna*
= wing, primary feather

Germanic
(2) *fethrō*
= feather

(spoken)
Latin
pinniōn-   *pennōn-*

Old
English
fether
= feather

Old
French
penne   *pignon*   Old
l = quill   *l* = feather French
                            penon
Middle   *l* = crest of
English   feathers,
                            long banner

Middle
English
fether

penne   *pinion*   *penon*
= quill

Modern
English

FEATHER   PEN   PINION   PENNON

New
Latin
Pterodactylus
= "wing-finger"

French
hélicoptère
= "spiral-wing"

PTERODACTYL   HELICOPTER

141

pətēr

1. The Indo-European word *pətēr* = "father" appears in Germanic *fadar*, Old Irish *athir*, Latin *pater*, Greek *patēr*, Tocharian *pacar*, and Sanskrit *pitár*, all meaning "father."

Unlike our word FATHER, the word *pətēr* did not primarily designate a man as the physical begetter of children. It was the formal title of the head of a household. The Indo-European social structure was rigorously patriarchal, and the *pətēr* was its embodiment.

The supreme deity was addressed as *Dyeu-pətēr*, which can be translated as "Sky-father"; this did not imply that he was the progenitor of the other gods, nor of men, but that he was their chief. (*See* **deiwos** = "god.")

After the dispersal of the Indo-Europeans, their original clan system disappeared or was modified by contact with other traditions. The word *pətēr* was then generally retained in the unspecialized and familiar sense of "male parent." But extensive traces of its original significance survived: most notably, in Roman law, the *patria potestās* = "father's power" included the right of life and death over his children and all the members of his household; a wife had the legal status of daughter to her husband.

2. Indo-European *pətēr* became Germanic *fadar*, with regular changes of *p* to *f* and of *t* to *d*. This appears in Gothic *fadar*, Old Norse *fadhir*, Old High German *fater* (whence Modern German *vater*), and Old English *fæder*, all meaning "father, progenitor," with little trace of the Indo-European juridical role. Old English *fæder* became Modern English FATHER, with the same change of *d* to *th* as in MOTHER and BROTHER.

3. A Latin adjective formed from *pater* was *paternus* = "of or relating to a father, fatherly." A Late Latin extended form of this was *paternālis*, adopted into English as PATERNAL. A noun formed from *paternus* was *paternitās* = "the fact or condition of being a father," adopted as PATERNITY.

4. The members of the Roman Senate, or ruling council of the republic, were collectively called the *Patrēs* = "Fathers," each originally being the head of an independent noble clan. From this came the adjective *patricius* = "belonging to a family of senatorial rank," later a medieval title of nobility. It was adopted into Middle English as *patricien*, now PATRICIAN.

5. Another Latin derivative of *pater* was *patrōnus* = "man who protects the interests of business dependents, lawyer who defends clients." In Medieval Latin it was used to mean "tutelary saint." It was adopted into Old French as *patron*, which was borrowed into Middle English as PATRON.

6. Formed from Greek *patēr* = "father, ancestor" was *patria* = (a) "paternal descent, family, clan" and (b) "ancestral country, homeland." From this in sense (a) came *patriarkhēs* = "head of a clan, tribal chief" (*arkhein* = "to rule"); in the Greek translation of the Bible this was used of the ancestral leaders of the Hebrews; in the early Christian Church it was used as a title

of bishops. It was adopted into Late Latin as *patriarca* and thence into Middle English as *patriarche,* now PATRIARCH.

Also from Greek *patria* was *patriōtēs* = "of the same homeland, fellow-countryman." This was adopted into Late Latin as *patriōta,* thence into Old French as *patriote,* and thence into English as PATRIOT.

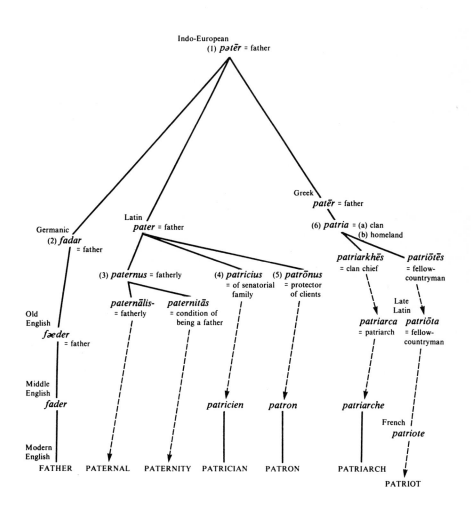

piskos

1.   The noun *piskos* or *peiskos* = "fish" is found only in the western and northern branches of the language family—Germanic, Celtic, Latin, and Slavic. It may therefore be a pre–Indo-European word that was separately borrowed at a very early date by all four of these branches; but more likely it is an original Indo-European word that in Greek, Sanskrit, etc., has been replaced by individual local borrowings.

   Piskos or *peiskos* appears in Germanic *fiskaz*, Old Irish *iasc* (with regular Celtic loss of initial *p*), Latin *piscis*, all meaning "fish"; and also in Russian *piskar'* and Polish *piskorz* = "kind of fish."

2.   Germanic *fiskaz* appears in Gothic *fisks*, Old Norse *fiskr*, Old High German *fisc* (whence Modern German *fisch*), and Old English *fisc*, becoming Modern English FISH.

3.   Latin *Piscēs* = "the Fishes" was the name of the twelfth constellation and sign of the zodiac. This was adopted into Middle English as PISCES.

   Formed from Latin *piscis* was the verb *piscārī* = "to fish," whence the agent-noun *piscātor* = "fisherman." This is the basis of the English adjective PISCATORIAL = "of or related to fishing."

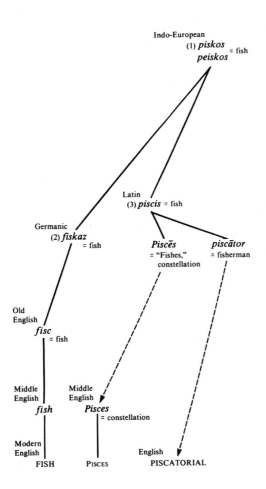

Indo-European
(1) *piskos*
    peiskos = fish

Latin
(3) *piscis* = fish

Germanic
(2) *fiskaz*
    = fish

Piscēs
= "Fishes,"
constellation

piscātor
= fisherman

Old
English
fisc
    = fish

Middle
English
fish

Middle
English
Pisces
    = constellation

Modern
English
FISH

Pisces

English
PISCATORIAL

pūr-

1. Indo-European *pūr-* = "fire" appears in Germanic *fūri* = "fire," Umbrian *pir* = "fire," Old Slavic *puria* = "glowing coal," Greek *pur* = "fire," Hittite *pahhur* = "fire," and Tocharian *por* = "fire."

2. With regular change of *p* to *f*, Indo-European *pūr-* became Germanic *fūri*, appearing in Old Icelandic *furr*, Old High German *fiur* (whence Modern German *feuer*), and Old English *fȳr*, all meaning "fire." Old English *fȳr* became Modern English FIRE.

3. Greek *pur* = "fire" had a derivative *pura* = "hearth, funeral pyre." The earliest Indo-European peoples inhumed their dead, but many of the later branches, including the post-Mycenaean Greeks of Homer's time, took to cremation in various times and places. Greek *pura* was borrowed into Latin as *pyra* and thence into English as PYRE.

Greek *pur* was also used to form the English prefix PYRO- as in PYROMANIAC, PYROTECHNICS.

146

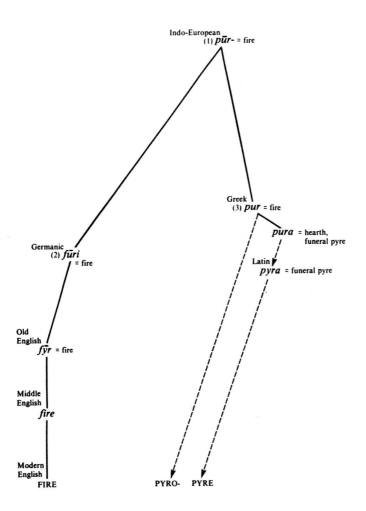

Indo-European
(1) *pūr-* = fire

Greek
(3) *pur* = fire

pura = hearth,
funeral pyre

Germanic
(2) *fūri*
= fire

Latin
pyra = funeral pyre

Old
English
fȳr = fire

Middle
English
fire

Modern
English
FIRE

PYRO-   PYRE

147

rē-

1. Indo-European *rē-*, also *er-*, = "to row" had derivatives *rētra-* = "oar" and *erəter* = "oarsman," appearing in Germanic *rō-* = "to row" and *rōthra-* = "oar," Old Irish *rāme* = "oar," Latin *rēmus* = "oar," Lithuanian *iriū* = "row," Greek *eretēs* = "oarsman" and *eretmos* = "oar," and Sanskrit *arítra* = "oar" and *aritár* = "oarsman."

This term is clear evidence for the use of paddles or oars by the earliest Indo-European community, living north and northeast of the Black Sea before 4000 B.C. The word *naus* = "boat or ship" has a very similar distribution (but has not survived by direct inheritance in English, although it is present in words borrowed from Greek and Latin such as *nautical* and *navy*).

2. Germanic *rō-* appears in Old Norse *rōa* = "to row," Middle High German *ruejen* = "to steer," and Old English *rōwan* = "to row," becoming Modern English ROW.

3. Germanic *rōthra* = "paddle, oar, steering-oar," appears in Old High German *ruodar* (whence Modern German *ruder*), Middle Dutch *rōder* (whence Modern Dutch *roer*), Old Frisian *rōther*, and Old English *rother*, all meaning "oar" or "steering-oar." Old English *rother* became Middle English *rother, ruder*. In the late Middle Ages, European shipbuilders began to make steering gear in the form of a vertical wooden blade hinged to the stern of the vessel. In Middle English this new device was still called by the old term *ruder* = "steering-oar," becoming Modern English RUDDER.

4. The word OAR is from Old English *ār*, also an old Germanic word, originally *airo*. This word looks as if it should be somehow related to Indo-European *rē-/er-*, but there is no straightforward connection in regular linguistic terms. Possibly, therefore, the words are unrelated.

5. From the fifth century B.C. until about the second, the chief warship used by the Greeks and Romans was a vessel using both sails and large numbers of rowers. The rowing arrangements involved either three separate decks of oars on each side or the seating of the rowers in three tiers of benches. In Greek this ship was called *trierēs,* in Latin *trirēmis* (*tri-* = "three" + *rēmus* = "oar"). This was adopted into English as TRIREME.

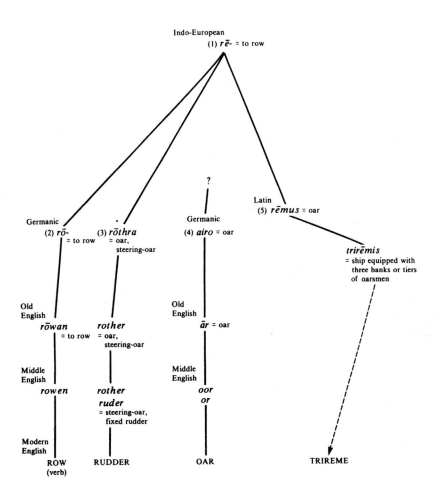

Indo-European
(1) *rē-* = to row

?

Latin
(5) *rēmus* = oar

Germanic
(2) *rō-*
= to row

(3) *rōthra*
= oar,
steering-oar

Germanic
(4) *airo* = oar

trirēmis
= ship equipped with
three banks or tiers
of oarsmen

Old
English
rōwan
= to row

rother
= oar,
steering-oar

Old
English
ār = oar

Middle
English
rowen

rother
ruder
= steering-oar,
fixed rudder

Middle
English
oor
or

Modern
English
ROW
(verb)

RUDDER

OAR

TRIREME

149

reidh-

1. Indo-European *reidh-* = "to ride, travel by horse" is widely attested in Germanic and Celtic, but little elsewhere. It appears in Germanic *ridan* = "to ride" and *raidaz* = "a riding," Gaulish *rēda* = "four-wheeled vehicle," Old Irish *riad* = "a journey," and Latvian *raidīt* = "send swiftly."

2. Germanic *rīdan* appears in Old Norse *rīdha,* Old High German *rītan* (whence Modern German *reiten*), and Old English *rīdan,* all meaning "to ride." Old English *rīdan* became Modern English RIDE.

3. Germanic *raid-* appears in Old Norse *reidh,* Middle Dutch *rēd,* Old Frisian *rēd,* and Old English *rād* = "the act of riding, a journey on horseback," also "a mounted expedition or attack." It became Middle English *rode,* Modern English ROAD. Only in the sixteenth century did the meaning "a made track or highway for horses and vehicles" emerge.

In medieval Scottish, Old English *rād* became *rade, raid,* keeping the sense of "a mounted expedition," especially "a sudden attack, a planned foray to inflict damage and carry off plunder." It was a word that found much employment in the perennial feudal, semiprivate warfare carried on in the border country between England and Scotland. In the sixteenth century, English writers wrote of English *roads* (and *inroads*) into Scotland, while Scottish writers wrote of Scottish *raids* into England.

After the seventeenth century, the word in this sense seems to have died out in both countries. It was revived by Sir Walter Scott. In World War I RAID suddenly came into vogue as a term used by the British Army for foot attacks on enemy trenches, and then gradually for larger attacks by land or sea. After that war, journalists used it for surprise swoops by police. In World War II it was used again by the soldiers, and later in the war especially of bombing attacks, or *air raids.*

4. Probably but not certainly connected is Germanic *raidjaz* = "prepared," appearing in Old High German *reiti,* Old Frisian *rēde,* and Old English *ræde* or *ge-ræde,* all meaning "prepared." Presumably, therefore, the Germanic adjective *raidjaz* meant "mounted, prepared for a ride, ready to fight." Old English *ræde* became Middle English *redy,* Modern English READY.

5. Italian *arredare,* Spanish *arrear,* Old French *areer,* and Norman French *araier* all mean "to set in order," especially "to draw up men for battle." It is reliably conjectured that they all descend from a Late Latin word *arrēdāre,* which has not survived in any recorded documents. This verb in turn would be a compound of *ad-* = "toward" + *rēdāre* = "to make ready," probably borrowed from a Germanic verb *raidjan* = "to prepare," closely related to *raidjaz* = "prepared," as in paragraph 4, above.

Formed from Norman French *araier* was the noun *arai* = "attire," also "state of readiness," also "battle order." These were borrowed into Middle English as *araien* (verb) and *araie* (noun), Modern English ARRAY.

150

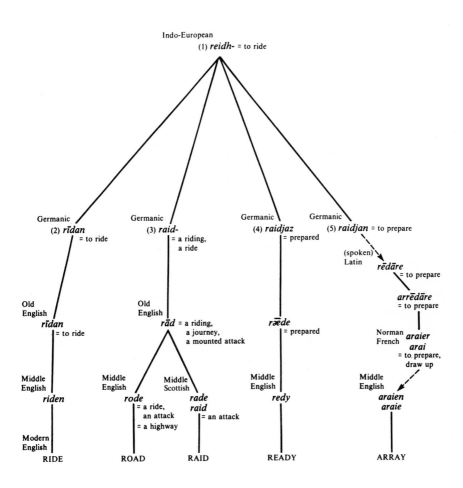

Indo-European
(1) *reidh-* = to ride

Germanic
(2) *rīdan*
= to ride

Germanic
(3) *raid-*
= a riding,
a ride

Germanic
(4) *raidjaz*
= prepared

Germanic
(5) *raidjan* = to prepare

(spoken)
Latin   *rēdāre*
= to prepare

arrēdāre
= to prepare

Old
English
rīdan
= to ride

Old
English
rād = a riding,
a journey,
a mounted attack

rǣde
= prepared

Norman   *araier*
French   *arai*
= to prepare,
draw up

Middle
English
riden

Middle
English
rode
= a ride,
an attack
= a highway

Middle
Scottish
rade
raid
= an attack

Middle
English
redy

Middle
English
araien
araie

Modern
English
RIDE

ROAD

RAID

READY

ARRAY

sal-

1. Indo-European *sal-* = "salt" appears in Germanic *saltam,* Old Irish *salann,* Latin *sal,* Latvian *sals,* Old Slavic *sol,* Greek *hals,* and Tocharian *sale,* all meaning "salt."

2. Germanic *saltam* appears in Gothic *salt,* Old High German *salz,* and Old English *salt, sealt,* becoming Modern English SALT.

3. Latin *sal* = "salt" formed the adjective *salīnus* = "being or related to salt." This was adopted into English as SALINE, the technical adjective of SALT.

   Latin *sal* = "salt" had another adjective *salārius* = "of or relating to salt." This was used as a noun, *salārium,* as the term for money paid to Roman soldiers as an allowance for buying salt (as a food preservative). *Salārium* thus came to mean "wages, regular pay"; it was adopted into Norman French as *salarie,* borrowed thence into Middle English as *salarie,* Modern English SALARY.

   The verb *salāre* = "to put salt on" is not recorded in any surviving Latin documents but is assumed to have existed as the ancestor of French *saler,* Spanish *salar,* and Italian *salare,* all meaning "to apply salt to." From Italian *salare* was formed the noun *salami* (originally plural) = "salted pork sausages." This word was later (twentieth century) borrowed into English as SALAMI.

   The reconstructed Latin verb *salāre* must also have had past participle *salātus* = "salted," from which a noun *salāta* was formed. This, too, is unrecorded, but must have existed in the Latin of the Roman Empire before it broke up into dialects (fifth century A.D.). *(Herba) salāta* would mean "salted vegetable," and was inherited as Portuguese *salada,* Spanish *ensalada,* Italian *insalata,* and Provençal *salada,* all meaning "cold dish of (raw) vegetables," no doubt of great variety but usually involving salt. Old French *salade,* as the ending *-ade* shows, was borrowed from Provençal *salada;* this borrowing marks the northward transmission of this typically Mediterranean dish. *Salade* was borrowed into Middle English in the fifteenth century, becoming Modern English SALAD.

4. Separately from the noun *sal,* Latin inherited the verb *sallere* = "to apply salt to," with past participle *salsus* = "salted." Here again a Latin noun has been reconstructed from its Romance descendants; Spanish *salsa,* Italian *salsa,* Provençal *salsa,* and Old French *sauce* all regularly descend from the unrecorded Latin word *salsa* = "salted relish" (of some unknown kind). The Old French word was borrowed into Middle English in the fourteenth century.

152

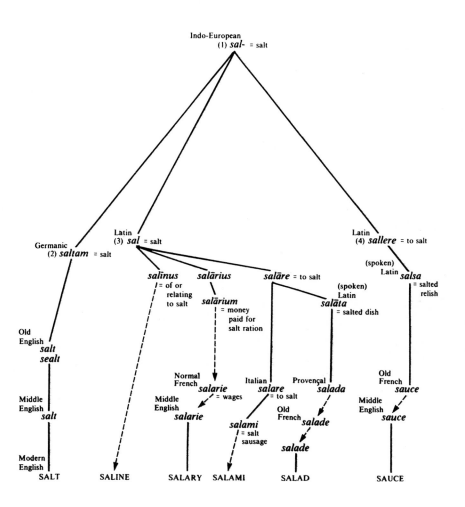

Indo-European
(1) *sal-* = salt

Germanic
(2) *saltam* = salt

Latin
(3) *sal* = salt

Latin
(4) *sallere* = to salt

salinus
= of or
relating
to salt

salarius

salare = to salt

(spoken)
Latin *salsa*
= salted
relish

(spoken)
Latin
salata
= salted dish

salarium
= money
paid for
salt ration

Old
English
salt
sealt

Normal
French
salarie
= wages

Italian
salare
= to salt

Provençal
salada

Old
French
sauce

Middle
English
salt

Middle
English
salarie

Old
French
salade

Middle
English
sauce

salami
= salt
sausage

Modern
English
SALT

SALINE

SALARY

SALAMI

salade

SALAD

SAUCE

153

sē-

1. The Indo-European verb *sē-* = "to sow," with its derivative nouns *sē-men* and *sē-tis* = "that which is sown, seed," appears in Germanic *sēyan* = "to sow" and *sēdiz* = "seed," Old Irish *síl* = "seed," Latin *sēmen* = "seed," Lithuanian *sèti* = "sow," Old Slavic *sěme* = "seed," and Sanskrit *síra-* = "sowing-plow" and *síta* = "furrow."

This widespread group of words is by itself good evidence that the Indo-European community was familiar with planting techniques. Notice that the basis of the group is the verb denoting the human activity of putting seed in the ground and that the words for "seed" are formed from it; this is the thinking of an agricultural people, not of plant-gatherers or botanists. Notice also that the metaphor of fertility, in which words meaning "plant-seed" are used to mean also "animal or human semen," apparently occurred already at the Indo-European level.

Agriculture, apparently initiated in the northern parts of the Middle East before 9000 B.C., was already old by the time of the Indo-Europeans. Archaeologically, the Early Kurgan people living on the southern Russian plains *c.* 4500 B.C. are probably the original Indo-Europeans. They were the first planters of barley and wheat in that part of the world, as well as being herders of cattle. The regular and unbroken inheritance of words like SOW and SEED from that day to the present is one of our most impressively direct links with the pioneers of farming.

2. Germanic *sēyan* appears in Gothic *saian,* Old High German *sāen* (Modern German *säen*), and Old English *sāwan,* all meaning "to sow." Old English *sāwan* became Middle English *sowen,* Modern English SOW.

3. The noun *sētis* regularly became Germanic *sēdiz,* with regular change of *t* to *d.* This appears in Old Norse *sāth,* Old High German *sāt* (Modern German *saat*), and Old English *sǣd,* all meaning "seed." The last became Modern English SEED.

4. The noun *sēmen* appears unchanged in Latin *sēmen* = (a) "plant-seed," (b) "animal semen." It was adopted into English, in the latter sense only, as SEMEN.

Formed from Latin *sēmen* was the verb *insēmināre* = (a) "to plant seed in the ground," (b) "to impregnate a female." This was adopted into English, also only in the latter sense, as INSEMINATE.

5. Another Latin word descended from this root is *satiō(n)-* = "the act of sowing." In later spoken Latin this word was used to mean "time for sowing, seed-time," also "favorable time of year." It was inherited in Old French as *seson* = "one of the four divisions of the agricultural year (spring, summer, autumn, winter)." This was borrowed into Middle English as *sesoun,* becoming Modern English SEASON.

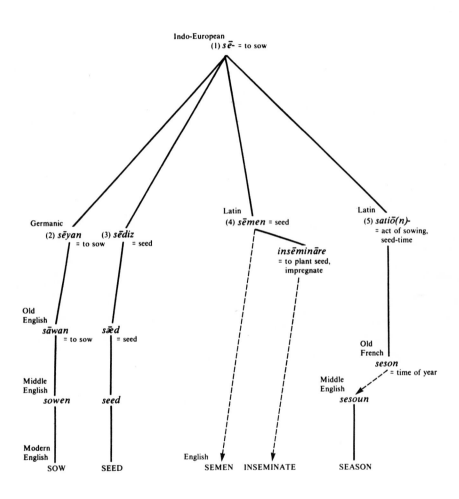

Indo-European
(1) *sē-* = to sow

Germanic
(2) *sēyan*
= to sow

(3) *sēdiz*
= seed

Latin
(4) *sēmen* = seed

insēmināre
= to plant seed,
impregnate

Latin
(5) *satiō(n)-*
= act of sowing,
seed-time

Old
English
sāwan
= to sow

sǣd
= seed

Old
French
seson
= time of year

Middle
English
sowen

seed

Middle
English
sesoun

Modern
English
SOW

SEED

English
SEMEN   INSEMINATE

SEASON

155

sed-

1. The Indo-European verb *sed-* = "to sit," with derivative nouns *sedlos, sēdyom, sedra* = "a sitting, a place to sit, a seat," appears in Germanic *sitan* = "to sit," *satjan* = "to set," and *setjam* = "a seat," Old Irish *sadid* = "sits," Welsh *sedd* = "sit," Latin *sedēre* = "to sit," Lithuanian *sedéti* = "to sit," Old Slavic *sĕdĕti* = "to sit," Greek *hedra* = "a seat", and Sanskrit *sīdati* = "sits."

2. Germanic *sitan* or *sitjan* appears in Old Norse *sitja*, Old High German *sizzan* (Modern German *sitzen*), and Old English *sittan*, all meaning "to sit." Old English *sittan* became Modern English SIT.

3. Germanic *satjan* = "to cause to sit," i.e., "to set, put, place," appears in Gothic *satjan*, Old Norse *setja*, Old High German *sezzan* (Modern German *setzen*), and Old English *settan*, all meaning "to place or put." The last became Modern English SET.

4. Germanic *setlaz* appears in Gothic *sitls*, Old High German *sezzal* (Modern German *sessel*), and Old English *setl*, all meaning "a sitting-down, a seat." Old English *setl* became Modern English SETTLE (noun). Formed from Old English *setl* was the verb *setlan* = "to put in a particular place," becoming Modern English SETTLE (verb), with many extended and generalized senses.

5. Germanic *sadulaz* appears in Old Norse *sodull*, Old High German *satal* (Modern German *sattel*), and Old English *sadol*, all meaning "seat for a rider on a horse." Old English *sadol* became Modern English SADDLE.

6. Germanic *sētjam* or *ga-sētjam* appears in Old Norse *sæti*, Old High German *gasazi* (Modern German *gesass*), and Old English *gesete*, all meaning "a sitting, a seat." Old English *gesete* died out. In the twelfth century, Old Norse *sæti* was borrowed into Middle English as *sæte, seete*, becoming Modern English SEAT.

7. Formed from Latin *sedēre* = "to sit" was the adjective *sedentārius* = "sitting" (of an occupation carried on at a desk, etc.). This was adopted into English as SEDENTARY. Also from Latin *sedēre*, with past participle *sessus*, was the noun *sessiō* = "a sitting." This was adopted into Old French as *session* and thence into Middle English as SESSION.

8. Greek *hedra* = "seat" had the compound form *kathedra*, also meaning "seat, chair" (*kata-* = "down"). This was borrowed into Latin as *cathedra*, used by Christians especially of a bishop's throne, and figuratively of the place where he presided over his diocese. In Medieval Latin the adjective *cathedrālis* occurred in the term *ecclēsia cathedrālis* = "church of the (bishop's) seat," i.e., the chief church of a diocese. This was borrowed into Old French as *eglise cathedral* and thence into Middle English as *cathedral church*. In the sixteenth century the phrase was reduced to the noun CATHEDRAL.

Latin *cathedra* was also inherited in Old French as *chaiere* = "seat," which was borrowed into Middle English as CHAIR.

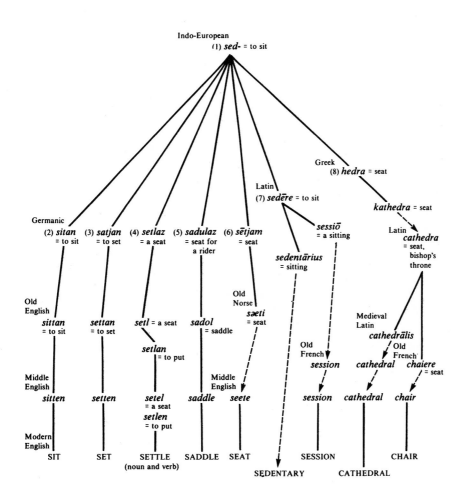

Indo-European
(1) *sed-* = to sit

Greek
(8) *hedra* = seat

kathedra = seat

Latin
(7) *sedēre* = to sit

Latin
cathedra
= seat,
bishop's
throne

sessiō
= a sitting

sedentārius
= sitting

Germanic
(2) *sitan*
= to sit

(3) *satjan*
= to set

(4) *setlaz*
= a seat

(5) *sadulaz*
= seat for
a rider

(6) *sētjam*
= seat

Old
English

sittan
= to sit

settan
= to set

setl = a seat

sadol
= saddle

Old
Norse
sæti
= seat

setlan
= to put

Medieval
Latin
cathedrālis

Middle
English

Old
French
session

Old
French
chaiere
= seat

Middle
English

sitten

setten

setel
= a seat
setlen
= to put

saddle

seete

session

cathedral

chair

Modern
English

SIT

SET

SETTLE
(noun and verb)

SADDLE

SEAT

SESSION

CATHEDRAL

CHAIR

SEDENTARY

157

seks

1. Indo-European *seks* or *sweks* = "six" appears in Germanic *seks*, Old Irish *se*, Latin *sex*, Lithuanian *šeši*, Old Slavic *sestĭ*, Greek *hex*, Tocharian *säk*, and Sanskrit *sát*, all meaning "six."

2. Germanic *seks* appears in Gothic *saihs*, Old Norse *sex*, Old High German *sehs* (whence modern German *sechs*), and Old English *sex, siex*, becoming Modern English SIX.

3. A compound formed from Latin *sex* = "six" was *sēmēstris* = "six-monthly" (*-mēstris* from *mēnsis* = month; *see* **men-** = "moon"). This was adopted into modern German as *semester* = "academic half-year," borrowed into English as SEMESTER, now used both strictly of an eighteen-week term and more loosely of various shorter periods of study.

4. Also formed from Latin *sex* was *sexāgintā* = "sixty," whence *sexāgēnārius* = "sixty years old," adopted as SEXAGENARIAN.

5. From the Latin ordinal adjective *sextus* = "sixth" was *sextans, sextant-* = "a sixth part of something." The sixteenth-century Danish astronomer Tycho Brahe devised an observing instrument based on an arc of sixty degrees, or one sixth of a circle, and named it (in New Latin) *sextans, sextant-*. This was adopted into English as SEXTANT, now primarily a navigational instrument.

6. Indo-European *seks* became Greek *hex*, with the regular change of *s* to Greek *h*. The geometric term *hexagōnon* = "six-angled figure" (*gōnia* = "angle"; *see* **genu** = "knee") was adopted into English (sixteenth century) as HEXAGON.

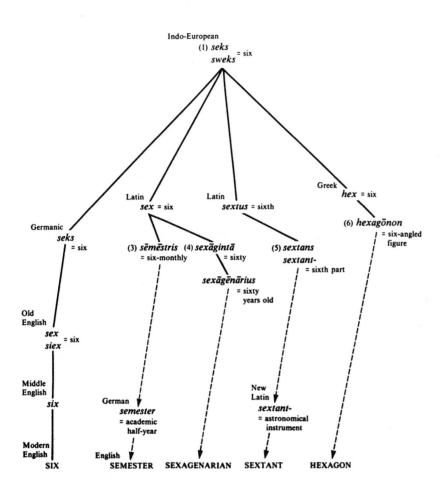

Indo-European
(1) *seks*
sweks = six

Germanic
seks
= six

Latin
sex = six

Latin
sextus = sixth

Greek
hex = six

(6) *hexagōnon*
= six-angled
figure

(3) *sēmēstris*
= six-monthly

(4) *sexāgintā*
= sixty

(5) *sextans*
sextant-
= sixth part

sexāgēnārius
= sixty
years old

Old
English
sex
siex = six

Middle
English
six

German
semester
= academic
half-year

New
Latin
sextant-
= astronomical
instrument

Modern
English
SIX

English
SEMESTER

SEXAGENARIAN

SEXTANT

HEXAGON

159

septm

1. Indo-European *septm* = "seven" appears in Germanic *sibun*, Old Irish *secht*, Latin *septem*, Lithuanian *septyni*, Old Slavic *sedmĭ*, Greek *hepta*, Hittite *šipta*, and Sanskrit *saptá*, all meaning "seven."

2. Germanic *sibun* appears in Gothic *sibun*, Old Norse *siau*, Old High German *sibun*, and Old English *seofon*, all meaning "seven," the last becoming Middle and Modern English SEVEN.

3. In the original Roman calendar, in which March was the first month, the seventh month was *September*. When January and February were added, September became the ninth month, but the now inappropriate name was never changed. It was adopted into Middle English as *Septembre*, becoming Modern English SEPTEMBER.

4. Formed from Latin *septuagintā* = "seventy" was *septuagēnārius* = "seventy years old," adopted into English as SEPTUAGENARIAN.

5. From Greek *hepta* = "seven" was the geometric term *heptagōnon* = "seven-angled figure" (*gōnia* = "angle"; *see* **genu** = "knee"); this was adopted as HEPTAGON.

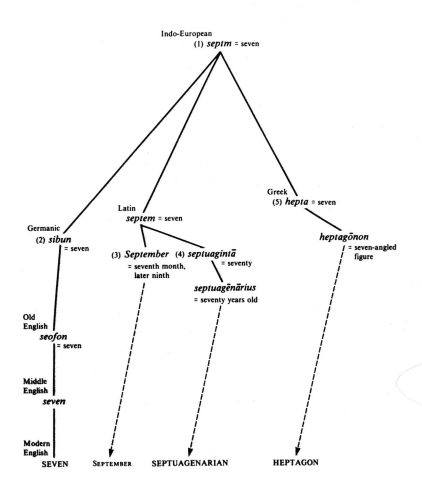

Indo-European
(1) *septm* = seven

Germanic
(2) *sibun*
= seven

Latin
septem = seven

Greek
(5) *hepta* = seven

(3) *September*
= seventh month,
later ninth

(4) *septuagintā*
= seventy

heptagōnon
= seven-angled
figure

septuagēnārius
= seventy years old

Old
English
seofon
= seven

Middle
English
seven

Modern
English
SEVEN   September   SEPTUAGENARIAN   HEPTAGON

161

stenə-

1. The Indo-European verb root *stenə-* = "roar, shout, groan, thunder" had a variant form *tenə-* without the initial *s* (a frequent type of alternation in Indo-European). This root appears in Germanic *thunaraz* = "thunder," Latin *tonāre* = "to thunder," Lithuanian *stenu* = "groan," Greek *stenein* = "to groan," and Sanskrit *stanati* = "thunders, roars."

The Indo-Europeans evidently regarded thunder as the voice of the weather god they called "Sky-father" (*see* **deiwos** = "god").

2. Germanic *thunaraz* appears in Old High German *donar* (Modern German *donner*), Old Frisian *thuner,* and Old English *thunor,* all meaning "thunder." *Thunor* became Middle English *thonre,* later *thondre,* then Modern English THUNDER.

3. Germanic *Thunaraz* was also used as the name of a thunder god, who appears to be a new Germanic creation, unrelated to the Indo-European *Deiwos;* he was bearded and had a hammer. In Old Norse his name was *Thunar,* later *Thorr.*

In late Roman times the fourth day of the week was called *Jovis diēs* = "Jupiter's day" (whence Modern French *jeudi,* Italian *giovedi*). When the Latin weekdays were adopted and translated by the Germanic peoples, they identified Jupiter with Thor because they both wielded the thunder. In Old English the day-name became *Thunres-dæg* (*thunres,* genitive of *thunor* = "thunder"). The Old Norse equivalent *Thōrsdagr* influenced the Old English word, which became *Thursdæg,* Middle English *Thuresday,* Modern English THURSDAY.

4. The root appears in Latin *tonāre* = "to thunder" (usually appearing with Jupiter as its subject). A spoken Latin word *extonāre* = "to thunder out, strike as if with thunder" (*ex-* = "out") is reconstructed from Romance descendants including Old French *estoner* = "to amaze, shock" (whence Modern French *étonner*). *Estoner* was borrowed into Middle English as *astonen* = "to amaze, shock." (a) From its past participle *astoned,* the verb was reformed as ASTOUND. (b) Separately, *astonen* picked up the *-ish* ending found in many verbs borrowed from French (*finish, vanish,* etc.) to produce the variant ASTONISH. (c) Separately again, *astonen* lost its initial vowel, and its verb ending, to produce the third variant STUN.

5. Closely related to Greek *stenein* = "to groan" is *Stentōr,* the name of a herald in the *Iliad.* The literal meaning of the name would be "he who shouts"; Homer gives him the epithet "bronze-voiced," and he became proverbial for loudness; hence the English adjective STENTORIAN.

162

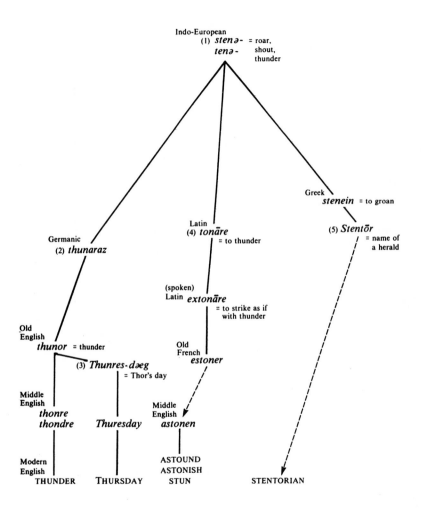

Indo-European
(1) *stenə-* = roar,
   tenə-   shout,
          thunder

Greek
stenein = to groan

(5) *Stentōr*
      = name of
      a herald

Latin
(4) *tonāre*
      = to thunder

Germanic
(2) *thunaraz*

(spoken)
Latin *extonāre*
      = to strike as if
      with thunder

Old
English
thunor = thunder

(3) *Thunres-dæg*
      = Thor's day

Old
French
estoner

Middle
English
thonre
thondre

Thuresday

Middle
English
astonen

Modern
English
THUNDER

THURSDAY

ASTOUND
ASTONISH
STUN

STENTORIAN

163

ster-

1. Indo-European *ster-* = "star" appears in Germanic *sterron-*, Cornish *sterenn*, Latin *stella*, Greek *astēr*, and Sanskrit *(s)tāra*, all meaning "star."

2. Germanic *sterron-* appears in Old High German *sterro*, Old Frisian *stera*, and Old English *steorra*, becoming Middle English *sterre*, Modern English STAR.

3. Latin *stella* is from a form of the root with a different noun suffix *(ster-la)*. The Late Latin adjective *stellāris* = "like a star, relating to the stars" was adopted into English (sixteenth century) as STELLAR. The Late Latin noun *constellātiō (con-* = "together") = "group of stars" was adopted into English as CONSTELLATION.

4. Besides the basic Greek form *astēr* was the form *astron* = "star, anything seen in the sky." Formed from this were the two nouns *astrologia (-logia* = "description") and *astronomia (-nomia* = "classification, arrangement"), both meaning "the science of the stars, observation and study of celestial phenomena." They were adopted into Latin as *astrologia* and *astronomia*, thence into Old French as *astrologie* and *astronomie*, and thence into Middle English as *astrologie* and *astronomie*, Modern English as ASTROLOGY and ASTRONOMY. Only in the sixteenth and seventeenth centuries did any clear distinction emerge between the two pursuits ASTROLOGY = "study of the stars for their occult influences on human affairs" and ASTRONOMY = "scientific study of the physical universe."

Greek *astron* was also borrowed into Latin as *astrum*, which was adopted into medieval Italian as *astro* = "star, constellation, any celestial event." From this in the fourteenth century astrologers coined the term *disastro* = "harmful event in the heavens, conjunction of stars and planets having a disruptive effect on human affairs" (*dis-* = "ill-, unfavorable"). This was borrowed into Middle English as *disastre* and thence into English (sixteenth century) as DISASTER.

Greek *astron* was also adopted into French in the late nineteenth century to form the science-fiction term *astronaute* = "star-sailor, human who voyages through the universe" (Greek *nautēs* = "sailor"). This was borrowed into English as ASTRONAUT, recently translated from fantasy into reality.

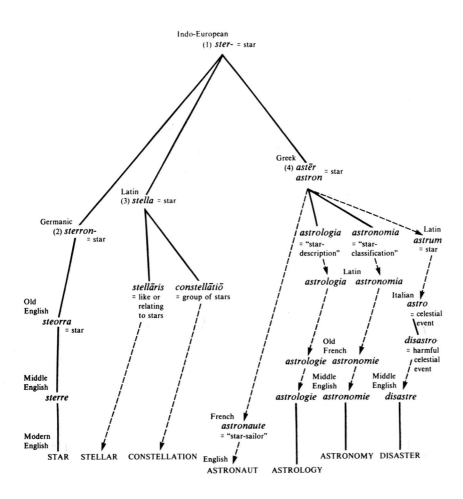

Indo-European
(1) *ster-* = star

Germanic
(2) *sterron-* = star

Latin
(3) *stella* = star

Greek
(4) *astēr* = star
astron

Old
English
steorra = star

stellāris = like or relating to stars

constellātiō = group of stars

astrologia = "star-description"

astronomia = "star-classification"

Latin
astrum = star

Latin
astrologia *astronomia*

Italian
astro = celestial event

Middle
English
sterre

Old
French
astrologie *astronomie*

disastro = harmful celestial event

Modern
English

Middle
English
astrologie *astronomie*

Middle
English
disastre

French
astronaute = "star-sailor"

STAR   STELLAR   CONSTELLATION   English
ASTRONAUT   ASTROLOGY   ASTRONOMY   DISASTER

165

sus

1. Indo-European *sus* or *sūs* = "pig" appears in Germanic *sū-*, Latin *sūs*, Greek *hus*, Tocharian *suwo*, and Avestan *hū*, all meaning "pig"; also in Lithuanian *suvēns* = "young pig." An extended form *sukos* appears in Celtic *sukkos* = "pig, pig's snout," and in Sanskrit *sūkara* = "pig." And an Indo-European adjectival form *suīnos* = "relating to pigs" appears, readapted as a noun, in Germanic *swīnam* = "pig."

   Alongside *sus*, referring to the adult animal, the Indo-European word *porkos* referred to the young pig. There can thus be little doubt that the original Indo-European–speaking people kept pigs, which in Anatolia were domesticated before 6500 B.C. At settlements of the Early Kurgan culture (Ukraine, before 4000 B.C.; thought to be early Indo-European–speaking people) bones of domesticated pigs have also been found.

2. Germanic *sū-* appears in Old High German *sū*, Old Saxon *suga*, Middle Dutch *soge*, and Old English *sugu* = "female pig." The last became Modern English SOW.

3. Germanic *swīnam* = "pig" appears in Gothic *swein*, Old Norse *suin*, Old High German *swīn*, and Old English *swīn*. The last became Modern English SWINE, now archaic as a term for the animal itself but remaining in current use as a term of abuse.

4. Celtic *sukkos* = "pig, pig's snout" appears in Middle Irish *soc* = "pig's snout, plowshare," Welsh *hwch* = "pig, sow," Cornish *hogh* = "pig," and British *hukk-* = "pig." (The change of initial *s* to *h* occurs elsewhere in Celtic. British is the language of the Celtic population of Britain, overrun by the Romans in the first century A.D. and by the Anglo-Saxons in the fifth century.) British *hukk-* is not recorded in any surviving document, but has been reconstructed by comparison with the other Celtic words cited above, and also as the source from which Old English *hogg* = "pig" must have been borrowed. It is thus one of the surprisingly small number of words known to have been borrowed by the Germanic invaders of Britain from the Celtic Britons. It became Modern English HOG.

5. Latin *sūs* = "pig" had the diminutive form *sūculus* = "pig." In three of the Romance languages there are comparable verbs meaning "to make dirty, to pollute": Catalan *sullar*, Provençal *solhar*, Old French *soillier*. On the basis of changes undergone by other Romance words inherited from Latin, these words are assumed to be descended from an unrecorded Latin verb *sūculāre* = "to make dirty," derived from the noun *sūculus* = "pig." Old French *soillier* was borrowed into Middle English as *soilen*, becoming Modern English SOIL (verb—not related to the noun SOIL = "earth, ground").

166

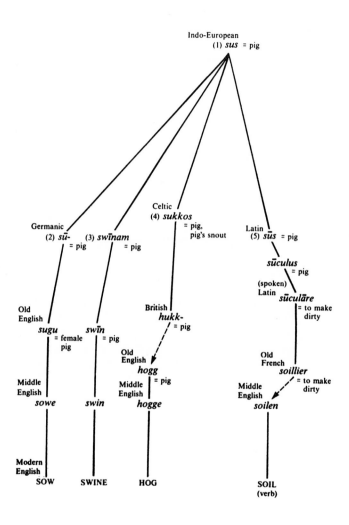

Indo-European
(1) *sus* = pig

Germanic
(2) *sū-*
= pig

(3) *swīnam*
= pig

Celtic
(4) *sukkos*
= pig,
pig's snout

Latin
(5) *sūs* = pig

sūculus
= pig

(spoken)
Latin *sūculāre*
= to make
dirty

Old
English
sugu
= female
pig

swīn
= pig

British
hukk-
= pig

Old
English
hogg
= pig

Old
French
soillier
= to make
dirty

Middle
English
sowe

swin

Middle
English
hogge

Middle
English
soilen

Modern
English
SOW

SWINE

HOG

SOIL
(verb)

167

swād-

1. The Indo-European word *swād-* = "sweet, pleasant" appears in Germanic *swōtjaz,* Latin *suāvis,* Greek *hēdus* (originally *swēdus*), and Sanskrit *svādus,* all meaning "sweet, pleasant, delightful to the senses or to the mind."

2. Germanic *swōtjaz* appears in Old Norse *soetr,* Old High German *suozi,* and Old English *swēte,* all meaning "sweet, delightful." The last became Modern English SWEET.

3. Latin *suāvis* = "sweet, delightful" was adopted into French as *suave* = "sweet," also "smoothly polite," borrowed into English as SUAVE.

4. Latin *suādēre* = "to advise (something) on someone," originally meant "to recommend something, to speak of something as being good." Its compound form *persuādēre* = "to urge (something) on someone" (*per-* being an intensive prefix) was adopted into English as PERSUADE; the object of the verb has changed from the thing urged to the person upon whom it is urged.

5. Closely related to Greek *hēdus* = "sweet, delightful" was *hēdonē* (originally *swēdonē*) = "pleasure." This was adopted into English (nineteenth century) to form the word HEDONISM, the theory that pleasure is the purpose of life.

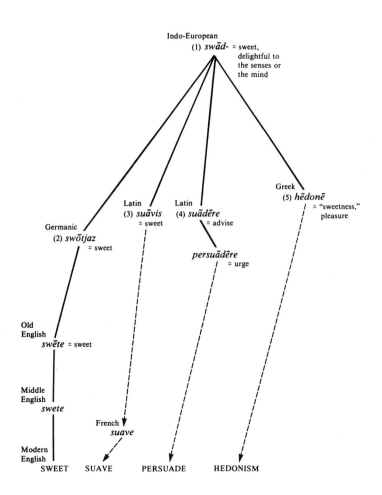

Indo-European
(1) *swād-* = sweet, delightful to the senses or the mind

Greek
(5) *hēdonē* = "sweetness," pleasure

Latin
(3) *suāvis* = sweet

Latin
(4) *suādēre* = advise

persuādēre = urge

Germanic
(2) *swōtjaz* = sweet

Old English
swēte = sweet

Middle English
swete

French
suave

Modern English
SWEET   SUAVE   PERSUADE   HEDONISM

169

sweid-

1. Indo-European *sweid-,* also *swoid-,* = "sweat" appears in Germanic *swaidaz,* Welsh *chwys,* Latin *sūdor,* Latvian *sviédri,* Greek *hidrōs,* and Sanskrit *svéda,* all meaning "sweat."

2. Germanic *swaidaz* appears in Old High German *sweiz* (whence Modern German *schweiss*), Old Frisian *swēt,* and Old English *swāt,* all meaning "sweat." Old English *swǣtan* = "to sweat" became Modern English SWEAT.

3. Formed from Latin *sūdor* = "sweat" was the verb *sūdāre* = "to sweat," with a compound form *exsūdāre, exūdāre* = "to sweat out." This was adopted into sixteenth-century English as EXUDE, originally a medical term meaning "to come out in droplets," now a part of the general vocabulary meaning "to ooze out or diffuse."

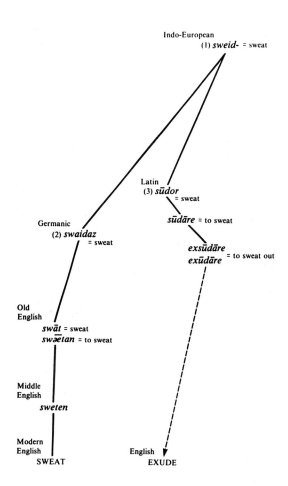

Indo-European
(1) *sweid-* = sweat

Latin
(3) *sūdor* = sweat

sūdāre = to sweat

Germanic
(2) *swaidaz* = sweat

exsūdāre
exūdāre = to sweat out

Old
English
swāt = sweat
swǣtan = to sweat

Middle
English
sweten

Modern
English
SWEAT

English
EXUDE

171

swesor

1. Indo-European *swesor* = "kinswoman" appears in Germanic *swistra,* Old Irish *siur,* Latin *soror,* Lithuanian *sesuõ,* Tocharian *šar,* and Sanskrit *svásar,* all meaning "sister, female relative."

Swesor did not originally mean "female sibling." It seems to have been a term applied to all the unmarried females within the extended family, or clan. When married, a woman was adopted into her husband's family relationships. Unmarried, she was a *swe-sor* = "she *(sor)* belonging to the *swe*"; the *swe* was some social grouping or category, possibly confined to women, within the patriarchal clan.

2. Germanic *swistra* appears in Gothic *swistar,* Old Norse *systir,* Old High German *swester* (whence Modern German *schwester*), and Old English *sweostor, swuster,* all meaning "sister," also sometimes "kinswoman." Old English *swuster* became Modern English SISTER.

3. *Swesor,* with change of *s* between vowels to *r,* became Latin *soror* = "sister," also "female cousin." From this was formed Medieval Latin *sororitās* = "sisterhood," especially "community of nuns or sisters." This was adopted into American English in the nineteenth century to form the word SORORITY = "association of university women," modeled on FRATERNITY.

4. An adjective form from *swesor* was *swesrinos* = "of or relating to a kinswoman." This appears in Latin *sobrīnus* = "cousin on one's mother's side" and *consobrīnus* (*con-* = "together"), a specific term for first cousins who are the children of two sisters. Later, *consobrīnus* came to be used more loosely for any cousin. It was so inherited in Old French as *cosin,* which was borrowed into Middle English as *cosin,* becoming Modern English COUSIN.

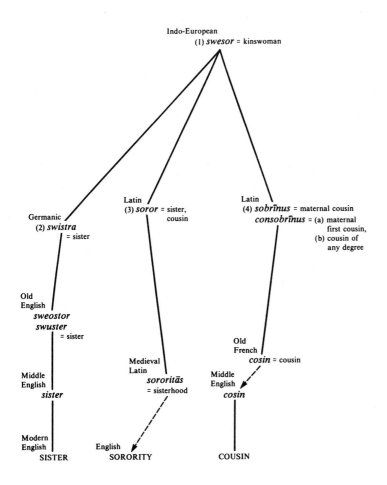

syū-

1. The Indo-European root *syū-, sū-* = "to sew" is regularly represented in most of the language groups: Germanic *siwjan* = "to sew" and *saumaz* = "a seam," Latin *suere* = "to sew," Lithuanian *siuvù* = "sew," Sanskrit *sīvyati* = "sews," *sūtra* = "thread."

Hand-sewing is presumably one of the oldest human technologies, going back long before the earliest reachable Indo-European community. The leather and textiles of that period have of course perished, but among the finds from the Kurgan III culture (Ukraine *c.* 3500–3000 B.C., thought to be an early Indo-European–speaking group) are thin copper awls, some of the first tools to be made from metal. The basic Indo-European word for "sew" was widely retained in core vocabularies from one end of the Indo-European world to the other, and a number of derivatives within the original language can also be recovered with certainty: *syūtos* = "sewn," *syūmen* = "thread," *syūdhla* = "awl or needle." (There were also other sewing terms, including *nētlom* = "needle," from which our word *needle* directly descends.)

The unbroken tradition of hand-sewing within the family has survived into the industrialized world without fundamental change (although the needle and thread are no longer homemade). This tradition is exactly reflected by the handing down from adult to child, through hundreds of generations, of the word *syū-*, SEW.

2. *Syū-* regularly appears in Germanic *siwjan* = "to sew," becoming Gothic *siujan*, Old High German *siuwan*, and Old English *seowian* or *siowan*, all meaning "to sew." The Old English word became Modern English SEW. The original pronunciation, as the spelling still anachronistically shows, was /sue/, and this survived until the seventeenth century. The reason for the irregular change to /so/ is unknown.

3. The root also appears in Germanic *saumaz* = "a seam," becoming Old High German *soum*, Old Icelandic *saumr*, and Old English *sēam*, all meaning "seam." The last became Modern English SEAM.

4. Indo-European *sū-* and *syūtos* appear in Latin *suere* = "to sew" and its past participle *sūtus* = "sewn." From the latter was formed the noun *sūtūra* = "(piece of) sewing." This was adopted into English as the technical word SUTURE, = "surgical stitching, etc."

5. The Sanskrit word *sūtra* = "thread" was also used to mean a "string" of observations or collection of rules; the *Sutras* are various ancient Hindu texts, for example, the *Kama Sutra,* or collection relating to love; hence English KAMASUTRA.

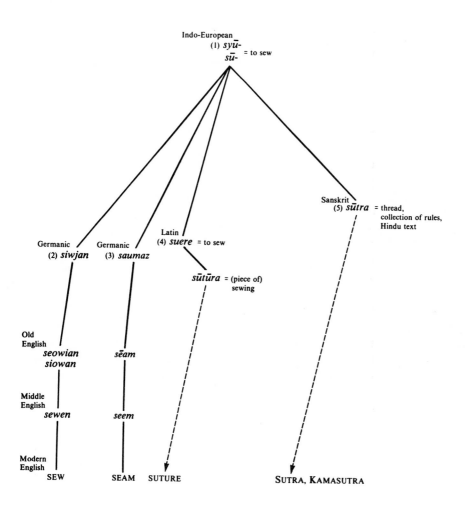

Indo-European
(1) *syū-*
sū- = to sew

Sanskrit
(5) *sūtra* = thread,
collection of rules,
Hindu text

Latin
(4) *suere* = to sew

Germanic
(2) *siwjan*

Germanic
(3) *saumaz*

sūtūra = (piece of)
sewing

Old
English
seowian
siowan

sēam

Middle
English
sewen

seem

Modern
English
SEW

SEAM   SUTURE

SUTRA, KAMASUTRA

175

ten-

1. Indo-European *ten-*, with its adjectival form *tenus, tnus* = "thin," appears in Germanic *thunniz*, Old Irish *tana*, Latin *tenuis*, Lithuanian *ténvas*, Old Slavic *tinŭkŭ*, and Sanskrit *tánus*, all meaning "thin."

This is a derived use of the root *ten-* = "to stretch," hence words meaning "something stretched out," "thin," and "string."

2. Germanic *thunniz* (with regular change of Indo-European *t* to *th*) appears in Old Norse *thunnr*, Old High German *dunni*, and Old English *thynne*, all meaning "thin." The last became Modern English THIN.

3. Latin *tenuis* = "thin, fine, attenuated" was adopted into English (seventeenth century) as TENUOUS.

4. Related to Latin *tenuis* is Latin *tener* = "delicate, soft, tender." This became Old French *tendre*, borrowed thence into Middle English *tendre*, becoming Modern English TENDER.

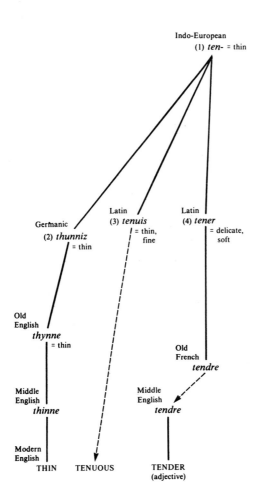

Indo-European
(1) *ten-* = thin

Germanic
(2) *thunniz*
= thin

Latin
(3) *tenuis*
= thin,
fine

Latin
(4) *tener*
= delicate,
soft

Old
English
thynne
= thin

Old
French
tendre

Middle
English
thinne

Middle
English
tendre

Modern
English
THIN   TENUOUS   TENDER
(adjective)

trei (I)

1. Indo-European *trei, treyes* = "three" appears in Germanic *thriyiz*, Old Irish *tri*, Latin *trēs*, Lithuanian *trȳs*, Old Slavic *troji*, Hittite *tri*, and Sanskrit *tráya-*, all meaning "three."

2. Germanic *thriyiz*, showing the regular change of Indo-European *t* to Germanic *th*, appears in Gothic *thrija*, Old Norse *thrír*, Old High German *drī* (whence Modern German *drei*), and Old English *thrī, thrie*, all meaning "three." Old English *thrie* became Modern English THREE.

   From Old English *thrī* there was formed an adverb *thriwa, thrige* = "three times." This became Middle English *thrie*, which was given a further adverbial suffix *-s* (as in *nights* = "at night"), becoming *thries*, and in Modern English, THRICE.

3. Latin *trēs* was inherited in Old French as *trei, treis* (becoming Modern French *trois*); this was borrowed into Middle English as *treye* = "three at dice or cards," becoming Modern English TREY, still in use among cardplayers.

   Latin *trēs* was inherited in Italian as *tre* = "three." The word *trio* = "group of three musicians" was formed from *tre* by analogy with *duo* = "two." It was borrowed into English (eighteenth century) as TRIO.

4. Related to Old Slavic *troji* = "three" is modern Russian *troe* = "three." Formed from this is *troyka* = "three-horse carriage or sleigh." This was borrowed into English (nineteenth century) as TROIKA.

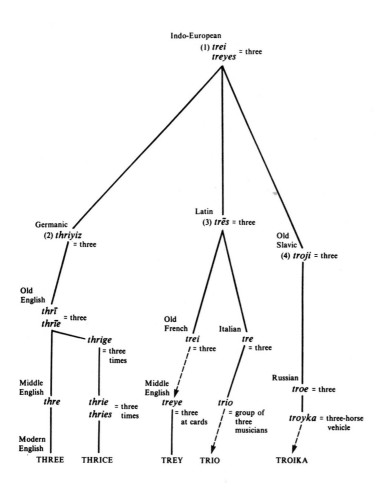

Indo-European
(1) *trei*
treyes = three

Germanic
(2) *thriyiz*
= three

Latin
(3) *trēs* = three

Old
Slavic
(4) *troji* = three

Old
English
thrī
thrīe = three

thrige
= three
times

Old
French
trei
= three

Italian
tre
= three

Middle
English
thre

thrie
thries = three
times

Middle
English
treye
= three
at cards

trio
= group of
three
musicians

Russian
troe = three

troyka = three-horse
vehicle

Modern
English
THREE

THRICE

TREY

TRIO

TROIKA

179

trei (II)

1. The ordinal adjective from *trei* = "three" was *trityos* = "third." This appears in Germanic *thrithyaz*, Latin *tertius*, Lithuanian *trẽčias*, Old Slavic *tretij*, Greek *tritos*, Tocharian *trit*, and Sanskrit *trtíya*, all meaning "third."

2. Germanic *thrithyaz* (with regular change of *t* to *th*) appears in Gothic *thridja*, Old Norse *thrithi*, Old High German *dritto* (whence Modern German *dritte*), and Old English *thridda*, all meaning "third." The Old English variant *thirdda*, first appearing in the Northumbrian dialect in the tenth century, later became the standard English form, giving Modern English THIRD (instead of *thrid*).

   Formed from Old Norse *thrithi* = "third" was *thrithjungr* = "third part" (*-ungr* is a noun suffix). From the eighth century to the tenth, large numbers of Norse people settled in northern England. The city of York was for a while the seat of an independent Norse principality. The large region later called Yorkshire was divided into three districts, each called a *thrithjungr* = "third part." Borrowed into late Old English this word became *thriding*. The districts were thus called the *North-thriding*, the *East-thriding*, and the *West-thriding*. By the twelfth century the implicit connection with "three" had been forgotten, and the names were being rendered as North *Riding*, East *Riding*, West *Riding*. They remained the basic administrative divisions of Yorkshire, each as big as a separate county, until abolished by the London government in the 1970s. Emigrant Yorkshiremen have carried their special term *Riding* into various countries. Long Island, New York, was in the seventeenth century divided into *ridings*. And the term has been permanently adopted in Canadian English as the name of an electoral district.

3. Formed from Latin *tertius* = "third" was *tertiārius* = "belonging to a third rank or grade." This was adopted into English (sixteenth century) as TERTIARY.

4. Also from *trei* are a number of derivatives in *tri-*, including Latin *triplus* = "threefold." This was inherited in Old French as *treble*, which was borrowed into Middle English (fourteenth century) as TREBLE. Latin *triplus* was later separately adopted into French as *triple*, which was also borrowed into English (sixteenth century) as TRIPLE.

5. Among the numerous other Latin compounds in *tri-* are *triangulum* = "three-angled figure," adopted into Middle English as TRIANGLE, and *tridens, trident-* = "three-tined spear" (*dent-* = "tooth"; *see* **dent-**), adopted as TRIDENT.

   Similarly, Greek *trigōnon* = "three-angled figure" (*gōnia* = angle; *see* **genu** = "knee") was adopted into mathematical New Latin (seventeenth century) to form the term *trigono-metria* = "triangle-measurement," whence English TRIGONOMETRY; and Greek *tripous, tripod-* = "three-footed vessel" (*pod-* = "foot"; *see* **ped-** = "foot") was adopted as TRIPOD.

180

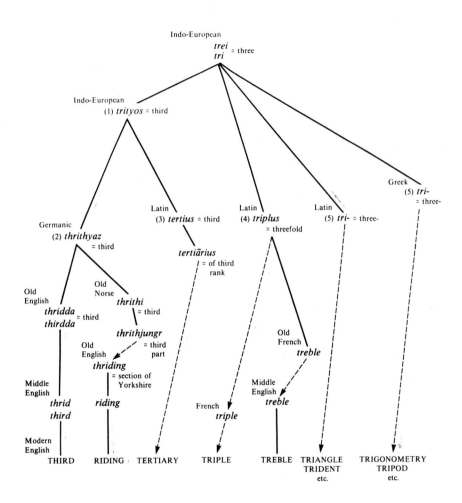

Indo-European
trei
tri = three

Indo-European
(1) *trityos* = third

Germanic
(2) *thrithyaz*
= third

Latin
(3) *tertius* = third

Latin
(4) *triplus*
= threefold

Latin
(5) *tri-* = three-

Greek
(5) *tri-*
= three-

tertiārius
= of third
rank

Old
English
thridda
thirdda = third

Old
Norse
thrithi
= third

thrithjungr
= third
part

Old
English
thriding
= section of
Yorkshire

Old
French
treble

Middle
English
thrid
third

riding

French
triple

Middle
English
treble

Modern
English
THIRD   RIDING   TERTIARY   TRIPLE   TREBLE   TRIANGLE   TRIGONOMETRY
                                              TRIDENT   TRIPOD
                                              etc.   etc.

181

uper

1. The Indo-European adverb/preposition *uper* = "over" appears in Germanic *uberi*, Celtic *for-*, Latin *super*, Greek *huper*, and Sanskrit *upári*, all meaning "over."

2. Germanic *uberi* appears in Gothic *ufar*, Old Norse *yfir*, Old High German *ubar* (whence Modern German *uber*), Old Frisian *over*, and Old English *ofer*, all meaning "over." Old English *ofer* became Modern English OVER.

3. Latin *super* = "over" was used as a prefix to form such words as *superfluus* = "overflowing," *superscribere* = "to write above"; these have been adopted into English as SUPERFLUOUS and SUPERSCRIBE, along with many others. *Super-* itself has been adopted as a prefix, forming new words such as SUPERCHARGER, SUPERMARKET.

4. Greek *huper* = "over, beyond" was likewise used as a prefix to form, for example, *huperbole* = "a throwing beyond, exaggeration," adopted into English as HYPERBOLE. The prefix HYPER- has also become productive in English: HYPERCORRECTION = "excessive correction"; HYPERVENTILATION = "abnormally deep breathing," etc.

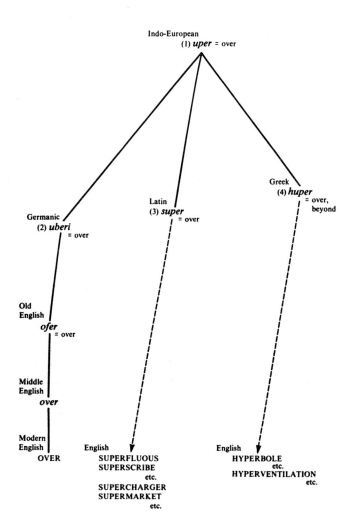

Indo-European
(1) *uper* = over

Germanic
(2) *uberi*
= over

Latin
(3) *super*
= over

Greek
(4) *huper*
= over,
beyond

Old
English
ofer = over

Middle
English
over

Modern
English
OVER

English
SUPERFLUOUS
SUPERSCRIBE
etc.
SUPERCHARGER
SUPERMARKET
etc.

English
HYPERBOLE
etc.
HYPERVENTILATION
etc.

183

upo

1. The Indo-European adverb/preposition *upo* = "under," also "up from under," appears in Germanic *upp* = "up," Old Irish *fo* = "under," Latin *sub* = "under," Greek *hupo* = "under," and Sanskrit *upa* = "at, by."

2. Germanic *upp* appears in Old Norse *upp,* Old High German *uf* (whence Modern German *auf*), and Old English *up, upp, uppe,* becoming Modern English UP.

    In Middle English the prepositional phrase *up on* appeared, becoming Modern English UPON.

3. Latin *sub* = "under, up from under" was freely used as a prefix, forming such compounds as *submergere* = "to sink under water" and *subscrībere* = "to write (one's name) under." Many of these have been adopted into English: SUBMERGE, SUBSCRIBE. The prefix itself has also been adopted, forming new English words such as SUBTROPICAL, SUBCULTURE, etc.

4. Greek *hupo* = "under" was also used as a prefix in such words as *hupogaios* = "underground," adopted into English as HYPOGEAL. This prefix, too, has been adopted into English: HYPODERMIC = "under the skin," etc.

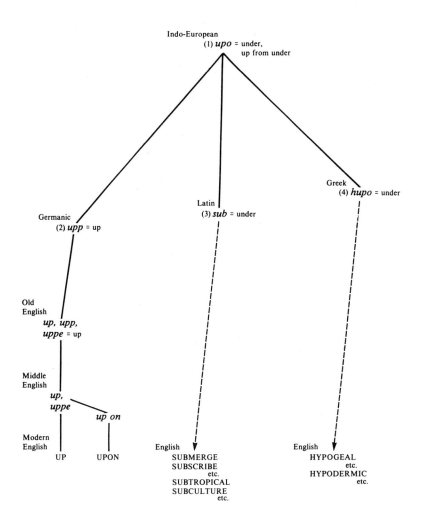

Indo-European
(1) *upo* = under,
up from under

Germanic
(2) *upp* = up

Latin
(3) *sub* = under

Greek
(4) *hupo* = under

Old
English
up, upp,
uppe = up

Middle
English
up,
uppe   *up on*

Modern
English
UP   UPON

English
SUBMERGE
SUBSCRIBE
etc.
SUBTROPICAL
SUBCULTURE
etc.

English
HYPOGEAL
etc.
HYPODERMIC
etc.

185

we/nes

1. The Indo-European pronoun of the first person plural was made up of two unrelated roots: *we* for the subjective case ("we"), and *nes, nos, ns* for the objective cases ("us").

   Indo-European *we, wē* appears in Germanic *wîz*, Lithuanian *vèdu*, Old Slavic *uě*, Hittite *wēs-*, Tocharian *wes*, and Sanskrit *vam, vayam*, all meaning "we."

2. Germanic *wîz* appears in Gothic *weis*, Old High German *wir* (Modern German *wir*), and Old English *we, wē*, all meaning "we." Old English *we* became Modern English WE.

3. Indo-European *nes, nos, ns* appears in Germanic *uns*, Old Irish *nar*, Latin *nōs*, Old Slavic *nā*, Greek *nō*, and Sanskrit *nas*, all meaning "we" or "us."

4. Germanic *uns* appears in Gothic *uns*, Old Norse *oss*, Old High German *uns* (Modern German *uns*), and Old English *us*, all meaning "us." Old English *us* became Middle English, Modern English US.

5. A possessive adjective from *ns* was *nseros* = "our." This became Germanic *unsaraz*, appearing in Gothic *unsara*, Old Norse *várr*, Old High German *unsēr* (Modern German *unser*), and Old English *ūre*, all meaning "our." Old English *ūre* became Middle English *oure*, Modern English OUR.

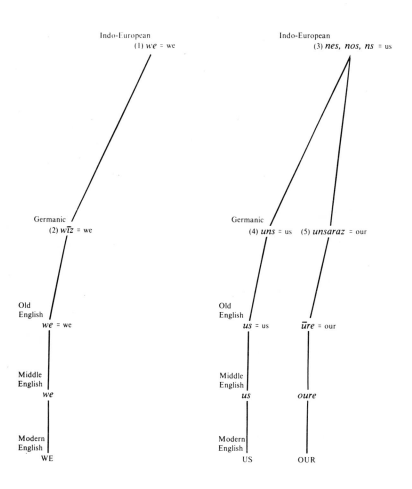

Indo-European
(1) *we* = we

Indo-European
(3) *nes, nos, ns* = us

Germanic
(2) *wīz* = we

Germanic
(4) *uns* = us   (5) *unsaraz* = our

Old
English
we = we

Old
English
us = us   *ūre* = our

Middle
English
we

Middle
English
us   *oure*

Modern
English
WE

Modern
English
US   OUR

187

wē-

1. Indo-European *wē-* = "to blow" appears in Old Irish *feth* = "air," Lithuanian *vejas* = "wind," Old Slavic *vejetŭ* = "blow," Greek *awesi* = "blows," and Sanskrit *vāti* = "blows."

Its derivative noun *wedhrom* = "wind," also "state of the wind, weather," appears in Germanic *wedram* = "weather," Lithuanian *vidras* = "storm," and Old Slavic *vedro* = "good weather."

Another derivative noun *wēntos* = "wind" appears in Germanic *windaz*, Welsh *gwynt*, Latin *ventus*, Tocharian *want-*, and Hittite *hu-want-*, all meaning "wind."

2. Germanic *wedram* appears in Old Norse *vedhr*, Old High German *wetar* (whence Modern German *wetter*), and Old English *weder*, all meaning "weather." Old English *weder* became Middle English *wethyr* (with the same change of *d* to *th* as in *mother, father*), and Modern English WEATHER.

3. Germanic *windaz* appears in Gothic *winds*, Old Norse *vindr*, Old High German *wint* (whence Modern German *wind*), and Old English *wind*, all meaning "wind." Old English *wind* became Modern English WIND.

Formed from Old English *wind* was *windwian* = "to ventilate threshed grain so that the chaff is blown off"; this was done with a device for throwing or tossing the grain up, in a suitable cross-draft. Old English *windwian* became Middle English *winwen*, Modern English WINNOW.

The Old Norse word *vindauga* = "window" literally meant "wind-eye," from *vindr* + *auga* = "eye." It was borrowed into Middle English as *windowe*, becoming Modern English WINDOW.

4. Latin *ventilāre* = "to expose to wind" is formed from *ventus* = "wind" in a similar manner to Old English *windwian* from *wind*. The meaning was also the same; *ventilāre* meant "to winnow threshed grain" and also "to sift out a subject, open it up for discussion." It was adopted into English as VENTILATE, at first meaning "to sift and discuss," and later also "to bring fresh air into a building, etc."

5. Also from this root, and presumably originally meaning "blower," is Latin *vannus* = "winnowing device." The basic form of this was a scoop or shovel by which the grain was shaken or tossed in the air, preferably in a cross-breeze, so that the chaff blew off and the grain remained.

This was borrowed into Old English as *fann* = "winnowing device," becoming Middle English *fanne*. In the sixteenth century this word began to be used also to mean a hand-held device for ventilating oneself with a cooling breeze. It became Modern English FAN.

6. Sanskrit *nirvāna* = (in Buddhism and Hinduism) "the state of absolute beatitude when the self and its passions have been extinguished"; its literal meaning was "the blowing out, extinction," from *nirvā-* = "to be blown out": *nir* = "out" + *vā-* as in *vāti* = "blows." This was borrowed into English in the nineteenth century as NIRVANA.

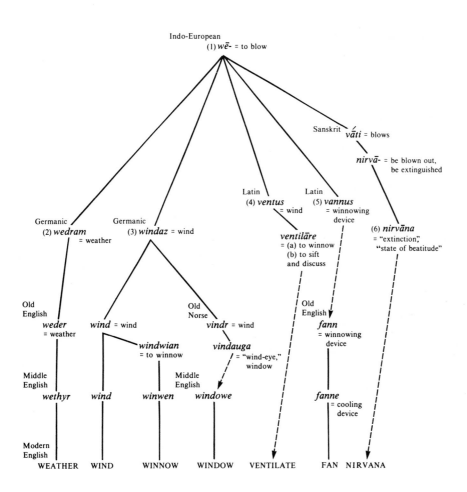

Indo-European
(1) *wē-* = to blow

Sanskrit *vāti* = blows

nirvā- = be blown out, be extinguished

Germanic
(2) *wedram*
= weather

Germanic
(3) *windaz* = wind

Latin
(4) *ventus*
= wind

Latin
(5) *vannus*
= winnowing device

(6) *nirvāna*
= "extinction,"
"state of beatitude"

ventilāre
= (a) to winnow
(b) to sift
and discuss

Old
English
weder
= weather

wind = wind

windwian
= to winnow

Old
Norse
vindr = wind

Old
English
fann
= winnowing
device

vindauga
= "wind-eye,"
window

Middle
English
wethyr

wind

winwen

Middle
English
windowe

fanne
= cooling
device

Modern
English
WEATHER   WIND   WINNOW   WINDOW   VENTILATE   FAN   NIRVANA

189

webh-

1. Indo-European *webh-* = "to weave" appears in Germanic *weban* = "to weave" and *wabjam* = "woven fabric," Greek *huphos* (from *wephos*) = "woven fabric," Albanian *venj* = "I weave," Tocharian *wap-* = "to weave," and Sanskrit *ūrna-vā́bhis* = "wool-weaver" (*ūrna-* = "wool"), a name for the spider.

The basic and probably original method of weaving starts with an upright frame, the loom, on which threads are vertically stretched. These upright threads are called the *warp* (this word is not related to the root *webh-;* it means "a throwing," i.e., the threads that are first set up or "thrown" on the loom). The textile fabric, or WEB, is made by weaving new threads horizontally through the warp threads; these crosswise threads are called the WOOF or the WEFT (*see* below).

2. Germanic *weban* appears in Old Norse *vefa,* Old High German *weban* (whence Modern German *weben*), and Old English *wefan,* all meaning "to weave." Old English *wefan* had past tense *wæf* and past participle *wefen;* it became Middle English *weven, wof, woven,* Modern English WEAVE, WOVE, WOVEN.

3. From Old English *wefan* was formed the noun *ōwef* = "off-weave" (*ō-* = "off"); this was an Old English term for the crosswise threads in weaving; it became Middle English *oof.* This word must often have been used in the expression *warp and oof* = "both upright threads and crosswise threads, i.e., the whole fabric of a textile"; by the sixteenth century, by assonance, this phrase became *warp and woof,* and the latter word became fixed as WOOF.

4. Formed from the Germanic verb *weban* was the noun *wefta* = "woven thread." This appears in Old Norse *veptr* = "weft," Middle High German *wift* = "fine thread," and Old English *wefta* = "cross-threads." The last became Modern English WEFT, synonymous with WOOF.

5. Also from Indo-European *webh-* is Germanic *wabjam* = "woven fabric." This appears in Old Norse *vefr,* Old High German *wappi,* and Old English *web,* all meaning "woven fabric." The last became Modern English WEB, now most often used to mean a spider's web, but still also used by weavers in the original technical sense.

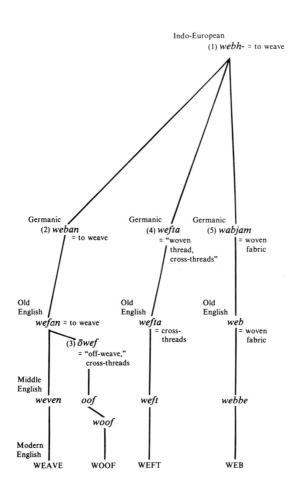

Indo-European
(1) *webh-* = to weave

Germanic
(2) *weban* = to weave

Germanic
(4) *wefta* = "woven thread, cross-threads"

Germanic
(5) *wabjam* = woven fabric

Old English
wefan = to weave

(3) *ōwef* = "off-weave," cross-threads

Old English
wefta = cross-threads

Old English
web = woven fabric

Middle English
weven   *oof*

woof

weft

webbe

Modern English
WEAVE   WOOF   WEFT   WEB

191

wed-

1. The Indo-European root *wed-* = "wet" has variant forms *wēd-, wod-, wōd-,* and *ud-,* and derivative nouns *wodōr, udōr* = "water." They appear in Germanic *wēt-* = "wet" and *watar* = "water," and in Old Irish *uisge,* Old Slavic *voda,* Greek *hudōr,* Hittite *wātar,* and Sanskrit *uda,* all meaning "water."

2. The root-form *wēd-* regularly became Germanic *wēt-,* appearing in Old Norse *vātr,* Old Frisian *wēt,* and Old English *wǣt,* al meaning "wet." From Old English *wǣt* came the verb *wǣtan* = "to make wet," becoming Middle English *weten,* with past participle *wette* = "wetted." This became the Modern English adjective WET. (If the Old English adjective *wǣt* itself had survived, it would have become Modern English *weet.*)

3. The noun form *wodōr* = "water" became Germanic *watar,* appearing in Old High German *wazzar* (whence Modern German *wasser*), Old Frisian *weter,* and Old English *wæter;* the last became Modern English WATER.

4. The root-form *ud-,* with a suffix *-ski-,* appears in Old Irish *uisge* = "water."

The art of distilling alcohol from wine, unknown to the Greeks and Romans, was probably discovered in the twelfth century by alchemists working at Salerno. The resulting liquor was named in Latin *aqua vītae* = "water of life." Thereafter it was manufactured in monasteries under conditions of secrecy, until in the sixteenth century hundreds of monasteries were abolished in the Reformation. Distillation then suddenly became known all across Europe, and the term *aqua vītae* was rendered into the various languages, becoming, for example, Swedish and Danish *akvavit.* The Gaels of Ireland and of Highland Scotland learned the technique at this time, and translated the name as (Irish) *uisge beathadh* and (Scottish) *uisge beatha,* both meaning "water of life" (for *beatha* = "life"; *see* **gwei-**). These were borrowed into Elizabethan English as USQUEBAUGH. This was later changed to *whiskybae,* and then shortened to WHISKY.

5. The root word *wod-* appears in Old Slavic *vod-,* as in Russian *voda* = "water." Distillation also began in Russia in the early sixteenth century. The liquor was called *vodka* = "little water," doubtless also a partial translation of *aqua vītae,* as above. VODKA was borrowed into English in the nineteenth century.

6. The noun form *udōr* appears in Greek *hudōr* = "water." This, in its Latinized spelling *hydr-, hydro-,* has been adopted into English as a word-forming element, as in HYDROELECTRIC, etc.

192

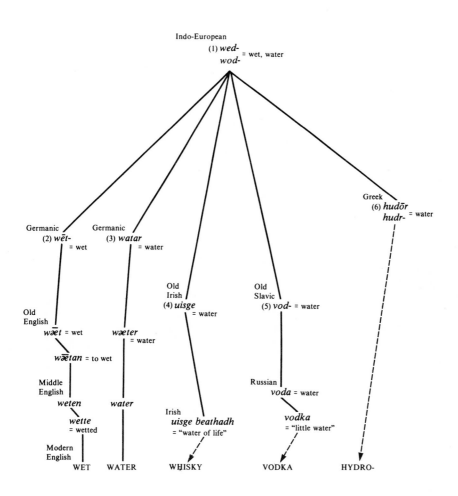

Indo-European
(1) *wed-*
wod- = wet, water

Greek
(6) *hudōr*
hudr- = water

Germanic
(2) *wēt-* = wet

Germanic
(3) *watar* = water

Old
English
wǣt = wet

wǣtan = to wet

Old
Irish
(4) *uisge* = water

Old
Slavic
(5) *vod-* = water

wæter = water

Middle
English
weten

wette = wetted

Russian
voda = water

water

Irish
uisge beathadh
= "water of life"

vodka
= "little water"

Modern
English
WET   WATER   WHISKY   VODKA   HYDRO-

193

wegh-

1. Indo-European *wegh-* = "to go, to travel, to ride in a vehicle, to carry by vehicle," with its derivatives *weghnos* = "vehicle," *weghos* = "a going, travel," *weghtis* = "a carrying, transportation," appears in Germanic *wagnaz* = "vehicle," *wegaz* = "road," *wigan* = "to carry," Old Irish *fēn* = "vehicle," Latin *vehere* = "to transport in a vehicle," Lithuanian *vežimas* = "vehicle," Old Slavic *vozŭ* = "vehicle," Greek *(w)okhos* = "vehicle, chariot," and Sanskrit *vahanam* = "chariot, ship" and *váhati* = "he carries in a chariot."

Wheeled vehicles may have been invented in Mesopotamia *c.* 4000 B.C., or by the Indo-European Kurgan people living in southern Russia at the same date. A further Indo-European contribution was probably the harnessing of the horse. The subsequent large-scale migrations of Kurgan elements south through the Middle East and west into Europe, almost certainly resulting in the dissemination of the Indo-European languages, was largely assisted by four-wheeled wagons, as shown by finds of pieces of vehicles buried in high-status graves and by numerous pottery models of vehicles, covering the period 3000–2000 B.C. The light war-chariot with two spoked wheels was developed before 2000 B.C. and thereafter was a favorite weapon of separate Indo-European warrior aristocracies.

(See also **ekwos** = "horse," **kwekwlos** = "wheel," and *yugom* = "yoke" [in **yeug-** = "to join"].)

2. Germanic *wagnaz* = "vehicle" appears in Old Norse *vagn*, Old High German *wagen* (whence Modern German *wagen* as in *Volkswagen* = "people's vehicle"), Middle Dutch *wagen*, and Old English *wægen*, all meaning "vehicle." Old English *wægn*, *wægen*, *wæn* became Modern English WAIN, surviving only in rural dialects in England, and in poetry. Later the English borrowed the Dutch word *wagen*, which became WAGON or WAGGON.

3. Germanic *wegaz* = "track, road, journey" appears in Gothic *wigs*, Old Norse *vegr*, Old High German *weg*, and Old English *weg* = "road, path"; the last became Modern English WAY.

4. Germanic *wigan* = "to transport, carry" had also the meaning "to lift on a balance or scale, to ascertain the weight of"; it appears in Old Norse *vega* = "to lift, weigh," Old High German *wegan* = "to move, weigh," and Old English *wegan* = "to carry, weigh"; the last became Modern English WEIGH, retaining only the secondary Germanic meaning except in the nautical phrase *to weigh anchor* = "to lift the anchor."

5. Germanic *wihtiz* = "a lifting, carrying," hence "a weighing, the amount something weighs," appears in Old Norse *vett*, *vætt*, Old Frisian *wicht*, and Old English *wiht* = "weight," becoming Modern English WEIGHT.

6. Latin *vehere* = "to transport in a vehicle" was also used in the passive *vehī* to mean "to travel in a vehicle." From it was formed the noun *vehiculum* = "a conveyance of any kind," which was adopted into English (seventeenth century) as VEHICLE.

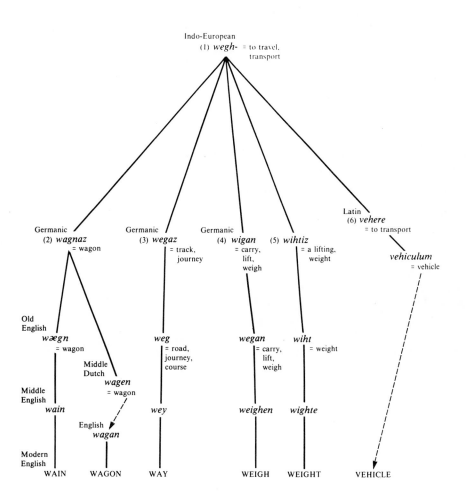

Indo-European
(1) *wegh-* = to travel, transport

Germanic
(2) *wagnaz* = wagon

Germanic
(3) *wegaz* = track, journey

Germanic
(4) *wigan* = carry, lift, weigh

(5) *wihtiz* = a lifting, weight

Latin
(6) *vehere* = to transport

vehiculum = vehicle

Old English
wægn = wagon

Middle Dutch
wagen = wagon

weg = road, journey, course

wegan = carry, lift, weigh

wiht = weight

Middle English
wain

English
wagan

wey

weighen

wighte

Modern English
WAIN   WAGON   WAY   WEIGH   WEIGHT   VEHICLE

weid-

1.   The Indo-European verb *weid-, wid-* meant "to see," especially in the sense "to see intellectually, to perceive, to understand," with derivatives in the perfect tense meaning "to have seen and understood," hence "to know," and further derivatives referring to knowledge. It appears in Germanic *wit-* = "knowledge," *wissaz* = "having knowledge," and *witan* = "to know," Latin *vidēre* = "to see," Old Slavic *viděti* = "see" and *věděti* = "to know," Greek *(w)eidenai* = "to know" and *(w)idea* = "appearance," and Sanskrit *vetti* = "knows" and *vēda* = "knowledge."

2.   Germanic *wit-* = "knowledge, understanding" appears in Gothic *un-witi* = "ignorance," Old Norse *vit* = "understanding," and Old English *wit, witt* = "understanding, intelligence." The last became Modern English WIT (noun), now usually meaning "verbal humor" but also retaining its original meaning "native intelligence."

   The Germanic noun *wit-nass-* = "knowledge, cognizance" appears in Old English *witnes* = "knowledge, legal attestation of a fact, testimony," becoming Modern English WITNESS.

   The Germanic verb *witan* = "to know" appears in Old English *witan,* now surviving only as an archaic word, WIT (verb) = "to know."

3.   Germanic *wissaz* (representing Indo-European *weidtos* = "provided with experience and understanding") appears in Gothic *-weis,* Old Norse *víss,* Old High German *wîs,* and Old English *wîs* = "having good judgment, wise"; becoming Modern English WISE.

4.   With Latin *vidēre* = "to see" was the noun *vīsiō* = "ability to see, sight, something seen." This was adopted into Old French as *vision,* and thence into (Middle) English as VISION. Similarly, Latin *vīsuālis* = "relating to sight" was adopted as VISUAL.

   Latin *vidēre* was also inherited into Old French as *veoir* = "to see," with past participle *veue* = "seen," also "something seen, a sight, a prospect." This was borrowed into Middle English as *vewe,* becoming Modern English VIEW.

5.   Greek *idea* (originally *widea*) = "appearance, form, ideal form, mental conception" was adopted into Latin as *idea* and thence into English (sixteenth century) as IDEA.

6.   Sanskrit *vēda* = "knowledge," also "sacred knowledge, sacred text," was used as the name of the four sacred scriptures of the Hindus, of which the oldest is the *Rigvēda* = "Praise-Scripture" (*ric* = "praise"). *Vēda* and *Rigvēda* were adopted into English (eighteenth century) as VEDA and RIGVEDA. The form of Sanskrit in which the *Vedas* are written is called VEDIC (most of the Sanskrit words cited in this book are in Vedic).

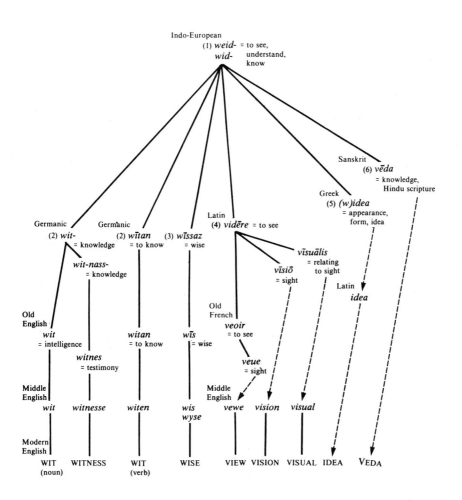

Indo-European
(1) *weid-* = to see,
wid- understand,
know

Sanskrit
(6) *vēda*
= knowledge,
Hindu scripture

Greek
(5) *(w)idea*
= appearance,
form, idea

Latin
(4) *vidēre* = to see

Germanic
(2) *wit-*
= knowledge

Germanic
(2) *wītan*
= to know

(3) *wīssaz*
= wise

wit-nass-
= knowledge

vīsuālis
= relating
to sight

vīsiō
= sight

Latin
idea

Old
English
wit
= intelligence

witan
= to know

wīs
= wise

Old
French
veoir
= to see

witnes
= testimony

veue
= sight

Middle
English
wit

witnesse

witen

Middle
English
wis
wyse

vewe

vision

visual

Modern
English
WIT
(noun)

WITNESS

WIT
(verb)

WISE

VIEW

VISION

VISUAL

IDEA

VEDA

197

wel-

1. Indo-European *wel-* = "to wish (for)" appears in Germanic *wilyan* = "to wish," *wilyon* = "desire," and *wel-* = "desirably," Middle Welsh *gwell* = "better," Latin *volō* = "I wish," Lithuanian *pa-vélmi* = "wish," Old Slavic *veljĕ* = "will," Greek *(w)leiein* = "wish," Avestan *var-* = "choose, wish," and Sanskrit *varayáti* = "wish for oneself" (with regular change of Indo-European *l* to Indo-Iranian *r*).

2. The Germanic verb *wilyan* appears in Gothic *wiljan,* Old Norse *volja,* Old Frisian *willa,* and Old English *willan,* all meaning "to wish," and also used as a "modal auxiliary" forming future tenses (as in *I will go*). The last became Modern English WILL (verb).

   The Germanic noun *wilyon* appears in Gothic *wilja,* Old Norse *vili,* Old High German *willo,* and Old English *willa,* all meaning "desire, wish." The last became Modern English WILL (noun).

3. The Germanic root *wel-, weil-* was used adverbially to mean "as one would wish, in accordance with one's preferences, desirably, satisfactorily." It appears in Gothic *waila,* Old Norse *vel,* Old High German *wola* (whence Modern German *wohl*), and Old English *well;* whence Modern English WELL (adverb).

   The Germanic noun *welom* = "happiness, prosperity, riches" appears in Old Saxon *wela* and Old English *wela, weola* = "prosperity, riches." The latter became Middle English *weal* (whence the archaic noun WEAL); from this also was formed the noun *welthe* (with abstract suffix *-th* modeled after *health*) = "riches," Modern English WEALTH.

4. From Latin *volō* = "I wish" was formed the Medieval Latin abstract noun *volitiō* = "wish, the act of wishing." This was adopted into French as *volition* and thence into English as VOLITION.

   From *volō* also was formed the noun *voluntās* = "desire, goodwill, consent, agreement, will"; hence the adjective *voluntārius* = "according to one's will, willing," which was adopted into (Middle) English as *voluntarie,* becoming Modern English VOLUNTARY.

   Closely related to *volō* was Latin *volup* = "pleasantly," with the noun *voluptās* = "pleasure," used especially of erotic pleasure. From this was formed an adjective *voluptuōsus* = "of or devoted to erotic pleasure," which was adopted into (Middle) English as VOLUPTUOUS.

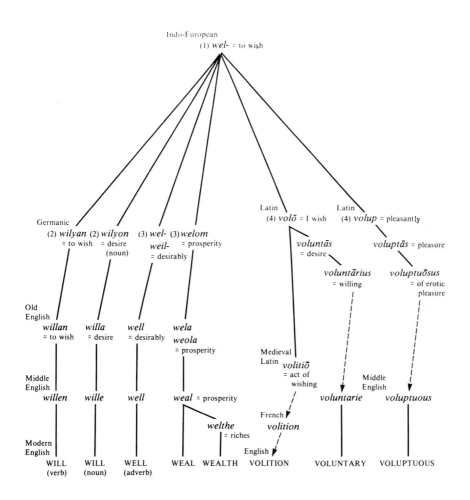

Indo-European
(1) *wel-* = to wish

Germanic
(2) *wilyan* (2) *wilyon* (3) *wel-* (3) *welom*
= to wish = desire *weil-* = prosperity
(noun) = desirably

Latin
(4) *volō* = I wish

Latin
(4) *volup* = pleasantly

voluntās
= desire

voluptās = pleasure

voluntārius
= willing

voluptuōsus
= of erotic
pleasure

Old
English
willan *willa* *well* *wela*
= to wish = desire = desirably *weola*
= prosperity

Medieval
Latin
volitiō
= act of
wishing

Middle
English
willen *wille* *well* *weal* = prosperity

voluntarie *voluptuous*

French
volition

Middle
English

welthe
= riches

English

Modern
English
WILL WILL WELL WEAL WEALTH VOLITION VOLUNTARY VOLUPTUOUS
(verb) (noun) (adverb)

199

wer-

1. Indo-European *wer-* = "to speak," with its derivative noun *werdhom* or *wrdhom* = "utterance, word," appears in Germanic *wurdam* = "utterance, word," Latin *verbum* = "utterance, word," Lithuanian *vardas* = "name," Greek *wereō* = "I shall say," *(w)rhēma* = "utterance, word," and *(w)rhētōr* = "public speaker," Hittite *weriya* = "to call," and Sanskrit *vratám* = "command."

2. Germanic *wurdam* appears in Gothic *waurd,* Old Norse *ordh,* Old High German *wort* (whence Modern German *wort*), and Old English *word,* all meaning "utterance, word." The last, also meaning "news, command, promise" and "unit of speech, individual word," became Modern English WORD.

3. From Latin *verbum* = "utterance, word" was formed the Late Latin adjective *verbālis* = "relating to words, expressed in words." This was adopted into (Middle) English as VERBAL.

Greek *rhēma* = "utterance, word" (which happens to be from the same Indo-European root, although this fact could not have been known in antiquity) was used in the grammatical sense "part of speech expressing action." The Roman grammarians adopted this technical concept and added it to the meanings of Latin *verbum,* which was thus adopted into Middle English as *verbe,* Modern English VERB. Similarly, Greek *epirrhēma* (*epi-* = "in addition")="additional word" was coined as the term for the part of speech that typically qualifies a verb. This was rendered into Latin as *adverbium* (*ad-* = "in addition"), which was likewise adopted into Middle English as *adverbe,* becoming Modern English ADVERB.

4. From Greek *rhētōr* = "public speaker" was formed the term *rhētorikē (tekhnē)* = "(the art of) public speaking." This was adopted into Latin as *rhētorica,* thence into Old French as *rethorique,* and thence into Middle English as *rethorik,* which was "corrected" in Modern English to RHETORIC.

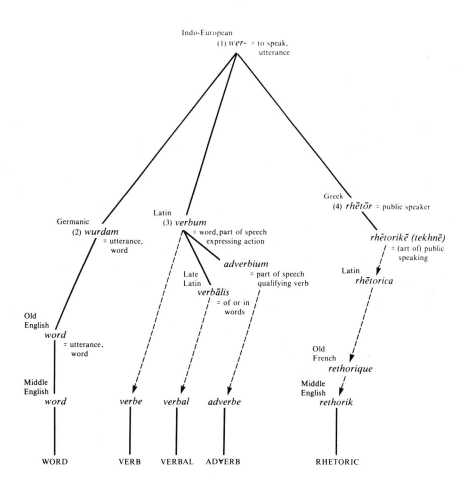

Indo-European
(1) *wer-* = to speak, utterance

Germanic
(2) *wurdam*
= utterance, word

Latin
(3) *verbum*
= word, part of speech expressing action

adverbium
= part of speech qualifying verb

Late Latin
verbālis
= of or in words

Greek
(4) *rhētōr* = public speaker

rhētorikē (tekhnē)
= (art of) public speaking

Latin
rhētorica

Old English
word
= utterance, word

Middle English
word

Old French
rethorique

Middle English
rethorik

WORD   VERB   VERBAL   ADVERB   RHETORIC

201

werg-

1. The Indo-European verb *werg-* = "to work," with its derivative noun *wergom* = "work," appears in Germanic *werkam* = "work" and *wurhtjo* = "artificer," Old Breton *guerg* = "efficacious," Greek *(w)ergon* = "work" and *(w)organon* = "tool," Armenian *gorc* = "work," and Avestan *varəz-* = "to work, make."

2. Germanic *werkam* appears in Old Norse *verk,* Old High German *werc,* and Old English *weorc, werk,* all meaning "work." The last became Modern English WORK.

3. Germanic *wurhtjo* appears in Old High German *wurhto,* Old Frisian *wrichta,* and Old English *wryhta,* all meaning "artificer, craftsman." The last became Modern English WRIGHT, now surviving chiefly in a few terms such as *cartwright* and *shipwright,* referring to crafts now all but obsolete, and in the literary (seventeenth-century) term PLAYWRIGHT; and in numerous English surnames.

4. From Greek *ergon,* originally *wergon,* = "work" was formed the adjective *energēs* = "working within, effective, operative" (*en* = "in"), from which Aristotle coined the noun *energeia* = "the ability to operate, the power of working." This was adopted into Late Latin as *energia* and thence into English as ENERGY, now defined in physics as a fundamental property of matter.

5. Greek *organon,* originally *worganon,* basically meant "tool, instrument." It was used in various specialized senses, including "musical instrument" and "part of the body regarded as a tool," such as the eye or the tongue. It was adopted into Latin as *organum* = "instrument, musical instrument," applied by early Christians especially to a church instrument in which pipes were played by means of a bellows. It was adopted into Old French as *organe,* and thence into (Middle) English as ORGAN, at first meaning only "pipe organ," later (fifteenth–sixteenth centuries) receiving also the Greek and Latin meanings of "specialized part of a plant or animal."

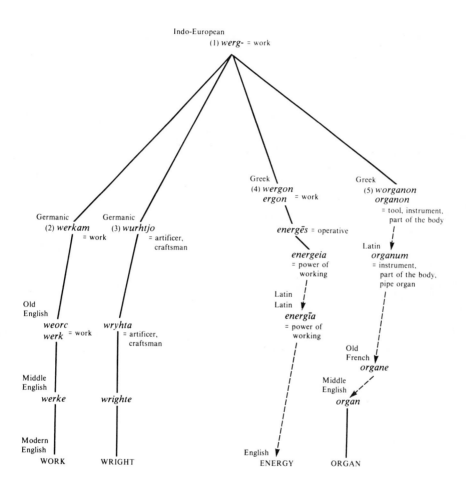

Indo-European
(1) *werg-* = work

Germanic
(2) *werkam*
= work

Germanic
(3) *wurhtjo*
= artificer,
craftsman

Greek
(4) *wergon*
ergon = work

Greek
(5) *worganon*
organon
= tool, instrument,
part of the body

energēs = operative

energeia
= power of
working

Latin
organum
= instrument,
part of the body,
pipe organ

Old
English
weorc
werk = work

wryhta
= artificer,
craftsman

Latin
Latin
energīa
= power of
working

Middle
English
werke

wrighte

Old
French
organe

Middle
English
organ

Modern
English
WORK

WRIGHT

English
ENERGY

ORGAN

203

wesperos

1.   Indo-European *wesperos* = "sunset," also "the evening star," appears in Germanic *westaz* = "west," Latin *vesper* = "evening, the evening star," Lithuanian *vãkaras* = "evening," and Greek *hesperos* = "evening, the evening star."

2.   Germanic *westaz* appears in Old Norse *vestr,* Old High German *west,* and Old English *west,* all meaning "west." Old English *west* became Modern English WEST.

3.   Formed from Latin *vesper* = "evening, the evening star" was *vespera* = "evening time," hence Late Latin *vesperae* = "evening service in the Christian Church." This was adopted into Old French as *vespres,* borrowed thence into Middle English as *vespres,* becoming Modern English VESPERS.

4.   Formed from Greek *hesperos* = "evening, the evening star" was *Hesperia* = "the western country," used by the Greeks to refer to Italy, and later by the Romans and others to refer to lands farther to the west. It was adopted into English as HESPERIA, remaining a poetic term for any western lands.

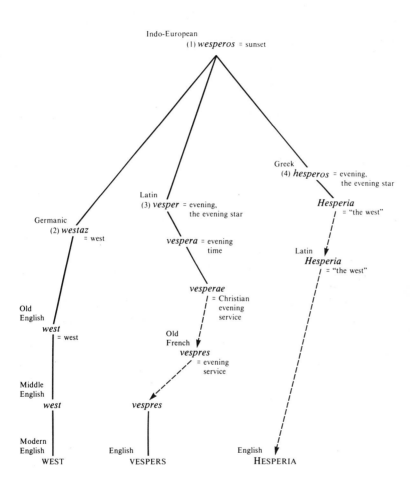

Indo-European
(1) *wesperos* = sunset

Germanic
(2) *westaz*
= west

Latin
(3) *vesper* = evening,
the evening star

Greek
(4) *hesperos* = evening,
the evening star

Hesperia
= "the west"

vespera = evening
time

Latin
Hesperia
= "the west"

Old
English
west
= west

vesperae
= Christian
evening
service

Old
French
vespres
= evening
service

Middle
English
west

vespres

Modern
English
WEST

English
VESPERS

English
HESPERIA

205

yeug-

1. The Indo-European root *yeug-* = "to join," with derivatives referring to the yoking of draft animals, especially the noun *yugom* = "a yoke," appears in Germanic *yukam* = "yoke," Old Welsh *iou* = "yoke," Latin *jungere* = "to join" and *jugum* = "yoke," Lithuanian *jùngiu* = "join" and *jùngas* = "yoke," Greek *zeugnūmi* = "join" and *zugon* = "yoke," Hittite *iugan* = "yoke," and Sanskrit *yunákti* = "harnesses, joins" and *yúgam* = "yoke."

The yoke is a heavy bar of wood, carved to fit rigidly over the necks of two draft animals, fastened around their necks, and attached to a pole between the animals by which they are made to pull a plow or vehicle. It has been used from the earliest times, especially with oxen, whose great strength makes them almost impossible to harness without the rigidity and weight of a yoke. The Indo-European word *yugom* is so widely and exactly represented as to be a guarantee that the earliest Indo-European–speaking people (probably before 4000 B.C.) possessed this fundamental device for harnessing ox power.

2. Germanic *yukam* appears in Gothic *juk,* Old Norse *ok,* Old High German *juch,* and Old English *geoc,* all meaning "yoke." *Geoc* (pronounced /yōk/) became Modern English YOKE.

3. In Latin *jungere* = "to join" the *n* is a "nasal infix." Jungere was inherited into Old French as *joindre,* with the stem *joign-,* which was borrowed into Middle English as *joinen,* becoming Modern English JOIN. From Latin *jungere* was also formed the abstract noun *junctiō* = "a joining"; this was adopted directly into English (sixteenth century) as JUNCTION.

4. From Latin *jugum* = "yoke" was formed the diminutive noun *jugulum* = "little yoke," hence "collarbone, neck." This had the Late Latin adjective *jugulāris* = "relating to the neck," which was adopted into medical English as JUGULAR, referring especially to two major veins in the neck.

To the Romans (as to others) the yoke was a symbol of domestication and servitude. A traditional practice of victorious Roman armies was to set up after the battle a symbolic yoke formed by two spears stuck in the ground, with a third forming the crosspiece, and to make the defeated enemy pass under it as a ritual of total surrender. The verb *subjugāre,* from *sub* = "under" + *jugum* = "yoke," meant "to send an enemy under the yoke," and thence also "to conquer," whether or not the ritual was used. This was adopted into English as SUBJUGATE.

5. Latin *conjux,* with stem *conjug-,* meant "spouse." It seems originally to have meant "yokefellow" (the prefix *con-* = "together"), and there are comparable nouns in Germanic, Greek, and Sanskrit. From it was formed *conjugālis* = "relating to marriage," adopted into English as CONJUGAL.

6. With the Greek noun *zugon* = "yoke" was the verb *zugoun* = "to yoke," hence an adjective *zugōtos* = "yoked." This was adopted into scientific

English (nineteenth century) as ZYGOTE = "cell formed by the joining of a sperm cell with an egg cell."

7.   Closely related to the Sanskrit verb *yunákti* = "joins, harnesses" is the noun *yógā* = "union, a harnessing, self-discipline." This was used as the name of several Hindu systems of spiritual self-discipline, some combined with physical exercises: borrowed as YOGA.

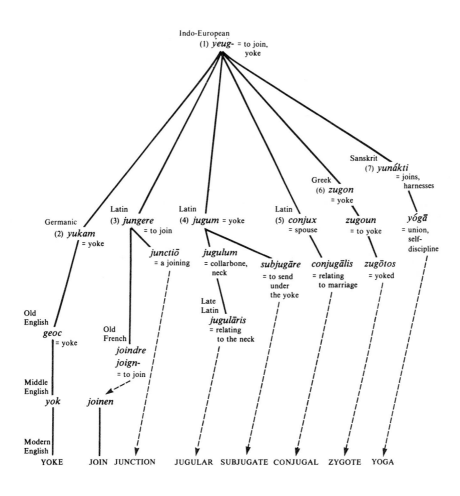

selection of sound-changes

(occurring at the beginnings of words)

Indo-European	Germanic	Celtic	Latin	Greek	Slavic	Sanskrit
p	f	(zero)	p	p	p	p
t	th	t	t	t	t	t
k	h	k	k	k	s	s
b	p	b	b	b	b	b
d	t	t	t	t	t	t
g	k	g	g	g	z	j
bh	b	b	f	ph	b	bh
dh	d	d	th	th	d	dh
gh	g	g	h	kh	z	h
s	s	s	s	h	s	s
m	m	m	m	m	m	m
n	n	n	n	n	n	n
r	r	r	r	r	r	r *or* l
l	l	l	l	l	l	l *or* r
w	w	w	v	(zero)	v	v

bibliography

language

The best introduction is in Calvert Watkins's two articles in *The American Heritage Dictionary* (New York, 1969).

A good summary is W. B. Lockwood, *Indo-European Philology* (London, 1969), with extensive further bibliographies.

The authoritative dictionary of Indo-European is Julius Pokorny, *Indogermanisches Etymologisches Wörterbuch* (Bern, 1959); for Latin, A. Ernout and A. Meillet, *Dictionnaire Etymologique de la Langue Latine* (Paris, 1959); for Greek, Hjalmar Frisk, *Griechisches Etymologisches Wörterbuch* (Heidelberg, 1960); and for other Indo-European languages, dictionaries published by Carl Winter of Heidelberg. For English, the authorities are *The Oxford English Dictionary* (Oxford, 1928); C. T. Onions, *The Oxford Dictionary of English Etymology* (Oxford, 1966); and *Webster's Third New International Dictionary* (Springfield, 1961). *The American Heritage Dictionary* (New York, 1969) contains an Appendix setting out virtually all of the Indo-European roots present in English.

archaeology

Marija Gimbutas's writings are essential, especially "Proto-Indo-European Culture: The Kurgan Culture During the Fifth, Fourth, and Third Millennia B.C.," published in a collection of conference papers, edited by George Cardona and others, entitled *Indo-European and Indo-Europeans* (Philadelphia, 1970); also see this volume for other articles and further bibliographies. Also essential are Gimbutas's two detailed studies of individual Indo-European peoples, *The Balts* (London and New York, 1963) and *The Slavs* (London and New York, 1971).

Volume 1, Number 1 of *The Journal of Indo-European Studies* (Spring 1973) contains a summary article by James Mallory, "A Short History of the Indo-European Problem," with further bibliography. See also other articles and issues of this journal.

index of english words

DEUCE	*dwō (I)*	FINGER	*penkwe (II)*
DI- (prefix)	*dwō (II)*	FIRE	*pūr-*
DIAGNOSIS	*gnō-*	FISH	*piskos*
DIAGONAL	*genu*	FIST	*penkwe (II)*
DIAMOND	*demə-*	FIVE	*penkwe (I)*
DIFFER	*bher-*	FOOT	*ped-*
DISASTER	*ster-*	FOREIGN	*dhwer-*
DIVINE	*deiwos*	FORENSIC	*dhwer-*
DOOR	*dhwer-*	FOREST	*dhwer-*
DOUBLE	*dwō (I)*	FORTNIGHT	*nekwt-*
DOZEN	*dwō (I)*	FORUM	*dhwer-*
DUAL	*dwō (I)*	FOUR	*kwetwer (I)*
DUET	*dwō (I)*	FOURTH	*kwetwer (II)*
DUODECIMAL	*dwō (I)*	FRACTION	*bhreg-*
DUPLICATE	*dwō (I)*	FRACTURE	*bhreg-*
		FRAGILE	*bhreg-*
		FRAGMENT	*bhreg-*
EAST	*aus-*	FRAIL	*bhreg-*
EASTER	*aus-*	FRATERNAL	*bhrāter*
EAT	*ed-*	FRATERNITY	*bhrāter*
EDIBLE	*ed-*	FRIAR	*bhrāter*
EGO	*eg/me*		
EGOTISM	*eg/me*		
EIGHT	*oktō*	GARDEN	*ghordhos*
ELEVEN	*oinos*	GENDER	*gen-*
ELUCIDATE	*leuk-*	GENEROUS	*gen-*
EN- (prefix)	*en*	GENTLE	*gen-*
ENDO- (prefix)	*en*	GENUFLECT	*genu*
ENERGY	*werg-*	GENUINE	*genu*
EOLITH	*aus-*	GENUS	*gen-*
EOHIPPUS	*aus-,*	GRAIN	*grənom*
	ekwos	GUEST	*ghostis*
EQUESTRIAN	*ekwos*	GYMNASIUM	*nogw-*
EQUINE	*ekwos*	GYMNAST	*nogw-*
ETCH	*ed-*	GYNECOLOGY	*gwenā*
EWE	*owis*		
EXUDE	*sweid-*		
		HART	*ker-*
		HAVE	*kap-*
FAGUS	*bhāgos*	HEART	*kerd-*
FAN	*wē-*	HEAVE	*kap-*
FARTHING	*kwetwer (II)*	HEAVY	*kap-*
FATHER	*pəter*	HECTARE	*kmtom*
FEATHER	*pet-*	HEDONISM	*swād-*
-FER (suffix)	*bher-*	HELICOPTER	*pet-*
-FEROUS (suffix)	*bher-*	HEMP	*kanabis*
FERTILE	*bher-*	HEPTAGON	*septm*
FIFTH	*penkwe (II)*	HESPERIA	*wesperos*

HEXAGON	*seks*	KERNEL	*grənom*
HIPPOPOTAMUS	*ekwos*	KIN	*gen-*
HOG	*sus*	KIND (noun)	*gen-*
HORN	*ker-*	KIND (adjective)	*gen-*
HORTICULTURE	*ghordhos*	KING	*gen-*
HOSPITALITY	*ghostis*	KNEE	*genu*
HOST (= army)	*ghostis*	KNEEL	*genu*
HOST (= entertainer)	*ghostis*	KNOW	*gnō-*
HOUND (noun)	*kwon*		
HOW	*kwo-*		
HUNDRED	*kmtom*	LADDER	*klei-*
HYDRO-	*wed-*	LEAN (verb)	*klei-*
HYPER- (prefix)	*uper*	LEAVE (noun)	*leubh-*
HYPO- (prefix)	*upo*	LIBIDO	*leubh-*
		LIGHT (noun)	*leuk-*
		LONE	*oinos*
I (pronoun)	*eg/me*	LONELY	*oinos*
ICEBERG	*bhergh-*	LOVE	*leubh-*
IDEA	*weid-*	LUCID	*leuk-*
IGNORANCE	*gnō-*	LUMINOUS	*leuk-*
ILLUMINATE	*leuk-*	LUNAR	*leuk-*
ILLUSTRATE	*leuk-*	LUSTER	*leuk-*
ILLUSTRIOUS	*leuk-*		
IMMORTAL	*mer-*		
IN (preposition)	*en*	MACHINE	*magh-*
IN- (prefix = in)	*en*	MADAM	*eg/me*
IN- (prefix = not)	*ne*	MAGNIFICENT	*meg-*
INCLINE	*klei-*	MAGNITUDE	*meg-*
INDOMITABLE	*demə-*	MAHARAJA	*meg-*
INFER	*bher-*	MAIN	*magh-*
INNOVATE	*newos*	MAJOR	*meg-*
INSEMINATE	*sē-*	MANTRA	*men-*
INTER- (prefix)	*en*	MARINE	*mori*
INTO	*en*	MARINER	*mori*
INTRAVENOUS	*en*	MARITIME	*mori*
		MARSH	*mori*
		MASTER	*meg-*
JOIN	*yeug-*	MATERNAL	*māter*
JUGULAR	*yeug-*	MATERNITY	*māter*
JUNCTION	*yeug-*	MATRIMONY	*māter*
JUPITER	*Deiwos,*	MATRON	*māter*
	pəter	MAXIMUM	*meg-*
		MAY (auxiliary verb)	*magh-*
		ME	*eg/me*
KAMASUTRA	*syū-*	MEAD	*medhu*
KENNEL	*kwon*	MEAN (noun)	*medhyos*
KERATIN	*ker-*	MEANS	*medhyos*

MECHANICAL	*magh-*	NICHE	*nizdos*
MEDIAN	*medhyos*	NIGHT	*nekwt-*
MEDIUM	*medhyos*	NINE	*newn*
MEGA- (prefix)	*meg-*	NIRVANA	*wē-*
MEGALO- (prefix)	*meg-*	NO	*ne*
MEMENTO	*men-*	NOCTURNAL	*nekwt-*
MENISCUS	*mēn-*	NOCTURNE	*nekwt-*
MENOPAUSE	*mēn-*	NOMINAL	*nomen*
MENSES	*mēn-*	NOMINATE	*nomen*
MENSTRUATE	*mēn-*	NON-	*ne*
MENTAL	*men-*	NONAGENARIAN	*newn*
MERE (= lake)	*mori*	NONE	*ne*
MESO- (prefix)	*medhyos*	NOON	*newn*
MESON	*medhyos*	NOSE	*nas-*
METROPOLIS	*māter*	NOSTRIL	*nas-*
MID	*medhyos*	NOT	*ne*
MIDDLE	*medhyos*	NOTION	*gnō-*
MIGHT (auxiliary verb)	*magh-*	NOUN	*nomen*
MIGHT (noun)	*magh-*	NOVEL (noun)	*newos*
MIND	*men-*	NOVEL (adjective)	*newos*
MINE (pronoun)	*eg/me*	November	*newn*
MISOGYNIST	*gwenā*	NUDE	*nogw-*
MNEMONIC	*men-*	NULL	*ne*
MONTH	*mēn-*		
MOON	*mēn-*		
MORASS	*mori*	OAR	*rē-*
MORTAL	*mer-*	OCTAGON	*oktō*
MOTHER	*māter*	OCTAVE	*oktō*
MUCH	*meg-*	October	*oktō*
MURDER	*mer-*	OCTOGENARIAN	*oktō*
MY	*eg/me*	OCTOPUS	*oktō*
		OF	*apo*
		OFF	*apo*
NAIL	*nogh-*	OFFER	*bher-*
NAKED	*nogw-*	OMPHALOS	*nobh-*
NAME	*nomen*	ONCE	*oinos*
NASAL	*nas-*	ONE	*oinos*
NAUGHT	*ne*	ONYX	*nogh-*
NAVE (= wheel hub)	*nobh-*	ORCHARD	*ghordhos*
NAVEL	*nobh-*	ORGAN	*werg-*
NEGATION	*ne*	ORTHODONTICS	*dent-*
NEGATIVE	*ne*	OUR	*we/nes*
NEO- (prefix)	*newos*	OVER	*uper*
NEST	*nizdos*	OVINE	*owis*
NESTLE	*nizdos*		
NEUTER	*ne*		
NEW	*newos*	PAJAMA(S)	*ped-*

213

PAL	*bhrāter*	RECOGNIZE	*gnō-*
PATERNAL	*pəter*	REFER	*bher-*
PATERNITY	*pəter*	REINDEER	*ker-*
PATRIARCH	*pəter*	REMINISCENCE	*men-*
PATRICIAN	*pəter*	RENOVATE	*newos*
PATRIOT	*pəter*	REVIVE	*gwei-*
PATRON	*pəter*	RHETORIC	*wer-*
PEDAL	*ped-*	RHINOCEROS	*ker-*
PEDESTRIAN	*ped-*	RIDE	*reidh-*
PEDICURE	*ped-*	RIDING	*trei (II)*
PEN	*pet-*	ROAD	*reidh-*
PENNON	*pet-*	ROW (verb)	*rē-*
PENTACLE	*penkwe (I)*	RUDDER	*rē-*
PENTAGON	*penkwe (I)*		
PERSUADE	*swād-*		
PHOSPHORUS	*bher-*	SADDLE	*sed-*
PINION	*pet-*	SALAD	*sal-*
PISCATORIAL	*piskos*	SALAMI	*sal-*
PISCES	*piskos*	SALARY	*sal-*
PODIATRY	*ped-*	SALINE	*sal-*
POLYGON	*genu*	SALT	*sal-*
PREMONITION	*men-*	SAUCE	*sal-*
PTERODACTYL	*pet-*	SEAM	*syū-*
PUNCH (= drink)	*penkwe (I)*	SEASON	*sē-*
PYJAMAS	*ped-*	SEAT	*sed-*
PYRE	*pūr-*	SEDENTARY	*sed-*
PYRO- (prefix)	*pūr-*	SEED	*sē-*
		SEMAPHORE	*bher-*
		SEMEN	*sē-*
QUADRANT	*kwetwer (I)*	SEMESTER	*mēn-, seks*
QUADRUPLE	*kwetwer (I)*	SEPTEMBER	*septm*
QUALITY	*kwo*	SEPTUAGENARIAN	*septm*
QUANTITY	*kwo*	SESSION	*sed-*
QUARANTINE	*kwetwer (I)*	SET	*sed-*
QUART	*kwetwer (II)*	SETTLE	*sed-*
QUARTER	*kwetwer (II)*	SEVEN	*septm*
QUEAN	*gwenā*	SEW	*syū-*
QUEEN	*gwenā*	SEXAGENARIAN	*seks*
QUICK	*gwei-*	SEXTANT	*seks*
QUINQUENNIAL	*penkwe (I)*	SISTER	*swesor*
QUINTESSENCE	*penkwe (II)*	SIT	*sed-*
QUINTET	*penkwe (II)*	SIX	*seks*
		SOIL (verb)	*sus*
		SORORITY	*swesor*
RAID	*reidh-*	SOW (noun)	*sus*
READY	*reidh-*	SOW (verb)	*sē-*
RECLINE	*klei-*	SQUADRON	*kwetwer (I)*

SQUARE	*kwetwer (I)*	TWENTY	*dekm,*
STAR	*ster-*		*dwō- (II)*
STELLAR	*ster-*	TWICE	*dwō- (II)*
STENTORIAN	*stenə-*	TWIN	*dwō- (II)*
STUN	*stenə-*	TWINE	*dwō- (II)*
SUAVE	*swād-*	TWO	*dwō- (I)*
SUB- (prefix)	*upo*		
SUBJUGATE	*yeug-*	UMBILICUS	*nobh-*
SUPER- (prefix)	*uper*	UN- (negative prefix)	*ne*
SURVIVE	*gwei-*	UNGUIS	*nogh-*
SUTRA	*syū-*	UNGULATE	*nogh-*
SUTURE	*syū-*	UNIQUE	*oinos*
SWEAT	*sweid-*	UNITE	*oinos*
SWEET	*swād-*	UNITY	*oinos*
SWINE	*sus*	UP	*upo*
SYNONYMOUS	*nomen*	UPON	*upo*
		US	*we/nes*
		USQUEBAUGH	*gwei-*
TAME	*demə-*		
-TEEN (suffix)	*dekm*	VEDA	*weid-*
TEN	*dekm*	VEHICLE	*wegh-*
TENDER	*ten-*	VENTILATE	*wē-*
TENUOUS	*ten-*	VERB	*wer-*
TERTIARY	*trei (II)*	VERBAL	*wer-*
TETRAHEDRON	*kwetwer (I)*	VESPERS	*wesperos*
THIN	*ten-*	VIEW	*weid-*
THIRD	*trei (II)*	VISION	*weid-*
THIRTY	*dekm, trei (II)*	VISUAL	*weid-*
THOUSAND	*kmtom*	VITAL	*gwei-*
THREE	*trei (I)*	VITAMIN	*gwei-*
THRICE	*trei (I)*	VIVID	*gwei-*
THUNDER	*stenə-*	VODKA	*wed-*
THURSDAY	*stenə-*	VOLITION	*wel-*
TOOTH	*dent-*	VOLUNTARY	*wel-*
TRANSFER	*bher-*	VOLUPTUOUS	*wel-*
TREBLE	*trei (II)*		
TREY	*trei (I)*		
TRI- (prefix)	*trei (II)*	WAGON	*wegh-*
TRIO	*trei (I)*	WAIN	*wegh-*
TRIPLE	*trei (II)*	WATER	*wed-*
TRIPOD	*ped-*	WAY	*wegh-*
TRIREME	*rē-*	WE	*we/nes*
TROIKA	*trei (I)*	WEAL	*wel-*
TUESDAY	*deiwos*	WEALTH	*wel-*
TWAIN	*dwō- (I)*	WEATHER	*wē-*
TWELVE	*dwō- (I)*	WEAVE	*webh-*

WEB	*webh-*	WISE	*weid-*
WEEVIL	*webh-*	WIT	*weid-*
WEFT	*webh-*	WITNESS	*weid-*
WEIGH	*wegh-*	WOOF	*webh-*
WEIGHT	*wegh-*	WORD	*wer-*
WELL (adverb)	*wel-*	WORK	*werg-*
WEST	*wesperos*	WRIGHT	*werg-*
WET	*wed-*		
WHAT	*kwo*		
WHEEL	*kwekwlos*	YARD	*ghordhos*
WHICH	*kwo*	YOGA	*yeug-*
WHISKY	*gwei-, wed-*	YOKE	*yeug-*
WHO	*kwo*		
WHY	*kwo*		
WILL	*wel-*	ZEUS	*deiwos*
WIND (noun)	*wē-*	ZOO	*gwei-*
WINDOW	*wē-*	ZOOLOGY	*gwei-*
WINNOW	*wē-*	ZYGOTE	*yeug-*

216